Christianity in India

Christianity in India

Christianity in India

Conversion, Community Development, and Religious Freedom

EDITORS
Rebecca Samuel Shah
Joel Carpenter

FORTRESS PRESS

MINNEAPOLIS

CHRISTIANITY IN INDIA

Conversion, Community Development, and Religious Freedom

Copyright © 2018 Fortress Press, an imprint of 1517 Media. All rights reserved. Except for brief quotations in critical articles or reviews, no part of this book may be reproduced in any manner without prior written permission from the publisher. Email copyright@1517.media or write to Permissions, Fortress Press, PO Box 1209, Minneapolis, MN 55440-1209.

Cover design: Laurie Ingram

Print ISBN: 978-1-5064-4791-9
eBook ISBN: 978-1-5064-4792-6

The paper used in this publication meets the minimum requirements of American National Standard for Information Sciences — Permanence of Paper for Printed Library Materials, ANSI Z329.48-1984.

Manufactured in the U.S.A.

For Vinay

and

Colleen Samuel

on the fiftieth anniversary
of their ministry

at

Divya Shanthi in Bangalore,
India (1969 - 2019)

Contents

Acknowledgments ix
Introduction xiii

Part I
Conversion and Identity

1. Saving the Soul of India:
Christian Conversion and the Rise of Hindu Nationalism
　　Rebecca Samuel Shah 3

2. Drinking a Cup of Nectar:
The Transformation of Lakshmibai Tilak
　　Sean Doyle 23

3. A "Willingness to Become Undone" in Relation to Others:
The Plural Life of C. F. Andrews
　　Bernardo A. Michael 48

4. Christian Conversion in India:
Political Exploitation or Personal Transformation?
　　Joshua Iyadurai 69

Part II
Indian Praxis, American Learning

5. American Evangelicalism, Social Action
and Christianity in India:
　　Aminta Arrington 107

6. What God Has Joined Together Let No One Separate:
Local Church and Development Agencies in God's Mission
    Darren Duerksen   125

Part III
Nationalism, Violence, and Freedom

7. Bollywood and the BJP:
An Analysis of Indian Identity in Karan Johar's Films
    Samuel Thambusamy   151

8. Human Rights and Freedom of Religion-
The Ground Experience:
Interviews with Dr. John Dayal and Rev. Vijayesh Lal
    Karuna M. John   179

9. Christian Response to Violence in India
    Vikas Ram and Kay Higuera Smith   198

10. Religious Freedom among the Marginalized
in Bangalore, India
    Rebecca Samuel Shah and Timothy Samuel Shah   228

11. The Burned Church:
Christians and Pluralism in India
    Paul S. Rowe   256

Bibliography   281

Contributors   301

Index   305

Acknowledgments

Behind every book there is a story, and so too with this one. This book is built on a project: a seminar held in India in June and July of 2015 for an interdisciplinary team of two dozen theologians, historians and social scientists from Canada, India, and the United States. Our task, as we made visits in Bangalore, Chennai and Delhi, was to find out more about Christianity in contemporary India and especially its role in the nation's economic and social development.

That was our intention, but what we discovered during our visits and conversations was that religious identity and loyalties, a perennially troubling topic in India, was again a hot controversy. With the recent election of the Hindu nationalist Bharatiya Janata Party (BJP) to a parliamentary majority, incidents of violence against Christians and Muslims were increasing dramatically. So, our conversation shifted considerably, and so too the topical thrust of this book.

We have many to thank for supporting this project and the book you are holding. First, we thank our organizational sponsors. We are grateful to the Nagel Institute for the Study of World Christianity at Calvin College, and particularly its program manager, Donna Romanowski, who guided this project from beginning to end, including this book's production and editing process. We must also thank our general sponsor, the Council for Christian Colleges and Universities, and particularly its vice-president, Rick Ostrander, for giving us encouragement and publicity.

The Religious Freedom Research Project (RFRP) of the Berkley Center for Religion, Peace and World Affairs at Georgetown University kindly loaned us Rebecca and Timothy Samuel Shah, who became the leaders of our seminar in India and the foremost intellectual shapers of this book. And we are grateful to the Oxford Centre for Religion and Public Life, whose founders, Vinay Samuel and Chris Sugden, helped to shape the very rich initial seminar for the study team in Bangalore

This project was fueled by the gifts and encouragement of several generous funding partners. Walter and Darlene Hansen provided major financial support and some gentle guidance as well, based on their extensive experience in India. We are thankful too for the gifts of Doug and Lois Nagel and Jacob and Barbara Smit, longtime encouragers and supporters of the Nagel Institute. And we owe special thanks for support from Calvin College's Paul B. Henry Institute for the Study of Christianity and Politics and its director, Kevin den Dulk, who accompanied our team in India for a week.

We were treated to warm hospitality and very open and frank conversations across India, ranging from banking and telecom executives to Dalit women in micro-finance collectives, from church bishops to local pastors and from national BJP officials to humble people serving in local works of mercy. And we must convey our gratitude to David Selveraj, director of the Visthar Academy of Justice and Peace Studies near Bangalore, who was our host there and a very kind yet challenging docent to us North Americans, some of whom were engaging India for the first time.

Our team had a dozen participants from North America and an equal number from India. Each of them helped to shape what you see in this book, whether or not they contributed a chapter to it. We are grateful to them, one and all.

This book is challenging in several respects, but the leaders at Fortress Press did not blink at agreeing to its publication. We are much beholden, therefore, to Will Bergkamp and Jesudas Athyal for their unflagging support. In the late stages of production, two copy editors extraordinaire, David and Maria denBoer, put us in their debt. We are also grateful to Jason VanHorn and his student, Christian Kammel for creating the map of India for the book.

We dedicate this book to Vinay and Colleen Samuel, our initial hosts in Bangalore. Their hearty energy for serving others, theological insights, and exemplary leadership inspire us beyond measure.

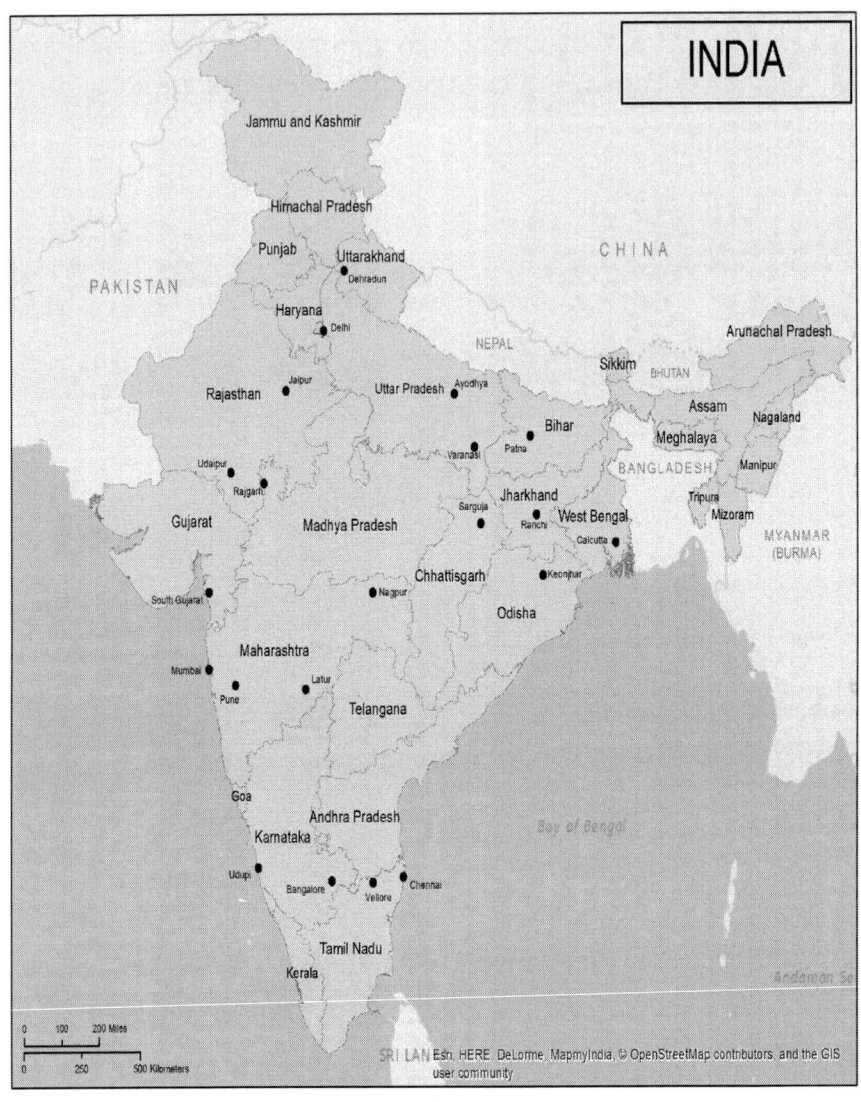

This map conforms to the Indian government's coordinates for boundaries.

Introduction

Anyone who offers a book on Christianity in India recalls the ancient Indian parable of the blind men and the elephant. Attempts to describe the essence of Indian Christianity are bound to give only a partial account. Christianity has been in India since the earliest centuries of the church, and all the main families of Christianity are present: ancient Orthodox communities, Roman Catholics, Protestants, Pentecostals, and locally initiated Christian movements. Over many centuries of presence in India, Christian traditions have put down deep roots in Indian culture. They are by no means alien life forms or mere holdovers from European colonialism and foreign missions. Indeed, says the pre-eminent historian of Indian Christianity, "nowhere in the world today are existing non-Western forms of Christianity older or more complex than in India."[1] Christianity is varied not only by tradition or movement in India but by its being rooted in many distinct regional and ethnic communities across this vast nation, from among the Adivasi peoples of the great Northeast of India[2] to the Christian communities within the Tamil, Telugu, and Kerala regions of southern India. The recent growth of Christianity—particularly Pentecostalism—in the Hindi heartlands of north-central India has been perhaps the most controversial recent development. While Christians in India make up a small minority, estimated to be about 3 to 4 percent of India's total population, the faith's 45 million adherents make Christianity India's

---

1 Robert Eric Frykenberg, *Christianity in India: From Beginnings to the Present* (Oxford: Oxford University Press, 2008), viii.

2 Adivasi refers to the tribal peoples of South Asia, thought to be the region's original inhabitants.

third-largest religion.³ And it has played a profound role, far beyond its numbers, in India's modern development.

We do not presume here to give a comprehensive overview of Christianity in India. There are some fine books that give historical and contemporary coverage.⁴ The purpose of this book is rather to draw attention to the contributions that Indian Christians have made to the advancement of India and to examine the contentious issues that arise whenever Indian Christianity is discussed today: conversion, community development, and religious freedom. These chapters draw on intimate and personal encounters with Christian individuals and organizations in India, past and present, and bring up to date the ongoing challenges of religious conversion and religious freedom in contemporary India.

Christianity's presence and practice in India today is highly controversial, and it has prompted increasing discrimination and violence. This book examines the volatile current situation and shows how Indian Christian communities contribute to their societies, even amid social pressure and violent persecution. Readers will come away surprised and sobered to learn how these initiatives for constructive social change often invite oppression. There has been a dramatic rise in social and legal pressure on religious minorities and violence against them since a Hindu nationalist central government came to power in 2014. Yet India, we have found, is an amazingly diverse nation, and much of its social, political, and economic progress results from the contributions made by its great variety of peoples and faiths. Efforts

---

3 Dyron Daughrity and Jesudas Athyal, *Understanding World Christianity: India* (Minneapolis: Fortress Press, 2016), 142-43.

4 There is a large and dynamic literature on Indian Christianity. Good places to start are with the two works cited above: Frykenberg's definitive history, *Christianity in India*; and Daughrity and Athyal, *Understanding World Christianity: India*, which mixes historical and contemporary treatments.

to suppress diversity and religious dynamism in the name of Hindu primacy can only hurt India.

First on the list of issues in this book is conversion. What do we make of its long history of controversy in India? Do Indian Christians promote conversion unfairly? Is it destructive of Indian identity and national solidarity? What is its effect on people who experience it? And what difference do Christian converts make in India's cities and villages? Members of the team that conducted the studies in this book included Americans and Canadians who brought their own theories and experiences about Christianity's social, cultural, and economic dynamics. They came away, however, having learned a great deal from their Indian teachers and guides. Two of our chapters ruminate on what North American Christians can learn from Indians about Christianity's basic mission, such as local churches' role in community development, Christian institutions' contributions to civil society, and the spiritual wellsprings of entrepreneurship. Finally, several of our chapters address the rise of Hindu nationalism, how Christians respond to violence, and the importance of religious freedom and pluralism for contemporary India.

The first part of this book gives a fresh view of conversion in India, past and present. Conversionary zeal is by no means the exclusive domain of Christian evangelists, as Rebecca Samuel Shah reveals in her opening chapter. Today's Hindu nationalists are fervently seeking to convert or re-convert non-Hindu people, particularly those of India's tribal minorities. Shah offers a brief history of Hindu revivalism since the late nineteenth century, and with it a summary of the ongoing controversies over conversion. Out of this revival and controversy arose Hindutva, the Hindu nationalist ideology that undergirds today's ruling force in India, the Bharatiya Janata Party (BJP).

Hindu revivalists were by no means the only Indians who led efforts at Indian cultural revival. Among the champions of traditional Indian art and thought were some elites who converted to Christianity in the late nineteenth century. Sean Doyle offers a study of Lakshmibai Tilak, a high-caste woman, celebrated Marathi[5] author, and wife of the Marathi literary giant Narayan Waman Tilak. Her conversion to Christianity challenges the dominant narratives about conversion in India, which assume that it must lead to cultural alienation and dislocation. Tilak's conversion inspired her to challenge the evils of caste while also doing much to revive her rich cultural and literary heritage.

Twentieth-century English missionaries frequently engaged in deep dialogue and friendships with Indian religious leaders. Not a few of them found that the first converts they made were themselves. Bernardo A. Michael explores the life of Anglican missionary and activist Charles Freer (C. F.) Andrews. Andrews's lifelong pursuit of cross-cultural and interreligious understanding led him into enduring friendships with many Indians from varied castes and religious traditions. This widely honored friend of Gandhi fostered an openness to Christianity among Indians and an openness to Hindu and Muslim faiths among the English.

Part I ends with an important study of converts to Christianity in India today. Joshua Iyadurai examines the conversion narratives of recent Brahmin converts. Their accounts undercut the Hindu nationalist stereotype of conversions as merely matters of socioeconomic gain made by people with little capacity for critical choice. The converts in this study are all well-educated and reasonably well-off economically. Their conversions are profoundly spiritual and display a high degree of personal agency and deliberative decision-making.

In the book's second part, North American members of our team share insights they gained from Indian Christians' belief and practice. Aminta Arrington discovered that Indians of varying theological views who work among the poor and marginalized see an integral relationship between evangelization and social transformation, and they unite them in both practice and theory. She argues that Indian Christians' integral

---

5 Marathi is an Indian language, spoken predominantly in some of the western Indian states.

thought and practice could provide a powerful theological corrective to American evangelicals, who tend to separate these two facets of the Christian gospel.

Darren Duerksen sees a similar dualism at work in the relationship between local churches and Christian development organizations (CDOs). His observations in India yielded both examples of this problem of separation and some solid counter-examples. He maintains that Christians, particularly in the West, need to rediscover the importance of the local church for God's mission in the world today and recapture a strong theological conviction that God intends for the local church to be a central agent in mission—CDOs' technical expertise notwithstanding.

The third and final part of this book addresses the issue of rising Hindu nationalism in India and the violence and threats to religious freedom that it seems to have inspired. Samuel Thambuswamy's chapter examines the role of Bollywood films in creating an Indian identity that privileges Hinduism. Focusing on Karan Johar's blockbuster films, he shows how the crafting of a "new India" image has played a key role in building support among the wealthy Indian diaspora for a Hindu nationalist agenda, and indeed for the BJP.

Anti-Muslim and anti-Christian communal violence is an every-week reality in India today. Few have done more to highlight and document this violence and to call those responsible to account than John Dayal, a Catholic layman who is a renowned journalist, author, and activist for religious freedom, and Vijayesh Lal, who now is the head of the Evangelical Fellowship of India (EFI), after serving as the EFI's religious freedom officer. Under his leadership, the EFI has trained dozens of local religious workers to give accurate reports of attacks on pastors, evangelists, parishioners, and church facilities. To highlight these reports, the EFI has established a monthly summary, circulated internationally. Writer and editor Karuna M. John interviews Dayal and Lal.

How do Indian Christians respond to these acts of violence? Vikas Ram and Kay Higuera Smith conducted extensive interviews with people in India who personally witnessed or experienced or whose close family suffered in one of the violent outbreaks or pogroms against Christians from the period of 1986 to the present, but especially from 2007 to 2015. Ram and Smith see suffering people seeking theological answers to their questions about suffering and responding with considerable courage and resilience as they press on with their callings.

Given the bitter reality of such persecution, observes Timothy Samuel Shah in the following chapter, it seems bizarre to hear Western intellectuals critique the idea of religious freedom as a universal human right and suggest that such matters ought to be settled "communally," according to local custom and belief. He argues that the poorest and most beset-upon of Indian society—women and Dalits—have been ill-served by such local customs and communal values. Shah follows the history of Indian case law and constitutional debates about conversion to show that the main argument for anti-conversion laws is that these impoverished people have no independent agency and thus need to be looked after by the elites. He finds these arguments to be badly flawed, to say the least. In the second half of the chapter, Rebecca Samuel Shah reflects on what she learned in eight years of research among Dalit women involved in micro-credit projects in a Bangalore slum. She found that those who were recent Christian converts displayed dramatically different—and more pro-development—values than those of the other women. Anti-conversion laws treated them like "hapless things," Shah says, but conversion, by contrast, is empowering and liberating.

Our book ends with a chapter by Paul S. Rowe, who muses about a church he visited in Delhi that had been burned by anti-Christian militants. He asks if the burned church is an indicator of the future of religious freedom in India. He explores the ways in which religious pluralism has strengthened civil society and made contributions to the democratic and liberal environment in India. Religious freedom and pluralism promote a stronger civil society in India, Rowe insists, and much would be lost if these conditions are discouraged. Indian Christians, he argues, have done far more to build civic institutions such as schools, hospitals, community development agencies, and other community-serving NGOs than their small minority status would suggest. They produce tremendous social capital for the nation, and their suppression would have tragic consequences. Christians are good for India, and that is something that any true nationalist should be able to recognize.

PART I
CONVERSION AND IDENTITY

Chapter 1

Saving the Soul of India

Christian Conversion and the Rise of Hindu Nationalism

Rebecca Samuel Shah

As a group of American and Indian scholars arrived at the Young Men's Christian Association (YMCA) in Delhi on a late June afternoon in 2015, they were greeted by green and orange buntings draped along the path toward the front door. Fluttering beside a print of Warner Sallman's *Christ at Heart's Door* in the entryway was a large saffron flag with an image of an open lotus flower, the symbol of the Bharatiya Janata Party (BJP). Within a few minutes it became clear that the YMCA guesthouse where the scholars had booked their rooms was also hosting a gathering of BJP staff from across the country. Volunteers and party workers had arrived to prepare for the next big election in the Christian-majority Northeast of India. This gathering was important because although the BJP had won handily in the general election, it suffered serious setbacks in the Northeast, which was governed by the Congress Party since 2001.

Enthusiasm and zeal to "evangelize" the Christian-dominated Northeast were palpable at the YMCA. Hordes of BJP foot-soldiers wrapped in saffron-colored shawls marched in and out of the building armed with their lotus-print book bags filled with party literature. To Western eyes the scene was not unlike a Christian missionary conference in the nineteenth and early twentieth centuries in London or Chicago, where hundreds of Christian missionaries were urged to head out to the far-flung "regions beyond" to win the world for Christ. BJP foot-soldiers attended numerous strategy sessions and gathered in doorways, along corridors, and on garden benches to discuss ways in which the "unreached" could be reached with the "gospel" of the BJP. Less than a year later, in May 2016, the party's "Look Northeast" plan yielded its first successful result: a rousing BJP victory against the Congress Party in the state of Assam. The party has since been able to build a strong base for the 2019 general election in Christian-majority states such as Nagaland, Mizoram, and Meghalaya.

A Clash of Proselytizations?

Expressions of Hindu nationalism, however, do not always assume the benign (if highly organized and assertive) form we witnessed at the Delhi YMCA. During a twelve-month period in India during 2016-17, a church was burned down or a cleric beaten, on average, about ten times a week.[1] Violent incidents of this kind are in turn justified as a kind of Hindu self-defense against provocation and even coercion on the part of missionizing and proselytizing Christians. They are based on allegations that conversion to Christianity in India is now—and throughout history has often been—the result of force, allurement, or threats of violence. As a result, over the past decade, more and more states in India have enacted anti-conversion laws, and pressure is mounting to pass a national anti-conversion law. Ironically called "freedom of religion" laws, these laws mainly seek to restrict the poor and outcastes from converting to Christianity. Most anti-conversion acts mention the need to "protect women and minors" and other

---

1   US Commission on International Religious Freedom, *2017 Annual Report*, released August 2017, http://www.uscirf.gov/sites/default/files/2017.USCIRFAnnualReport.pdf, accessed February 13, 2018.

susceptible communities from the vulgarity of forced conversions. These laws specify doubled penalties for such attempts.

For example, on August 2, 2017, the state government of Jharkhand proposed the "Jharkhand Freedom of Religion Bill 2017." The bill criminalizes conversions that occur by "force, inducement, or fraud." It is noteworthy, though, that the definitions of these three terms are left ambiguous in the bill. For example, the promise of "everlasting life" may be construed as an "inducement" and warrant severe punishment, including up to three years' imprisonment and a fine of 50,000 rupees (around US$800)—a significant sum for most Indian Christians.

At the same time, there is little embarrassment about the use of inducements or incentives to proselytize and promote conversion in the other direction—that is, from Christianity to Hinduism. In March 2014, the Indian Supreme Court ruled that anyone who "reconverted" (a word pregnant with significance) to Hinduism, even if his parents, grandparents, or great-grandparents were Christian, could return to the "fold of the community and regain his membership (and therefore benefits) that were available to members of Scheduled Castes."[2] These benefits include grants for housing, education, vehicles, and reserved seats in government colleges and legislative bodies, among others.

Undoubtedly, the acts of witness, evangelism, propagation, and sharing the faith's main message are important parts of both Islam and Christianity. They are, it seems, particularly integral to Christian faith. Over the years, conversions to both faiths have become a bone of contention in India and Sri Lanka, but in recent years, the target of anti-conversion legislation seems largely to be Christianity.

---

2 K. P. Manu, *Malabar Cements Ltd vs Chairman, Scrutiny Committee for Verification of Community Certificate,* February 26, 2015, Bench: Dipak Misra, V. Gopala Gowda, https://indiankanoon.org/doc/98912765/, accessed February 9, 2018.

The Makings of a New Hinduism

One of the most striking developments in the past twenty years has been the growing influence of the sociopolitical ideology known as Hindutva. The politics of Hindutva, as represented by the agenda and policies of India's ruling party, the BJP, cannot be separated from large grassroots movements like the Vishwa Hindu Parishad (VHP) and the Rashtriya Swayamsevak Sangh (RSS). These paramilitary organizations, with their well-knit networks of *shakas*, or cells, in the hundreds of villages throughout India, provide the organizational backbone of the BJP—a grassroots strength and presence not available to any other political party. The recent win in Northeast India can in part be attributed to the influence of RSS-funded schools like the Ekal Vidyalaya and the Vanavasi Kalyan Ashram, which helped to soften negative attitudes toward the RSS and BJP by conducting free tutorials for school children among the poor, mainly Christian tribal communities. Such efforts are in fact part of a long-term strategy of religious, cultural, and political proselytization whereby Indian Tribals or Adivasis ("forest dwellers")—who generally do not come from Hindu backgrounds in any meaningful sense—are aggressively recruited to Hinduism and the Hindutva ideology.

In current and popular perspective, both in India and in the West, the Hindutva ideology of the BJP and of those in the *Sangh Parivar* (family of Hindu-nationalist organizations) are assumed to be "Hindu" and closely aligned to "Hinduism" in the religious and non-native[3] sense of the word. Many today think of Hinduism as a single, easily identifiable "world religion"[4] that we read about in school text books and see represented in the media.

---

3 For more on the distinction between "religious" and "native" definitions of the term "Hindu," refer to Robert Frykenberg's *Constructions of Hinduism: At the Nexus of History and Religion* (New Delhi: Critical Quest, 2009).

4 This categorization of Hinduism began in 1893 at the first World's Parliament of Religions, which took place in Chicago. To explore more of the origins and concept of "Hinduism" as a single world religion, see Richard King, "Orientalism and the Modern Myth of 'Hinduism,'" *Numen* 46, no. 2 (1999): 146-85.

However, it was not until the aggressive propagation of a reconstructed "neo-Hinduism" in the nineteenth century that the term "Hinduism" came to signify a unified and inclusive religious entity in India and the West. The historian Robert Frykenberg points out that the concept of "Hinduism" that is used today across the world in popular parlance was first used to describe anyone or anything native to the entire region of South Asia.[5] The term "Hindavi," as it was known in Arabic and Persian, was used to distinguish between the native (holder of the faith) and the unbeliever who was referred to as "kafir." Frykenberg writes that when early Europeans came to South Asia, they described what they saw by distinguishing between people who were indigenous—"Hindoo"—and people who were not. It was not uncommon for indigenous Christians to be called "Hindoo Christians" or, similarly, native Muslims to be called "Hindoo Muslims."[6] Therefore, the term "Hindu," before the revisions of the nineteenth century, referred to anything or anyone native to India.

Modern Hinduism we see today and the one that took shape over the nineteenth and early twentieth centuries does not necessarily correspond neatly with the vast diversity and dynamism of religious traditions in India. Furthermore, in a continent where thousands of deities are worshiped and where followers of Buddhism, Jainism, Islam, Zoroastrianism, Judaism, and Christianity trace their ancestry back thousands of years, it is probably insuperably difficult to think of neo-Hinduism as the one overarching, all-inclusive religious system of the subcontinent.

To a great extent, the modern neo-Hindu reform movement was shaped by high-caste Brahmins who were responsible for reading and translating religious texts and laws for the British scholars and elites.[7] Romila Thapar suggests that the new Hinduism fortified with strong Brahmanical teachings was now combined with elements of "upper

---

5 Frykenberg, *Constructions of Hinduism*, 525.

6 Ibid.

7 King, "Orientalism and the Modern Myth of 'Hinduism,'" 172.

caste belief and ritual [and] with one eye on Christian and Islamic models."⁸ Hindu reformers were faced with the challenge of how to make Hinduism more comparable to the Judeo-Christian (and even Islamic) conception of the nature of religion and thus undertook an effort to verify the historical accuracy of deities and sacralize their purported birthplaces such as Ayodhya for Lord Rama or Mathura for Lord Krishna.⁹ From their effort to emulate Abrahamic faiths, these reformers also sought to reconstruct Hinduism so as to marginalize and even condemn the idol-worship of ordinary believers and instead place greater emphasis on a canon of Hindu scriptures that they were developing. They thus devoted great energy to arguing for the authority, antiquity, and coherence of that body of Hindu writings, particularly the Vedas. Other additions to the new version of Hinduism formulated and propagated by the Hindu reformers included the support of the ecclesiastical authority of the Brahmins as well as the legitimacy and urgency of proselytization.¹⁰

One episode helps to illustrate how the Hindu reform movement was transformed from a relatively isolated and parochial intellectual initiative to a major cultural and political phenomenon with far-reaching international impact. This was the appearance of a young Hindu reformer, Swami Vivekananda, at the first World's Parliament of Religions in Chicago in 1893. Vivekananda arrived uninvited, but his address is seen by many as the "turning point"¹¹ in the modern Hindu revival. In the first sentence he uttered to the gathering, he asserted that Hinduism was the "mother of all religions":¹² "I thank you in the name of the mother of all religions; and I thank you in

---

8 Romila Thapar, "Syndicated Moksha?" *Seminar*, no. 313 (September 1985): 21.

9 King, "Orientalism and the Modern Myth of 'Hinduism,'" 173.

10 Ibid., 172.

11 Jyotirmaya Sharma, *Hindutva: Exploring the Idea of Hindu Nationalism* (New Delhi: Viking, 2003), 75.

12 Ibid., 76.

the name of millions and millions of Hindu people of all classes and sects. . . . I am proud to belong to a religion which has taught the world both tolerance and universal acceptance."[13]

On the double assumption that Vivekananda enjoyed the authority to speak on behalf of millions of Hindus and that these Hindus constituted a single community sharing a univocal tradition, he announced that Hinduism had taught and continued to teach the world about tolerance and had always welcomed people of different faiths to its shores. On the one hand, Vivekananda's statement at once unified and elevated Hinduism to the level of a tutor with a single, authoritative message. On the other hand, it demoted other faiths to the status of inferior pupils, who could, at best, merely learn from this ancient and tolerant faith.

While Vivekananda thus found a global platform to reconceive and reconstruct Hinduism, it in fact remained a highly disparate set of beliefs and practices that had for millennia defied self-definition and order, and where literally thousands of deities were worshiped. Indeed, Hindu faith and practice was less a monolith than a subcontinental swirl of rituals, festivals, and devotional practices. But Vivekanada was undeterred; building on the work of previous modernist Hindu reformers, he sought to turn Hinduism into something that deserved global respect and recognition. He recast it as a religious tradition that, he would argue, outdid all other religious traditions across every conceivable dimension. In Vivekananda's reconstruction, Hinduism became, all at once, supremely ancient, authoritative, coherent, flexible, reasonable, inclusive, and tolerant.

Over time, many Western elites became convinced that the "Hinduism" as reconstructed by Vivekananda and others was a single ancient and inclusive religion and that it represented most, if

---

13 Swami Vivekananda, "Paper on Hinduism," first World's Parliament of Religions, Chicago, September 19, 1893, http://www.viveksamity.org/user/doc/CHICAGO-SPEECH.pdf, accessed July 20, 2017.

not all, the peoples of South Asia.[14] In their eyes, notes historian Christopher Bayly, this synthesized version of Hinduism with its sacred scriptures, ecclesial structures, and focus on a single Supreme Being seemed to parallel their own Christian and Jewish traditions in some respects but also to surpass them in other ways, particularly in its putative inclusiveness, flexibility, and tolerance. Bayly notes that the rhetoric around the new "Hinduism" conveyed an underlying unity of Hinduism by resonating with the preconceived beliefs of Westerners. For Westerners, by and large, a single, unified religion required a single, coherent textual tradition revolving around the interpretation of an ancient, authoritative set of sacred scriptures. Vivekananda and other reformers convinced a growing number of Westerners that Hinduism was a coherent, respectable religion *according to Western standards*.[15] In the eyes of the Hindu reformers, the fact that Westerners could recognize and respect Hinduism as a powerful and ancient tradition that even outperformed Western religions on their own preferred terms enhanced the prestige and social power of their reconstructed "Hinduism."

This view of Hinduism as a supremely coherent and ancient religion and one, moreover, that represented most Indians, was particularly welcome at a time of increasing national struggle and unrest. This reconstruction made it possible for Hinduism to go from being a site of contestation and fluidity among profoundly opposed local traditions and practices to be a coherent and inspiring focus of cultural unity, national identity, and anti-colonial political mobilization. It also made Westerners doubt the necessity or reasonableness of Christian missionary efforts. Why would any Indian need another religion if their indigenous and ancient religion is so similar to, if not superior to, Christianity? Why would Indians need to go beyond their cultural and religious boundaries to find a non-native religion? Within the terms set by the modern Hindu reformers and many of their Western interlocutors, the questions appeared to answer themselves.

---

14   Frykenberg, *Constructions of Hinduism*, 523-50.

15   Christopher A. Bayly, *Indian Society and the Making of the British Empire* (Cambridge: Cambridge University Press, 1987), 162.

Hindutva

To an outsider looking in, this version of unified Hinduism might have seemed remarkably tidy and perhaps even boring, having been stripped of its fanciful and colorful mythologies and rituals. Yet this version of Hinduism is the progenitor of the political ideology and nationalistic religion of Hindutva. Indeed, Hindutva is the political and nationalist child of the reconstructed Hinduism formulated and propagated by Vivekananda and his fellow modern reformers of the nineteenth and early twentieth centuries. Vivekananda passed away in 1902. Only two decades later, Hindutva was already a fully formed ideology and social movement, with the foundation of the Hindu-nationalist mother-ship, the RSS, in 1925.[16]

Perhaps the clearest understanding of what motivated the founders of Hindutva to establish the RSS and later the BJP comes from sociologist Ashis Nandy. At the heart of the Hindutva project, he argues, is a profound disappointment, even disgust, with the weakness and deficiencies in Hinduism. Vinayak Damodar Savarkar was the Marathi intellectual and anti-colonialist firebrand who coined the term "Hindutva." In fact, Savarkar frequently compared Hinduism *unfavorably* with the Semitic religions—Christianity, Judaism, and Islam—because in his mind the former lacked a uniform and well organized structure that was "capable of being a sustaining ideology for an imperious state."[17] He thus saw Hinduism as "effeminate, spineless and non-martial and, thus, as vulnerable to the more aggressive faith such as Islam and Christianity."[18] Nandy suggests that RSS leaders like Savarkar

---

16 Beginning with the formation of the Arya Samaj in 1875, the Hindu Sabha in 1909, the Hindu Mahasabha in 1915, the Hindu Sanghatan in 1921, and finally the Rashtriya Swayamsevak Sangh (RSS) in 1925 with its political wing, the Jana Sangh in 1951, a consolidated network of strident and secretive groups arose that exists to promote the ideology of Hindutva.

17 Ashis Nandy, *The Romance of the State and the Fate of Dissent in the Tropics* (New Delhi: Oxford University Press, 2003), 80.

18 Ashis Nandy, *Creating a Nationality: The Ramjanmabhumi Movement and Fear of the Self* (Delhi: Oxford University Press, 2010), 83.

secretly admired the masculine strands of the Semitic faiths, especially European Christianity. Hindu nationalists firmly believed that Hinduism had been weakened because the pure and rational Vedic religion had become sullied by beliefs and practices that were fantastical and ignorant. Dayanand Saraswati, a Hindu reformer who in the nineteenth century founded the Vedic-centered reformist movement known as the Arya Samaj, reserved his harshest criticism for the native Indian religious movements such as Buddhism, Jainism, and various forms of Hindu metaphysics. He also attacked Hindu sects, known as Vaishnavites, that worshiped Lord Vishnu. Saraswati deplored the fact that "the Jain idols were always naked and represented a being who was seated in a contemplative mood and renounced the world, while on the contrary the Vaishnava idols symbolized gods having by their sides goddesses, who were dressed out in fine style and excited lascivious thoughts by their lewd charms and licentious looks."[19] Saraswati blamed Hindu mythology and idol worship for making Indians superstitious and ignorant. He also argued that practices such as wearing *rudraksha* beads (holy beads), burning incense, or smearing one's forehead with a tilak or covering one's body in ashes made Indians weak and unable to fight to preserve their culture and their national life. They were no different, he said, from "donkeys and pigs and other animals who wallow in dust."[20]

The other reason for the formation of Hindutva was to bring order to a religion that had been given over to indolence and chaos. Hindus, the reformers felt, needed to be roused to defend and fight for their land and their culture. Hinduism, in its current irrational form, was a chaotic and disorganized faith divided by its numerous schools of philosophies, thousands of deities, and its fascination with myths and legends. Hindu reformers such as Saraswati, Aurobindo, Vivekananda, and Savarkar[21] believed that these weaknesses and flaws

---

19   Sharma, *Hindutva*, 32.

20   Ibid., 31.

21   For more on motivating forces behind the work of Saraswati, Aurobindo, Vivekananda, and Savarkar, see Sharma, *Hindutva*.

in popular Hinduism had made Hindus "incapable of resisting the more organized, rational faiths."[22]

As historian Robert Frykenberg suggests, these efforts were a part of a calculated institutional, ideological and political agenda. While working to revise the structure, beliefs, and practices of Hinduism, Hindu reformers infused the new faith with a political and nationalistic emphasis.[23] And historian Romila Thapar suggests that efforts to codify Hinduism into a single religious rubric created what she terms "Syndicated Hinduism."[24] Over the years, Syndicated Hinduism provided the means for Hindu nationalists to propagate their ideology through cultural and political organizations such as the RSS and the Hindu Mahasabha and, much later, the Vishwa Hindu Parishad, the BJP, and the Bajrang Dal.

Syndicated Hinduism's importance has become particularly apparent within communities of transnational Hindus—the Hindu diaspora—who are seeking a version of their faith that they can respect and propagate as a "peer competitor" with Christianity and other world religions. Thapar maintains that the diaspora communities with their tremendous wealth and influence continue to provide the basis and support for Syndicated Hinduism.[25] We see versions of a sanitized and Westernized Hinduism in films that are directed toward the growing numbers of Indians living in the United States and the United Kingdom. Indeed, Syndicated Hinduism has become an influential, transnational, syndicated enterprise. Once the RSS and its sister organizations were shadowy and secretive. This was particularly so in the aftermath of

---

22 Nandy, *Creating a Nationality*, 83.

23 Robert Eric Frykenberg, "Constructions of Hinduism at the Nexus of History and Religion." *Journal of Interdisciplinary History* 23, no. 3 (1993): 548.

24 The concept of Syndicated Hinduism comes from Thapar, "Syndicated Moksha?" 14-22.

25 Romila Thapar, "Syndicated Hinduism," in *Hinduism Reconsidered*, ed. Gunther D. Sontheimer and Hermann Kulke (New Delhi: Manohar, 1991), 77.

the assassination of Mahatma Gandhi, whose murderer enjoyed close links to several individuals actively involved in the RSS and the Hindu Mahasabha. Today, however, the RSS enjoys unprecedented respect, visibility, and reach. The organization has thousands of units spread uniformly over the country. Its members sit in parliament. The BJP, while politically powerful, has always remained dependent on fringe groups such as the RSS and the Shiv Sena.

Conversion

At the heart of any form of religious traditionalism or revivalism, whether Christian, Hindu, Buddhist, Muslim, Jain, or Sikh, is the perceived threat of change to established rituals, practices, social order, and what one may term the "traditional way of life." The prospect of large numbers of Hindus converting from the religion and culture of their birth to either Christianity or Islam represents an existential threat that is simultaneously cultural, religious, national, and geopolitical. It represents a sword of Damocles hanging over Hindu values, traditions, and customs that are ingrained in the social and religious fabric of Indian life. Additionally, in the eyes of Hindu nationalists, conversion to either Christianity or Islam represents the corruption of an Indian's proper identity and the betrayal of loyalty. Conversion to Christianity is not only seen as a rejection of a person's Indian identity but also as the taking on of a foreign identity.

Large-scale conversions to Christianity in the late nineteenth and early twentieth centuries sparked these fears and helped to intensify movements of Hindu counter-mobilization and counter-proselytization to an extreme degree. In 1871, the Indian Census showed that the majority of Catholic as well as Protestant adherents in India were non-Brahmin and were drawn from the lowest castes. By 1931, for example, a vast number of outcastes[26] in Andhra Pradesh had converted

---

26   In this chapter the terms "outcaste," "depressed classes," and "untouchable" are used interchangeably. All these terms refer to a people who exist beyond the boundaries of a caste and who, despite legislation to prevent exclusion, remain on the margins of Indian society even today.

to Christianity. In some areas of the state there were converts in every untouchable hamlet.[27] In Guntur district alone, 57 percent of the district converted to Christianity. Malas and Madigas, the main untouchable caste groups, made up most of the converts in the state and by 1900 constituted an established and flourishing Christian community with ordained ministers and established churches.

Christian mission movements since the early 1800s were designed and geared to evangelize the upper castes and were based on the then popular notion of "Sanskritization," which presupposed that the lower sections of the community imitated the lifestyle of the higher, more dominant castes. A majority of mainstream Christian missions believed that Christianity would percolate downward from the upper castes to the lower castes and therefore much effort was put into evangelizing the upper castes during the early 1800s. The dramatic results of mass conversions of non-Brahmin, and the lowest untouchable caste groups, to Christianity during the 1870s was received with "mixed emotions"[28] by Protestant missions at the time. In 1928, Dr. John Mott, chair of the International Missionary Council, suggested that American Methodist Bishop and missionary to India J. Waskom Pickett[29] (then editor of the journal *Indian Witness*) conduct an "impartial scientific survey of

---

27 G. A. Oddie, "Christian Conversion among Non-Brahmins in Andhra Pradesh: With Special Reference to the Dornakal Diocese, c.1900–36," in *Religion in South Asia: Religious Conversion and Revival Movements in South Asia in Medieval and Modern Times*, ed. G. A. Oddie (New Delhi: Manohar, 1991), 95-124.

28 Susan Billington Harper, *In the Shadow of the Mahatma: Bishop V. S. Azariah and the Travails of Christianity in British India* (Grand Rapids, MI: Eerdmans, 2000), 185.

29 Between 1930 and 1931, Bishop Pickett conducted a seminal study in collaboration with (and with the generous financial backing of) the Institute of Social and Religious Research. To date, Pickett's Study of Mass Movements remains the single largest database amassed on Dalit Christianity and its social and economic impact. For more information, see J. Waskom Pickett, *Christian Mass Movements in India: A Study with Recommendations* (New York: Abingdon Press, 1933).

ten or a dozen Christian conversion movements"[30] taking place in India. To be clear, Mott's motive was not enthusiasm for these mass conversions but rather the opposite: he feared that these movements were either not very deep or authentic or would prove an obstacle to the evangelization of India, or both.

The mass movements of conversion to Christianity in the middle of the eighteenth and nineteenth centuries presented a dramatic departure as thousands of outcastes moved from Hinduism to Christianity. Yet the clear majority of the converts to Christianity were the least "Hindu" of Indians—Dalits (outcastes) and Adivasis (tribal communities) who had lived on the periphery of traditional religious life. Writing in 1906 after studying the outcastes in India, Abbe Dubois, a French ethnographer, notes, "The idea that he was born to be in subjection to other castes was so ingrained in his mind that it never occurs to the Pariah to think his fate is anything but irrevocable."[31] Yet as Bishop J. Waskom Pickett's seminal study of the spiritual and social impact of the mass movements of conversion to Christianity[32] indicated, conversion promoted a radically positive sense of worth and will in the converts, so that over time a virtuous cycle was created where the empowered and mobilized converts were able to transform their lives and the lives of their families and community. "Christians have acquired a new concept of themselves," Pickett observed, and "this or a like concept has been accepted by their neighbors. Confirmation of this theory is provided by the decline of the use of the old term by which Christians in this area were known before their conversion. The term 'Chura' is falling into disuse. Hindu, Moslem, and Sikh informants told us that they seldom or never refer to the Christians in their villages by the old caste name."[33]

---

30   G. Arthur McPhee, *The Road to Delhi: Bishop Pickett Remembered, 1890-1981* (Bangalore: SIACS Press, 2005), 185.

31   John C. B. Webster, *A History of Dalith Christians in India* (San Francisco: Mellen Research University Press, 1992), 23.

32   Pickett, *Christian Mass Movements in India.*

33   Ibid., 149.

The idea that Christianity could transform the economic and social lives of its adherents was nothing new. Since the nineteenth century, conversionary forms of Protestantism had been consistently associated with lower levels of alcohol consumption and drug use. In many countries, revivalist Protestants helped spur the temperance movement in reaction to a rapid increase in the supply and consumption of distilled alcohol. Historians suggest that temperance was associated with economic uplift in both frontier and urban communities[34] and Protestant activists helped spread temperance worldwide.

Although conversions to Christianity had occurred steadily in India from the sixteenth century on, it was not until the middle of the eighteenth century that the population of Indian Christians rose dramatically. As a primarily rural phenomenon, it was not uncommon for an entire village comprising a few hundred people to come to Christ at the same time.[35] At the start of World War I there were more than a million outcaste converts to Christianity and many more followed during the next two decades. Perhaps it was the spectacular size and speed at which vast numbers of outcaste Hindus became Christians that prompted Hindu nationalists to cast aspersions on the validity of these conversions and to assume that they occurred because of material or instrumental reasons and that the converts were merely "rice Christians."

The opposition of Hindu reformers and later Hindu nationalists to the outcaste conversions to Christianity was intense. Groups such as the Arya Samaj engaged in aggressive counter-missionary efforts, sometimes using the traditional Hindu cleansing or purification ceremony known as to convert—or reconvert—Christians to Hinduism. Opposition also came from Mahatma Gandhi, who shared with Hindu reformers such

---

34 For more on this issue, see Jack S. Blocker, *American Temperance Movements: Cycles of Reform* (Boston: Twayne Publishers, 1989); Robert D. Woodberry, "The Origins of the Temperance Movement: A Comparative Historical Analysis," paper presented at the national meeting of the American Sociological Association, New York, August 16-20, 1996.

35 Pickett, *Christian Mass Movements in India.*

as Vivekananda a nationalist pride in the unity and respectability of Hinduism and an optimism about its potential to be reformed. Gandhi styled himself a defender of the rights of the depressed classes, and he was open to the influence of religion in political life (and thus stood in contrast to Jawaharlal Nehru, who saw religious mobilization as an inherent threat to the secular India he envisioned). Also, at this stage in his life, Gandhi knew a great deal about the teachings of Christ and enjoyed Christian hymns and prayers, thanks in no small part to close friends such as C. F. Andrews who knew him from his time in South Africa. Nevertheless, despite being more than familiar with the Christian gospel and sympathetic to the person of Jesus Christ, whom he venerated, Gandhi mounted increasingly intense public attacks on Christian missions, accusing them of "co-opting"[36] untouchables (outcastes) into the Christian fold.

Specifically, Gandhi demanded that Christian missions confine their work with untouchables to social and economic uplift and not interfere—as he saw it—in areas of religious confession and commitment. For many mass movement converts who were untouchables, Gandhi's position was deeply unsettling,[37] for he was taking a skeptical view of conversion:

> I believe that there is no such thing as conversion from one faith to another in the accepted sense of the term. It is a highly personal matter for the individual and his God. . . . It is a conviction daily growing upon me that the great and rich Christian missions will render true service to India, if they can persuade themselves to confine their activities to humanitarian service without the ulterior motive of converting India or at least her unsophisticated villagers to Christianity and destroying their social superstructure which notwithstanding its many defects has stood now from time immemorial.[38]

---

36 Harper, *In the Shadow of the Mahatma*, 302.

37 M. Judith Brown, "Who is an Indian?" in *Missions, Nationalism, and the End of Empire*, ed. Brian Stanley and Alaine M. Low (Grand Rapids, MI: Eerdmans, 2003), 111-31.

38 Ibid., 125.

Even as Mahatma Gandhi publicly excoriated Christian missions for what he saw as unfairly luring the poor away from Hinduism, Indian Christians such as the first Indian Anglican Bishop, V. S. Azariah, urged missionaries to redouble their efforts to evangelize the outcastes since "the widespread and deep unrest among the depressed classes . . . constitutes a Call of God to the Christian Church which it cannot ignore."[39] Azariah had spent most of his tenure as bishop trying to rescue the untouchables from the "social superstructures" of caste and enforced exclusion. He worked hard to eradicate caste-centeredness of Indian culture within the church and replace it with what he called a "new brotherhood."[40] He insisted—and faced tremendous resistance from his congregants—that converts from different caste groups were required to attend the same churches, drink from the same communion cup, go to the same school, and eat together in public celebrations like weddings and harvest festivals.

The presumption of Gandhi—and more recently of Mohan Bhagwat, the leader of the RSS, who has publicly questioned the motivation of Mother Teresa's service to the poor—is that Christians manipulate the disadvantaged to receive and adopt a religious message in exchange for material help.[41] But for Azariah and for the many Indian Christians who work among the poor, Christianity alone embodies a life of dignity and hope for a future free of degradation and subservience. Conversion offers them a social and religious identity rooted in a personal faith in a loving God rather than in an identity that is dependent on one's social position or the recognition of higher castes. In the words of one of the converts who came to

---

39 Harper, *In the Shadow of the Mahatma*, 3.

40 Ibid., 249.

41 Rajendra Sharma, "Conversion Was Mother Teresa's Real Aim, RSS Chief Mohan Bhagwat Says," *The Times of India,* February 24, 2015, http://timesofindia.indiatimes.com/india/Conversion-was-Mother-Teresas-real-aim-RSS-chief-Mohan-Bhagwat-says/articleshow/46348555.cms, accessed February 8, 2018.

Christ in the early 1930s: "I wanted to become a Christian, so I could be a man. None of us was a man. We were dogs. Only Jesus could make men out of us."[42]

Nationalism

In India today, the ideologies of Vivekananda and Savarkar have become increasingly and unconsciously absorbed and enjoy a growing public impact. Indeed, the highest levels of government reflect their influence. Consequently, there are increasing demands on non-Hindus—particularly Christians and Muslims—to prove their devotion to the *maatrebhoomi* (motherland). Since the new Hinduism is now regarded as *the* religion of India with the exclusive authority to speak for all Indians, any conversion from Hinduism is a betrayal of the "motherland," a loss of one's Indian identity, and a threat to national unity. Referring to the Hindu nationalist family of organizations, which includes groups such as the RSS and Bajrang Dal, Ainslie Embree writes:

> National unity, they argue, means an integrated, homogenous society; and this can only be found by recognizing that Indian culture and Hindu culture are synonymous terms. This means, of course, that the place of the religious minorities is at once called into question, for the essence of Islam and Christianity—the belief in salvation through membership in a collective social body—seems to be a denial of national unity.[43]

The Hindu nationalist movement's emphasis on the acceptance of and tolerance for other religions by Hinduism is an essential aspect of their political ideology. Recalling Vivekananda's speech to the World's Parliament of Religions where he spoke of "tolerance and acceptance" of Hinduism, which is the "mother of all religions." By focusing on tolerance, the Hindu nationalist can effectively deny differences between Hinduism and other religious traditions and particularly between Christianity and Islam.[44] However, Hinduism, notes Embree, is neither truly tolerant nor gently absorptive:

---

42   Pickett, *Christian Mass Movements*, 36.

43   Ainslee T. Embree, *Utopias in Conflict: Religion and Nationalism in Modern India* (Delhi: Oxford University Press, 1992), 47.

44   Ibid., 23-24.

> Political issues involving the rights of minorities were being obscured by the assertion that Hinduism was uniquely tolerant and willing to absorb other systems into itself. That the Islamic community in India wanted neither to be absorbed or tolerated seems to have occurred to a very few exponents of Hindu tolerance, but neither is it self-evident that Hinduism is tolerant and absorptive in the sense that has so often been claimed.[45]

In Embree's view, Hinduism's relationship to other religions is not one of liberal toleration or gentle absorption but rather one of "encapsulation."[46] By this he means that historically Hinduism has remained at its core relatively uninfluenced and unchanged by its encounters with other religious traditions and cultures. When a religious tradition such as Islam arrived in India, Hinduism encapsulated it—in the sense of enclosed and contained it—but remained the dominant and unchanging religion and culture within India. The implication is that Hinduism as the mainstream religious culture of India does not so much seek to foster a tolerant mutual understanding or co-existence with the religious Other as to dominate and colonize the religious Other within an overarching cultural and religious framework whose superior antiquity, wisdom, and tolerance all must accept without question. Indeed, this approach is even more domineering and effective precisely because it is carried on under the rubric of a professed, self-congratulatory tolerance and gentle absorption.

In fact, however, as Mahatma Gandhi himself illustrates, Hinduism displays a profound intolerance of those who seek to question and change their religious identity and tradition and to transcend caste and religious boundaries. This intolerance is something outcaste converts constantly discover and experience. If all this is true, then the compelling motivation of the BJP to win over the entire Christian Northeast is more than simply political. It is rooted in a deep desire to secure the wholesale and ultimate allegiance of a non-Hindu religious community. For the Hindu nationalists cannot accept that the non-Hindu religious

---

45   Ibid., 25.
46   Ibid., 24.

identity of Northeast Christians as well as other Indian Christians—which revolves around a commitment to a God who is above and beyond the Indian nation-state and to a transnational community that is not circumscribed by the territory of Bharat—is fully compatible with complete and proper loyalty as full citizens of the Indian nation. In a sense, then, the deeper Hindu nationalist objection to Christianity is not that it is geo-politically too "colonial" or neo-colonial or foreign. Rather, the objection is that Christianity is too culturally anti-colonial in that it refuses to be absorbed or encapsulated by neo-Hindu nationalism as a subservient internal colony. To put it another way, Christianity refuses to pay obeisance to the cultural metropole the Hindutva brigade aspires to construct.

Chapter 2

Drinking a Cup of Nectar
The Transformation of Lakshmibai Tilak

Sean Doyle

In the late nineteenth century in a hill station situated by the Western Ghats of Maharashtra, near Pune, a high-caste Hindu woman named Lakshmibai Tilak (1868-1936) found herself in a difficult predicament. Her family had been suddenly displaced due to a plague outbreak, and after being quarantined in an isolation camp, the Tilaks were fortunate to find temporary housing in a predominantly Muslim area. Lakshmibai, intensely scrupulous in matters of traditional purity, was deeply troubled that in their new location there was no one suitable in terms of caste status to draw water for her, thus risking defilement were she to drink provisions obtained by ritually impure hands. Frustratingly, she also could not acquire water for herself without public embarrassment because this would be beneath her dignity due to her elevated social station. Her husband Narayan Vaman Tilak (1861-1919), who had recently converted to Christianity, tried to reassure her that it was true religion to care properly for one's body by slaking thirst with available water, but she was in mounting inner turmoil over the situation.

Lakshmibai eventually swallowed, in sheer desperation, a mouthful from a pot that a Muslim woman had procured for them, despite her initial feeling of violent nausea at the supposedly unclean act. Her body reacted to the water with convulsing and vomiting, as though she had consumed virulent poison. Nevertheless, Lakshmibai would later refer to this deeply affecting experience as sipping a cup of nectar because the harrowing decision to drink was the first in a series of breakthroughs whereby her caste and purity sensibilities were radically transformed under the influence of Narayan's Christian faith upon her social conscience. She subsequently converted to Christianity and threw herself into charitable outreach with her husband to low-castes and Dalits, to prostitutes, to plague victims, and to people of other faiths. Simultaneous with this profound shifting of beliefs, Lakshmibai also increasingly grew in her self-understanding as a woman of great creativity, able to make worthwhile literary contributions of equal merit as those of her husband, a well-regarded Marathi poet.

Lakshmibai's progression from a person with a deep consciousness of social stratification to one who willingly breached traditional boundaries of caste and gender is a fascinating case study of the influence of Christian social values and ethics. Indeed, the Christian message of equality and dignity before God, embodied in the actions of her husband Narayan, was the primary catalyst for Lakshmibai's religious conversion, her compassion and charity toward the marginalized, and her development as a woman writer. The deep impulses driving Lakshmibai to promote cultural renewal were sparked and nurtured through her shift in religious identity. Her conversion to Christianity did not result in an unmooring from her cultural and literary heritage, but rather it inspired her to cultivate her skills and plumb the depths of her indigenous birthright. She immersed herself in the Marathi milieu and through artful words and reforming actions contributed to the rich renewal that was taking place in Maharashtra. The story of her striking personal transformation challenges the dominant narratives about conversion in India that assume it must lead to cultural alienation or dislocation.

Social and Intellectual Context in Nineteenth-Century Maharashtra

Lakshmibai's conversion to Christianity and reassessment of societal divisions took place amid dramatic social and religious reformations in nineteenth-century Maharashtra. Many Hindus were undergoing a deep cultural negotiation between their own traditional assumptions regarding caste and gender and the newly infused values coming from abroad. Within the British-controlled Bombay Presidency, colonial administrators and especially Christian missionaries began to disseminate new egalitarian ideas into the cultural stream of Western India. The Bombay Education Society opened primary and high schools, as well as the Elphinstone College, named after an educational reformer who believed in the promotion of modern English values.[1] And the American Marathi Mission, composed of Protestant Congregationalists, opened the first school for girls in 1818. The introduction of Western concepts of liberal humanism and Christian charity among many of the Maharashtrian intelligentsia challenged the unquestioned acceptance of the traditional social and religious hierarchies.[2]

A growing number of these English-educated elites found themselves at a crossroads and began to reformulate their beliefs. They sought cultural and religious renewal through efforts for reform, to address the perceived inequalities and injustices suffered by the outcastes, the poor, and women.[3] Such appraisals and critiques of the social status quo were spread by the growth of Marathi newspapers and magazines,[4] whose patrons included Western-educated Indian

---

1 Stanley Wolpert, *Tilak and Gokhale: Revolution and Reform in the Making of Modern India* (Berkeley: University of California Press, 1962), 6.

2 Rosalind O'Hanlon, *Caste, Conflict, and Ideology: Mahatma Jotirao Phule and Low Caste Protest in Nineteenth-Century Western India* (New York: Cambridge University Press, 1985), 89.

3 Matthew Lederle, *Philosophical Trends in Modern Maharashtra* (Bombay: Popular Prakashan, 1976), 421.

4 Wolpert, *Tilak and Gokhale*, 6-7.

intellectuals who debated the "social change, political tutelage, and scientific advances" that accompanied British rule.[5]

Christian social teachings also made their mark upon the minds of these Western-educated Hindu men and women. The earliest social reformers in India were the Bengali leaders of the Brahmo Samaj, such as Ram Mohan Roy, who advocated for a "purified" monotheism influenced equally by Christ's ethical teachings and by an iconoclastic interpretation of the Vedas. Roy and the Brahmos championed the uplift of women, openly criticized polygamy and sati, and sought to undercut social stratifications. They deemed these traditions to be obstacles to the growth of national unity and solidarity. So, they organized inter-caste marriages and social functions that mixed diverse groups of peoples.[6] When Keshub Chunder Sen, an influential Brahmo who was also impressed by the person of Christ, visited Bombay in 1864, a Monotheistic Association arose that developed into the Prarthana Samaj (Prayer Society). The Prarthana Samaj's members thought of the Samaj as a protest movement within Hinduism that called for a return to social patterns from antiquity that antedated the later hierarchical accretions.[7]

R. G. Bhandarkar (1837-1925) argued strenuously during the meetings of the Prarthana Samaj for women's rights and abolitionist reforms.[8] Another pivotal member, M. G. Ranade (1842-1901), was a compelling voice for the remarriage of Hindu widows, so that they would not be left in destitution. The Samaj set up an orphanage and a shelter for the homeless, and they embarked upon pioneering educational work for women and the depressed classes.[9] In addition, the Samaj

---

5   O'Hanlon, *Caste, Conflict, and Ideology*, 50.

6   K. R. Shirsat, *Narayan Vaman Tilak: Poet and Patriot* (Bombay: Bombay Tract and Book Society, 1979), 10.

7   Lederle, *Philosophical Trends*, 82.

8   Ibid.

9   Ibid., 84-86. Although the majority of these reformers were Brahmin men, there also were prominent women such as Ramabai Ranade and

retrieved the egalitarian emphases of the Marathi poet-saints (*bhaktas*) of the past, such as the seventeenth-century Tukaram, who asserted that love (*bhakti*) for a personal God was of singular importance, rather than caste identification or requirements. They believed that one who is deeply devoted to God, even if he or she is an untouchable, has the spiritual status of a true Brahmin.[10]

While a great many of the Maharashtrian reformers came from the Brahmin social order, there were voices from the lower castes that were just as provocative. The *Shudra* reformer Jyotirao Phule (1827-90), inspired by his education in a Scottish mission school in Pune and subsequent work in their orphanage, established schools for girls and for untouchable children.[11] Mission schools were often important conduits to Indian social reformers of the values of equality and the dignity of all. Though not a full-fledged convert to Christianity, Phule was a Hindu reformer deeply influenced by the example and teachings of Jesus Christ.[12] Phule developed a conception of humanity that was based on the view that the monotheistic God was ruler of all, providing people with rationality, dignity, equal rights, and respect regardless of birth status. He instituted the "Society for the Teaching of Knowledge to Mahars, Mangs and Other People," founding village and night schools, promoting instruction in occupational skills, and launching essay and debating competitions meant to promote greater confidence and expressiveness in Dalit youths.[13] In 1873, Phule initiated the Satyashodhaka Samaj (Society for Truth Seekers), which openly challenged Brahminical domination and the disenfranchisement of

---

Pandita Ramabai Sarasvati who worked for the social uplift of Indian females of all castes.

10 O'Hanlon, *Caste, Conflict, and Ideology*, 225.

11 Roger Hedlund, *Indian Christianity: An Alternative Reading* (New Delhi: Christian World Imprint, 2016), 86.

12 Ibid., 89.

13 O'Hanlon, *Caste, Conflict, and Ideology*, 234-36.

the masses by circulating pamphlets and books such as the incendiary *Slavery, Priestcraft Exposed*.[14]

During such radical challenges to the socially sanctioned hierarchy in late nineteenth-century Maharashtra, it was not so improbable that Lakshmibai would be drawn to dispute the traditional mores. Many Hindus from diverse strata of society were questioning such assumptions. What was distinct about Lakshmibai was that as a high-caste Chitpavan Brahmin woman, her encounter with Christianity went beyond mere influence. She became a convert. She was introduced to the social teachings of Christ not in an indirect manner through exposure to a Hindu reform movement but directly to the implications of the Christian gospel through the embodied love and compassion for others that her husband showed. He managed to retain his broad Indian cultural identity while reaching out charitably to the marginalized. This transformative encounter with Christ's ethics through the actions of her husband Narayan profoundly reoriented her understanding of caste and gender distinctions—and herself.

Lakshmibai's Restrictive Upbringing

To appreciate the extent of the personal transformation enacted in Lakshmibai's life, it is essential to sketch her austerely conservative upbringing. By her own admission, movingly recounted in her beautiful autobiography *Smriti Chitre* (Memory Sketches), every aspect of Lakshmibai's social conditioning in a Hindu village prepared her to maintain distance from others, to view interaction with lower castes as polluting, and to adopt the traditionally prescribed role of a Hindu woman. Her father Narayan Gokhale was fixated on purity boundaries, going to great lengths to protect himself from any desecrating contact. He announced his decision to remain perpetually "holy" to his family with these words: "A low-caste Mahar (outcaste) was rinsing his mouth; a drop of his water splashed on me, and I am defiled. Pour water

---

14   Lederle, *Philosophical Trends*, 126.

over me, but do not touch me. I must bathe again."¹⁵ The young Lakshmibai was bewildered that her father even considered himself tainted at the touch of a Brahmin, a man of his own high caste. "What then of Marathas or even lower castes!" she exclaimed.¹⁶ If any visitors entered the home, Lakshmibai's mother was required to sprinkle water over their footprints after they departed; the children were even asked to wash thoroughly the salt and pepper before they were consumed during meals.

When Lakshmibai was eleven years old, her proposed marital union with Narayan Tilak, orchestrated by her sister's husband since her father "would never have found a son-in-law 'holy' enough to please him," was nearly called off. There was concern that according to strict religious sensibilities the Gokhale and Tilak lines might not auspiciously mix in marriage, although they were from the same Chitpavan Brahmin community.¹⁷ Lakshmibai's uncle, who was a Khambete in lineage, adopted her in a formal ceremony, so that the marriage could proceed according to proper caste specifications.

Whereas Lakshmibai's father was deeply concerned with ceremonial cleanliness, her new father-in-law Wamanrao Tilak was religious in a different manner. Lakshmibai made the following assessment: "his estimation of a person depended on goblins, sorcery, demon-possession, luck, planets, horoscopes, and the length and shape of fingers and toes."¹⁸ Wamanrao invoked the possession of himself by a fierce goddess every Friday night, and this deity proceeded to identify Lakshmibai and Narayan as sources of bad fortune for the Tilak family. Their inauspicious birth-status "under an evil star" was often blamed, usually by the direct accusations of the goddess, for

---

15 Lakshmibai Tilak, *I Follow After: An Autobiography*, trans. E. Josephine Inkster (Madras: Oxford University Press, 1950), 2. This is the standard English translation of Lakshmibai's *Smriti Chitre*.

16 Ibid., 3.

17 Ibid., 8-9.

18 Ibid., 15.

the tragic incidents that Wamanrao experienced, including the loss of a job and the death of his eldest daughter.

Sadly, Lakshmibai's father-in-law's disapproval extended even to his own wife Janakibai, who loved poetry and often composed lyrics for herself and read the book of Proverbs, provided by some missionary women. In a fit of rage, he seized all her poetic and biblical material and consigned it to the flames. He exulted in his traditionally sanctioned authority over Janakibai, treating her "like a slave, to the point of making her chop wood when she was pregnant."[19] A particularly troubling episode in Narayan's early life occurred after his beloved mother Janakibai had traveled a long distance in the hot season to join Wamanrao, who, away from home on business, had sent for her because of his "impending death." He was feigning sickness to test her, wanting to see if she would respond to his call.[20] Desiring to serve him, though exhausted from the journey, she requested his assistance in lifting a heavy brass water pot down from her head. Wamanrao became enraged, shouting, "I am not your servant." In full view of Narayan, he grabbed her by the throat, threw her to the ground, and proceeded to kick his wife savagely. She died eight days later.

These family tensions and tragedies during Lakshmibai's formative years planted deep-seated convictions about maintaining rigid caste distinctions and the determination of one's status at birth. Lakshmibai's grandson would later write: "this was the impression she carried from *both* the houses."[21] The roles of women were limited to serving the overbearing domestic and religious concerns of their scrupulous

---

19   Meera Kosambi, *Crossing Thresholds: Feminist Essays in Social History* (Ranikhet: Permanent Black, 2007), 115.

20   H. L. Richard, *Following Jesus in the Hindu Context: The Intriguing Implications of N. V. Tilak's Life and Thought* (Pasadena: William Carey Library, 1998), 12.

21   Lakshmibai Tilak, *Agadi Step by Step: Testimony of Lakshmibai Tilak in Her Own Words*, ed. Ashok Tilak (Nasik: M. A. Tilak, 1968), 39. Italics mine.

husbands, with little freedom or encouragement to develop their own creative impulses.

Lakshmibai's Conversion

In her autobiography, Lakshmibai would assert that it was Narayan's growing Christian faith that had a gradual but decisive influence upon her. He challenged her viewpoint on caste and purity boundaries and affirmed her self-estimation as a woman of creative and artistic potential. His own conversion had been remarkably literary. On a train journey, Narayan encountered a missionary who, after appreciatively discussing Sanskrit literature, turned the conversation to Christ and gave him a copy of the New Testament. Narayan was awestruck by the Sermon on the Mount: "it became impossible to leave these jewel-like sentences, so filled with love, mercy, and truth." His desire to learn about the life of Christ grew, and he began to carry on correspondence with Baba Padamanji, the first Marathi novelist and a noted Christian advocate for the social uplift of widows. In 1895, Narayan was baptized in Bombay and discipled in his new faith by members of the American Marathi Mission, the oldest missionary society in India from the United States.[22] When news of his baptism reached his relatives, they reacted with deep sadness and mourning. Narayan, knowing the social stigma associated with his acceptance of Christianity in Chitpavan Brahmin society, requested that they keep a vigilant watch on his wife, so that the shame would not drive her to commit suicide. They responded by declaring, "Whether she lives or dies you have now nothing to do with her."[23] Lakshmibai returned to her parents' home after her husband's conversion, and a long period

---

22 See Richard, *Following Jesus in the Hindu Context*, 19-24, for more information on the details of Narayan's religious shift. Baba Padamanji had written an autobiography in Marathi of his conversion to Christianity titled *Arunodaya* in 1888. It is likely that Tilak had read this and other works by Baba Padamanji prior to their correspondence.

23 Tilak, *I Follow After*, 134.

of separation commenced. Narayan sent sporadic letters and financial provisions but kept his distance from Lakshmibai.

Influenced by his new faith, Narayan developed a deep antipathy to caste pretensions, and he began mixing freely with persons of different faiths and socioeconomic statuses. Despite being deeply disturbed at the news that her husband was willing to eat with Muslims and lower-castes, Lakshmibai eventually was persuaded by Narayan in 1899 to reunite with him in Ahmednagar, upon hearing his assurance that a Brahmin's house had been rented for her, where the utensils, water, and food would not meet polluting lower-caste hands. When Lakshmibai's Hindu servants found out that her husband was a Christian, they informed the Tilaks, ironically, that they could not wash her pots or draw her water any longer, or they would risk being fined and reprimanded for not abiding by caste restrictions. With no other recourse, Narayan arranged for them to live in a private compound owned by Christian missionaries; there, Lakshmibai had a separate room where she could maintain ritual purity and perform the worship of her gods. She recounted that there were constant sounds of prayers, singing, and Bible reading that she could hear coming from Narayan's living area throughout the day.

One day, Lakshmibai saw a large rat eating the food she had offered to her deities. In addition to the absurdity of her gods allowing such a repulsively impure action, there was something even more horrifying about the situation. Observing a few more rodents consuming the food and then violently convulsing, she realized that they were plague rats. The Tilaks were hastily quarantined and relocated to the predominantly Muslim urban area where she drank her cup of "polluted water." She recounts the effects of the traumatic experience:

> Secretly in my heart I continued to cry, "Oh God! What have I done today? Today what are my ancestors saying about me in heaven? What can I do to make amends for such a sin?" By not one or two but thousands of such thoughts was my mind overwhelmed. My eyes were tight shut at the time, yet all at once I felt as if a light was shining about me. I do not use the word "Light was shining" as a

form of speech. I truly experienced a brilliant light like that of the sun. My perturbation came to an end, and thoughts that had never had entrance there began to whirl through my mind.[24]

Lakshmibai's initial considerations included such questions as to why, if there really were caste distinctions, God gave all humans intelligence, moral sensibilities, joy, birth, and death. Why were there differentiations between humans in terms of caste, whereas the animal species knew no such social markers? As she continued to ponder these issues, Lakshmibai began to recognize that the Shudras (low-castes) and Dalits were not innately defiled and Brahmins were not inherently pure.[25] The implications of this line of reasoning were that from now on, having drunk this cup of "nectar,"[26] she could eat and drink from anyone's provisions and affirm the equality of all, without any caste-based prejudices, as she embraced a new code of conduct that emulated the ethics of Christianity much more than the customs of her traditional upbringing.[27] Narayan later wrote in a letter to his son Dattu: "Water, poluted [*sic*] by a Mohomedan touch was poison to her. But even poisons used properly, sometimes prove magic cures. This poison completely up-rooted her *jatibheda* (case distinction)."[28]

Over the next few months, through hearing Narayan's passionate Marathi poems of devotion (*bhakti*) to Christ, which she grew to enjoy, and his daily recitations of biblical passages in her mother tongue, there was a steady change in her heart. After his conversion, Narayan produced a continuous stream of hymns and devotional verses (called *abhangs* in Marathi) that retained the aesthetics and themes of traditional *bhakti* spirituality but glorified Christ instead of the Hindu deities. *Bhaktas*

---

24   Ibid., 191.

25   Anuradha Sharma, "Dalit Women Writings: Breaking the Stereotypical Annotations of 'Being an Untouchable,' *International Journal of English Language, Literature, and Humanities* 2, no. 5 (2014): 62.

26   Tilak, *I Follow After*, 188.

27   Sharma, "Dalit Women Writings," 62.

28   Tilak, *Agadi Step by Step*, 30.

wrote poems and songs in their vernacular languages to express their passionate longing for God. They were seeking a way to cultivate an awareness of God's presence in the deepest core of their persons. *Bhaktas* gloried in their belief that the love of God extended even to the lowest. Some, such as the eminent seventeenth-century poet Tukaram, whom Narayan held in great honor, openly mocked hierarchical social distinctions. Narayan's compassion for the downtrodden and disenfranchised, originally cultivated by his appreciation for the Marathi *bhakti* tradition, had been further accentuated and deepened by his Christian faith. He adapted the forms of classical Marathi literature to express his devotion to Christ in a way that was compatible with his love for Indian culture.[29]

Narayan, as an educated upper-caste Maharashtrian, would have been aware of the various social reform movements that were developing in Hindu society at the time of his conversion to Christianity. It is worthwhile to consider what drew Narayan to a full Christian conversion experience, rather than participating in one of the modernizing Hindu societies that contact with Christianity had prompted. He had been particularly struck by Jesus's Sermon on the Mount, with its dramatic reversals of common social and ethical expectations toward values reflecting the kingdom of God. Given his innate distaste for traditional orthodox Hindu caste and gender specifications, as well as his deep-seated resentment of his father's treatment of his beloved mother, it is perhaps unsurprising that he would have wanted a complete identification with Jesus Christ through joining the Christian community. The vision of the kingdom of God outlined in Christ's teaching was so compelling to Narayan that he was willing to abandon the *dharmic* codes of his traditional upbringing. Narayan may have regarded the ethics of Christ as the necessary component of the social revolution that he felt India required. Nonetheless, he sensed that his new faith

---

29   Richard, *Following Jesus in the Hindu Context*, 68-71. The missionaries J. C. Winslow and Justin Abbott were profoundly influenced by Narayan's contextualized expression of Christ-devotion, leading them to stress the importance of Indian cultural forms for Christian mission in India.

could be expressed in a way that honored the sensibilities and aesthetics of classical Marathi cultural forms. He did not choose to jettison *bhakti*, *abhangs*, or *satsangs*; rather, he could remain true to his deepest identity as a Maharashtrian man while worshiping the Christ whose kingdom-values so captivated him. Gauri Viswanathan makes a striking assessment that is helpful in better understanding Narayan's religious aims: "Tilak conceived of Christianity as embodying a necessary vision of the future, with the power to purge Hinduism of its most hated features, yet at the same time adapted to India as a truly indigenous religion in its own right."[30] Tilak's conversion to Christianity could thus be viewed as having nationalistic and even anti-colonial dimensions, as he yearned deeply for a reformed Indian society.[31]

Lakshmibai found the deeds and attitudes of the loving Christ, who was the subject of her husband's Marathi devotional lyrics, to be attractive, particularly given her recent shift in sensibilities. Lakshmibai struggled with her own restrictive upbringing that she eventually reacted against, particularly when she observed the growing faith of her husband. Without his daily example of breaching caste-restrictions and serving the marginalized, she might not have chosen to make a complete conversion; but the exposure to Narayan's new *bhakti* to Christ became deeply appealing to her, transforming her ideals and social inclinations. She suddenly announced, to everyone's surprise, her desire to undertake baptism as a professing Christian, thereafter receiving her first communion in 1900. Having drunk the cup of nectar that shattered her previous inhibitions, a series of deep personal transformations were set in motion.

Lakshmibai's Increased Compassion for the Poor and Suffering

Perhaps the most touching aspect of Lakshmibai's post-conversion life was her desire to raise and provide for low-caste and Dalit children, some of whom were impoverished orphans. Lakshmibai's

---

30 Gauri Viswanathan, *Outside the Fold: Conversion, Modernity, and Belief* (New Delhi: Oxford University Press, 2001), 40.

31 Hedlund, *Indian Christianity*, 93.

internalization of the ramifications of the Christian values of social equality brought her to a place where her willingness to break caste and purity restrictions rivaled that of Narayan's. One day, while giving away alms to beggars, Lakshmibai struck up a conversation with a dark-skinned girl of around twelve years who survived a famine but had no one to care for her; she called herself "Nakoshi because no one wants me."[32] Lakshmibai, who renamed her Houshi ("desired"), embraced her as a daughter; there was no concern at all as to the orphan's caste or family background. Houshi was immediately given two saris and money for bangles and welcomed into the Tilak home.

Next, Lakshmibai brought an emaciated beggar girl into their residence from the Mang caste, which was among the lowest in Maharashtrian society. She was renamed Daya, meaning "mercy." Such a selfless act of charity would have been completely unthinkable to Lakshmibai at an earlier stage in her life. When some Christian women paid a visit to Lakshmibai, they were astonished at her having taken the Mang child in. Lakshmibai replied, "Mang, Mahar, Brahman, all are the same." The women responded, "You have outstripped us. We cannot go so far as that."[33] Lakshmibai, who once was a most scrupulous Brahmin woman regarding caste consciousness, came to a point where she felt that conceptions like "I am pure, you are polluted" were meaningless. Her new faith pushed her beyond the threshold of mere charity into deep personal involvement in the lives of others. One scholar of Dalit literature remarks that her compassion for these outcaste children, with whom she had arrived at a common sense of humanity and equality, was "in fact an elevation of human kind."[34]

The Tilaks sent both Houshi and Daya to school to receive an education at one of the highest quality girls' schools in Pune. They both recognized the enrichment and liberation that comes from learning, and they wanted this empowerment for their daughters. Such a decision was progressive in Maharashtrian culture, for the

---

32 Tilak, *I Follow After*, 196.

33 Ibid., 209.

34 Sharma, "Dalit Women Writers," 63.

instruction of low-castes and Dalits had traditionally been proscribed, and the provision of education for women was not viewed as socially respectable, even for higher-castes.[35] Lakshmibai's advocacy for the liberation of females from the perceived oppressions of traditional society extended beyond providing literacy to her girls. She had a deep concern for those ensnared in prostitution, whether temple Devadasis or young widows forced into the practice to survive. From 1908 on she began giving public talks and writing on the subject to increase awareness of the plight of these exploited women. She also actively promoted her view that men, when they already had a wife who was still living, should not take another spouse.[36] Indeed, once Lakshmibai had taken the initial step in questioning caste and purity barriers, it was an entirely natural development for her to critique the patriarchal subjugation that many Hindu women faced.[37] Lakshmibai had become a champion for the full emancipation of women after her conversion to Christianity. She spoke on behalf of Indian women with authority and authenticity as someone who had grown up in an oppressive environment. Her solidarity with women of all backgrounds dramatically increased after she became a Christian. Lakshmibai's son testified that "she related to the women around her as a daughter, sister, mother and grandmother, and served all those she came across in every way she could. There was no distinction of high and low, and never any repugnance on her part."[38]

One time, as a local famine escalated, the American Marathi Mission was unable to attend to all the children in need. Incredibly,

---

35 Jyotsna Kapur, "Putting Herself into the Picture: Women's Accounts of the Social Reform Campaign in Maharashtra," *Manushi: A Journal about Women and Society* 56 (1990): 29.

36 Lakshmibai Tilak, *Sketches from Memory*, trans. Louis Menezes (New Delhi: Katha, 2007), 389.

37 Padma Anagol, "Feminist Inheritances and Foremothers: The Beginnings of Feminism in Modern India," *Women's History Review* 19, no. 4 (2010): 526.

38 Tilak, *Sketches from Memory*, 386.

the Tilaks decided to feed, clothe, and house twenty-two young boys. Lakshmibai washed their clothes and even nursed a few of the babies. Narayan arranged for some to begin learning a trade, such as working for a printing press. The missionaries tried to dissuade them from taking on such a heavy burden, but Lakshmibai writes that "it was seeing the helpless, neglected state of the children that had driven us to undertake the responsibility for them, and so long as no provision was made for them, we would not give them up."[39] After more than a year of personal sacrifice, the Tilaks were able to place the boys in a Christian boarding school. Despite coming from relatively affluent Brahmin families, the Tilaks perpetually gave away their money and resources to those in need, so much so that they often found themselves in financial discomfort.

The Tilaks went through a harrowing experience in 1903 when their biological daughter Tara contracted the plague and nearly died. Lakshmibai agonized over why God would allow their beloved little girl to suffer in this way. Because of this brush with death, she subsequently joined her husband in relief work during several severe epidemics in Maharashtra, where they faithfully and at great personal risk cared for the sick and dying, irrespective of the social standing of the victims. To better respond to such health emergencies, Lakshmibai decided to invest her money in receiving nurse's training at the regional hospital. Soon news reached the Tilaks of a neglected plague camp, where there was no one willing to attend to the victims. Since they had already been exposed to the disease through Tara, they made the courageous decision to enter the quarantined site to provide aid. They washed the desperate people, giving them sponge baths. As there were none to remove the corpses of those who had succumbed to the plague, Lakshmibai volunteered to carry out this traditionally defiling work. She was even willing to clean the putrid latrines in the camp. She recounts: "people of every religion and every caste were there, and on hearing that we were working among them, the fear of the camp

---

39 Tilak, *I Follow After*, 213.

became less, and more and more plague patients began to come."⁴⁰ When influenza followed on the heels of the plague, the Tilaks started a dispensary, and Lakshmibai prepared and distributed medicinal herbs, as well as oil and matches. Their provisions were received by Brahmans, Mangs, and Mahars alike. Hardly a mere "passive object" under the sway of missionaries and male converts, Lakshmibai burst into vital, active agency for the uplift of her community, across many sectors of society, as a direct result of her multiple religious, social, and personal transformations.⁴¹

The fact that Lakshmibai brought so many orphans and destitute children into her home and assumed a maternal role for them illustrated that the Tilaks were not just enacting a detached form of charity that occasionally condescended to help the impoverished, but rather they were deeply identifying with the pain of the poor and displaying an authentic, vibrant sense of compassion. These were the embodied kingdom-values that had entranced Narayan upon reading the Sermon on the Mount for the first time. The reshifting of social sensibilities was so complete in Lakshmibai that she would willingly enter a plague ward and wash the victims with her own hands. This was a deep conversion that had been enacted in their lives, and its effects led Lakshmibai, particularly, to engage in actions that would have made her shudder in horror of defilement at an earlier stage in her life. Their internalization of the Christian gospel propelled them into becoming effective change agents in society. In addition, as high-caste elites, they were uniquely positioned to make a real impact within their culture and to challenge the status quo, for they were not outsiders or Western missionary activists, but Indian participants invested in vibrant social reform.

Lakshmibai's Increased Confidence in Literary Endeavors

In addition to propelling outreach to the poor and suffering, Lakshmibai's transformed social and religious sensibilities nurtured a

---

40 Ibid., 230.

41 Anagol, "Feminist Inheritances and Foremothers," 526.

newly awakened creative impulse. She reminisces in her autobiography about her first public testimony, written for her by Narayan, in which she stood frozen for nine minutes in front of the patient audience, only to burst forth with a spontaneous, moving speech in her own words. Impressed, Narayan now hoped that his wife could build upon her potential and polish her skills to become a recognized author, poet, or orator. But Lakshmibai herself was less confident about her literary capacities. Upon her first attempt at composing poetry, her instinct was to hide it away from Narayan's sight, but he discovered that his wife had disposed of her writing in the wastebasket. Pulling out the discarded paper, he was overjoyed at the quality of the lyrics and he locked them away in the cupboard where they would be safely preserved.

Unlike his father, Narayan was deeply appreciative of his spouse's literary efforts. Perhaps recalling his mother's thwarted poetic endeavors, he encouraged Lakshmibai to develop her proficiencies and to offer submissions to regional competitions, thus affirming his wife as a woman of creativity. Later, he sent her compositions to various magazines for publication. As she grew in self-assurance, her opportunities for public speaking increased, as did her full participation in the Christian community. Their conversion to Christianity, which stresses the written word, motivated the Tilaks to respect and treasure each other's self-expression. Although, Lakshmibai had originally resented Narayan's change in religious outlook and struggled as a Hindu woman to maintain a marital relationship with him, she acknowledged the healthy change in their marriage that followed his conversion.[42] Whereas the younger Narayan was self-involved and could at times be neglectful of her, and he had a fiery disposition that could flare in anger, Lakshmibai observed the incrementally improving effect that Christianity had upon her husband's patience and character. Though raised by a traditional and at times oppressive father, Narayan sought to protect his wife, care for her wellbeing, and nurture their relationship, often going to great

---

42 Anju Kapur, "Theorizing Women Writing in India," *South Asia Bulletin* 14, no. 1 (1994): 115.

lengths not to offend her earlier religious scruples and encouraging her later pursuits in social reform. Indeed, the religious conversions of the husband and wife had a positive effect on the entire Tilak family and spurred further intellectual achievement in Lakshmibai. Leena Chandorkar has succinctly summarized the deep impact Narayan had upon Lakshmibai's emerging view of egalitarianism in society and the family:

> In Lakshmibai Tilak's progress towards autonomy, her husband's contribution was considerable. Rev. Tilak was a liberal who converted to Christianity as a protest against Hindu religious orthodoxy but also subconsciously as a rebellion against his father who symbolized the oppressor in his mind. His father's cruel treatment of his mother not only made Rev. Tilak look for peace in a new religion but also for a more just and non-exploitative society free of class, caste, race and gender bias. His encouragement to his wife ran parallel to the social work that he did for people of all castes and religions. Lakshmibai Tilak's awareness of herself as an autonomous being grew alongside the erosion in her mind of casteism and racism.[43]

As a poet of great standing in the community, Narayan helped to organize a two-day Poet's Conference in 1907. He encouraged Lakshmibai to submit a poem of her own, which was well-received on its own terms by the literary critics at the gathering. Her acclaimed lyric poems were eventually collected and published under the title *Bharali Ghagar* (The Filled Pitcher).[44] She then took up the project of creating a social novel, ransacking Narayan's books looking for appropriate words and spellings in Marathi. Though she admits the process was slow, her motivation and ability to write kept improving, so much so that she was asked to deliver the presidential address at the Christian Litterateurs Conference in Nagpur. Whenever she would recite her compositions before *semmelan*s (gatherings of poets), her son recalls that "peace descended the next instant—one could have heard a pin

---

43 Leena Chandorkar, *Eye Me Myself: A Study of Six Women's Autobiographies* (Delhi: New Century Publications, 2002), 184.

44 Laksmibhai Tilak, *Bharali Ghagar* (Mumbai: K. B. Devale, 1948).

drop."⁴⁵ It is important to note that Narayan persuaded Lakshmibai to cultivate her literary skills in the indigenous language and aesthetic sensibilities of Marathi rather than in English. The Tilaks were proud of their Maharashtrian cultural inheritance and their conversion to Christianity compelled them to dig even deeper into this heritage and produce further contributions to the contemporary Marathi renaissance and renewal. They continued to value and fiercely uphold their Indian cultural identity after becoming Christians.

At the time of her husband's death in 1919, Lakshmibai recounts that "a confidante who had kept me company when Tilak and I were separated, upon his conversion, now came running to my assistance. And who was this, that I'm speaking of, now? Poetry. That was my confidante."⁴⁶ Narayan had been working on an epic that he called the *Khristayan*, which would recount the story of Christ's life and ministry in the literary style and aesthetics of the classic Marathi *bhakti* (devotional) tradition. However, the epic was not even a fourth of the way completed at the time of his passing. Narayan had only gotten as far as Christ's birth and childhood in the narrative. Lakshmibai took up the challenge of finishing the epic herself, evidencing her developed literary voice that had grown through the years. The goal of completing the *Khristayan* became a source of focused attention and artistic commitment for her. She added sixty-four more chapters to it and drew Narayan's narrative of Christ's redemptive work to a close.⁴⁷ The epic was praised for its poetic craftsmanship, and Lakshmibai felt a sense of spiritual completion. She describes her fulfillment in this way:

> Before I completed the *Khristayan*, I asked myself, "What service have I rendered by becoming a Christian?—my own spiritual uplift? —my own good?—and what besides that? But when I started and finished the *Khristayan*, this riddle was solved. I got the inspiration

---

45   Tilak, *Sketches from Memory*, 385.

46   Ibid., 364

47   Lakshmibai Tilak and Narayan Tilak, *Kristayan* (Nasik: Devadatta Tilak, 1938).

to become a Christian because I had this mission to complete. Now I think my conversion to Christianity is truly fruitful.[48]

Lakshmibai was most highly praised for her riveting autobiography, released in four installments between 1934 and 1936, which was a seminal prose work in women's literature in India. The *Smriti Chitre* (Memory Sketches), written in colloquial, humorous Marathi,[49] has been acknowledged for its importance in the standard historical surveys of Marathi literature and universally esteemed for its winsome style: "the realistic language, the authentic detail of a woman's life and thought, were a revelation on the modern Marathi literary scene."[50] Although at the outset of the work Lakshmibai presents Narayan as the focal point of the narrative, in truth the majority of the account relays her struggles to come to terms with her husband's conversion, both before and after their reunion, and her gradual change in attitude toward the people around her. In fact, it quickly becomes clear that this "biography" of her husband is actually the autobiography of Lakshmibai, with her as the central protagonist.[51] The genre of the autobiography was not popular in Indian literature at the time; it has been claimed that only fourteen autobiographies were written in Marathi from 1818 to 1935.[52] Lakshmibai's was deemed the most successfully realized because of its delicately crafted narrative, conveying the full range of human emotions, including confusion, turmoil, joy, and compassion.[53]

---

48 Tilak, *Agadi Step by Step*, 46.

49 Susie Tharu and K. Lalita, eds., *Women Writing in India*, vol. 1, *600 B.C. to the Early Twentieth Century* (Delhi: Oxford University Press, 1993), 309.

50 Eleanor Zelliot, "A Bibliographical Essay on Women in Maharashtra," in *Images of Women in Maharashtrian Society*, ed. Anne Feldhaus (Albany: State University of New York Press, 1998), 258.

51 J. Kapur, "Putting Herself into the Picture," 30.

52 Mahadev Apte, "Home as the Extension of Self in Marathi Autobiographies," in *House and Home in Maharashtra*, ed. Irina Glushkova and Anne Feldhaus (Delhi: Oxford University Press, 1998), 43.

53 Suma Chitnis, "Exploring Tradition and Change among Women in Marathi Culture," in *Faces of the Feminine in Ancient, Medieval, and Modern India*, ed. Mandakranta Bose (New York: Oxford University Press, 2000), 265.

Many literary scholars have remarked that *Smriti Chitre* played a singularly pioneering role, paving the way for subsequent endeavors in women's writing in India by establishing a groundbreaking precedent in female Marathi autobiography.[54] Whereas the male authors of Lakshmibai's generation tended to write in more highly stylized or even pretentious prose, her language crackles with homespun sayings, proverbs, colloquial dialogue, and anecdotes that convey the natural way of speaking among Maharashtrian women.[55] In fact, it has been observed that underneath the unadorned prose of *Smriti Chitre* lies the vital message of social egalitarianism.[56] One critic has described how Lakshmibai, raised in a restrictive environment, was now a trailblazer among women who took to the "pen" in order to "get out of the tight hold of the patriarchal prescription of the feminine culture represented by the metaphor of the "needle."[57]

As Lakshmibai was advancing in years, her son arranged a public homage in Nashik to be paid to her in 1935. The first two installments of the autobiography had already been published, and the purpose of the gathering was to pay tribute to the completion of the highly anticipated third section. Lakshmibai had earned public recognition through hard work, persistence, and determination, as well as the encouragement of her late husband. Her son joyfully recounted that "her words were now of such worth that hundreds of people had gathered in the theatre, an hour before the event commenced. Every seat was taken. Many had to stand outside."[58] Various organizations placed garlands around her neck in honor of her many contributions to society. The aspiring writer who used to scribble on the floor at night

---

54 Chandorkar, *Eye Me Myself*, 93.

55 Ibid., 96.

56 Ibid., 178.

57 Ranjana Harish, "Pen and Needle: The Changing Metaphors of Self in Autobiographies by Women in Post-Independence India," *Indian Literature* 46, no. 4 (2002): 165.

58 Tilak, *Sketches from Memory*, 392.

using a matchstick when she was struck with poetic inspiration was now esteemed by many of the literati of Maharashtra as a significant, compelling voice.

Whereas the external dimensions of Lakshmibai's conversion to Christianity were most clearly seen in her charitable outreach to the destitute and marginalized, the internal dimensions of this transformation were vividly displayed in her literary productivity. Raised in an environment where her mother expended her energies to satisfy the purity demands of her father and joined by marriage to a father-in-law who squelched all poetic aspirations of Narayan's mother, it is remarkable that Lakshmibai progressed so far in her writing endeavors. This was due in no small measure to the encouragement of her Christian husband, who took immense pride in her efforts and gains in literary output. The core egalitarian values that Narayan, and then Lakshmibai, embraced through their conversions fed her urge for creative self-expression. By completing Narayan's unfinished epic *Khristayan*, she embraced her husband's valuing of the Marathi poetic *bhakti* tradition and used it as a means of conveying her devotion to Christ. She even broke ground in the genre of Marathi autobiography, giving voice to her own introspections and memories of her life with Narayan. These pursuits were fueled by the personal dignity and worth that Lakshmibai had experienced because of her emerging new religious identity.

Conclusion

Even at the time of her death in 1936, when Lakshmibai struggled with influenza and debilitating stomach pains, the effects of her conversion were evident. The doctors decided an operation was needed to remove an intestinal obstruction, and a constant stream of visitors came to spend time with her during the preparation for and recovery from the procedure. As one might expect, "it was a very mixed crowd—there were schoolboys and girls, a learned circle of friends, rich and poor and as many other kinds of people as there could be."⁵⁹ Lakshmibai told her son that she had more writing projects she soon wished to undertake, but her condition worsened after the operation and she passed away peacefully a few days later. Her funeral was attended by people of "every religion and all opinions, Europeans and Indians, men and women from Nashik and beyond."⁶⁰

Lakshmibai's compelling life story involves several personal transformations, most especially her expanding interaction with those of a lower social station and her rising sense of compassion for those around her, as well as her increasing awareness of herself as a woman of full personhood and artistic competence. These developments were nurtured by her adoption of a Christian belief system and its charitable ethic, particularly through the influence, encouragement, and example of her husband Narayan. She broke out of the traditional settings and constraining boundaries reserved for women and actively entered the spheres of education, social work, and especially literature, often partnering with Narayan in these endeavors. Her grandson recalls: "She wrote *bhajans* like him, delivered *kirtans* like him, composed *abhangs*, completed his great Christian epic the *Khristayan*, and lastly wrote down his epoch-making life story the *Smriti Chitre*."⁶¹ The young daughter of the "holy" Gokhale, who in his scrupulousness washed after contact with fellow Brahmins, had grown into a woman willing to adopt outcastes and selflessly serve plague victims. Instead of being a cup of bitter poison, the drinking of the water drawn by a Muslim woman that momentous day became a cup of sweet nectar, setting Lakshmibai free from caste barriers and initiating a journey of faith, self-expression, and charitable concern for the poor and downtrodden.

Lakshmibai's story is a fascinating historical case study of conversion to Christianity as a catalyst for cultural renewal. Her new faith challenged

---

59   Ibid., 398.

60   Ibid., 400.

61   Tilak, *Agadi Step by Step*, 45-46. These Marathi terms refer to religious hymns, singing sessions, and poetic compositions.

her to uplift her community and to make valued contributions to Marathi literature. Her legacy was unique: there are not many examples in this period of female high-caste converts to Christianity who challenged orthodox Hindu social values through economic and social outreach to the disenfranchised, while at the same time actively maintaining and cultivating their Indian identity.[62] The Tilaks had a deep conviction that a religious awakening grounded in Christian social ethics and built on the rich religious tradition of *bhakti* would enable India to embark on a new era of reform and change. Lakshmibai's implicit critique extended not only to traditional Hinduism, but also to colonial Western (and even missionary) power, for despite the influence of modernity upon her, she remained deeply committed to her Marathi cultural heritage rather than capitulating to English cultural forms. Although Indian feminists such as Meera Kosambi and Padma Anagol rightly appreciate Lakshmibai's seminal influence on women's literature and social conscience in India, there needs to be a deeper appreciation of the dynamics of religious conversion in Lakshmibai's self-appraisal and social sensibilities. Her embracing of the Christian message and her shift in religious identity were the primary impulses that led to her active promotion of cultural renewal, through collective social uplift and through the individual production of Marathi-language works. Her Christian faith inspired both her appreciation for traditional *bhakti*-spirituality and her emergence as a modern Maharashtrian woman of dignity and value.

---

62 Perhaps the closest parallel would be that of Pandita Ramabai Sarasvati, also of Maharashtra.

Chapter 3

A "Willingness to Become Undone" in Relation to Others

The Plural Life of C. F. Andrews

Bernardo A. Michael

A "Willingness to Be Undone" and the Cultivation of Humanity
What does it mean to be a citizen in today's world? This is a question that has repeatedly surfaced in my own life as I have journeyed across national and cultural boundaries in India, Nepal, and the United States. As older affiliations of belonging and loyalty were tested, stretched, and even rendered undone, there was a growing realization that the highs and lows I have experienced on this journey revolve around questions of difference. I have been compelled to reassess and reimagine my location in the world across the familiar ties formed by family, faith, community, region, and nation. The Nagel Institute of World Christianity's India seminar in 2015 on religious change and economic development reinforced these questions as we traveled across the country engaging organizations, communities, and individuals involved in interfaith work, development, and nation building.

Near the end of this seminar, we met with Ashis Nandy, the renowned social theorist and political psychologist. Nandy reminded our group of the instances of profound cooperation that exist among religious communities in India. This could be evidenced even at such a contested site as the ancient city of Ayodhya where, in 1992, Hindu radicals had destroyed the Babri Masjid, one of the city's oldest and most prominent mosques that had been under dispute for more than a decade. Nandy pointed out that it was Muslims who had traditionally provided the flowers and dresses for the idols of the 3,500 Hindu temples in Ayodhya.[1] Nandy insisted that these ties of collaboration and mutual exchange inform the daily relations of religious communities across the Indian subcontinent. Such ties of mutual dependence can be traced back millennia as Jews, Christians, Parsis, and Muslims migrated to the subcontinent, established roots, and found ways to communicate with each other. Such instinctual practices of daily accommodation and hospitality have persisted in South Asia alongside the persistent presence of social inequalities, exclusion, and conflict.[2] During the seminar, we were exposed to such examples where organizations, communities, and individuals came together to co-produce new spaces of shared living and learning in the fields of education, micro-finance and credit, social work, and interfaith dialogue.

Such spaces are fragile and face the real danger of being eroded as extremist versions of religious and cultural nationalism flex their muscles once more on the Indian subcontinent, and where bouts of religious violence have spared none of the modern nations: Bangladesh, India, Pakistan, and Sri Lanka. And in recent years it has become clear that religious, racial, and cultural nationalisms are arising all over the world—in China, the Philippines, Poland, France, Russia, Great Britain, and the United States as well as in South Asia and

---

1 Ayodhya is reputed to be the birthplace of the Hindu god Ram and the setting of the great Hindu epic the Ramayana. Presentation by Ashis Nandy, New Delhi YMCA, July 29, 2015.

2 For a study on this, see Dilip Menon, *The Blindness of Insight: Essays on Caste in Modern India* (Delhi: Navayana, 2006). Menon argues that communalism in India is a deflection of the central issue of violence and inegalitarianism within Hindu society.

the Arab world. So, in spite of many heart-warming local instances of individuals and communities living, learning, and sharing across profound differences, what hope is there for a broader citizenship that is diverse, inclusive, and equitable? All over the world today we see visions of an opposite kind, with parties and leaders coming to the fore with unitary definitions of society, religion, nationhood, and "us first" ideologies and policy goals. Is any meaningful dream of building pluralistic political communities dead?[3]

I hope not, for our existence today is inescapably plural, and only an embrace of plurality can provide the foundational materials for crafting societies where our differences and our shared humanity are simultaneously recognized and celebrated. The noted American philosopher Martha Nussbaum once wrote about the three capacities essential for the cultivation of healthy humanity in today's world. First is an ability to critically examine oneself and one's traditions. The second is the capacity to transcend narrow group loyalties and to extend to strangers the moral concern we typically reserve for friends and kin. Finally, we need to develop a "narrative imagination" that makes parabolic, plot-line connections out of sequences of human actions and their consequences.[4] Adopting such a stance has become increasingly critical in today's world where the advancement of social and cultural understanding has lagged, giving rise to all kinds of tensions and relentless cycles of violence.

The Indian subcontinent, especially, has witnessed many episodes of communal tension and violence, especially against minorities, of which the horrific ethnic cleansing that marked the partitioning of India and Pakistan was only the most dramatic. India's ruling elite tried

---

3 The notion of pluralism indicated here draws inspiration from the work of the Harvard Pluralism Project. See "From Diversity to Pluralism," http://www.pluralism.org/encounter/challenges, accessed August 22, 2015.

4 Martha Nussbaum, *Cultivating Humanity: A Classical Defense of Reform in Liberal Education* (Cambridge, MA: Harvard University Press, 1997), 9-11. See also Inga Clendinnen, *True Stories* (Sydney: ABC Books, 1999), 6.

to finesse these tensions by weaving an ostensibly secular fabric for the nation's public affairs, but religious fundamentalisms have risen to challenge its legitimacy. The rise of the Hindu Right in Indian politics is the main case in point. It has an older and more complicated history that emerged during colonial rule and the social reform and nationalist movements in the nineteenth and twentieth centuries. Empire, masculinity, and religious nationalism came together to forge a political culture that valued expressions of Hindu religious commitment at the cost of religious pluralism and a secular polity.[5] Hindu nationalism capitalizes on the fact that the officially secular fabric of the Indian nation, upheld in the Constitution, has always been framed within a majoritarian view of India's national identity and history that posits a primarily Hindu character and substance. A coterie of right-wing Hindu organizations, sometimes referred to as the *Sangh Parivar*, arose to advance this perspective as a social and political ideology.[6] This development has boded ill for minorities in general and for religious communities such as Muslims and Christians. Hindu Right propaganda

---

5   This history has been wonderfully captured in the recent work of Peter van der Veer, especially his *Imperial Encounters* (Princeton: Princeton University Press, 2001).

6   The Sangh Parivar is made up of a constellation of organizations, the most prominent being the Bajrang Dal, the Rashtriya Swayamsevak Sangh (RSS), and the Bharatiya Janata Party (BJP). For a brief overview of the RSS and BJP and their ideological agendas, see Safdar Hashmi Memorial Trust (SAHMAT), *Secularism Alert* (Delhi: SAHMAT, 1998). The movement's chief ideologues remains Madhavrao Sadashiv Golwalkar and Vinayak Damodar Sarvarkar, whose early twentieth-century writings championed the idea that India's unique Hindu character could be traced to its geography, culture, and history. See Madhavrao Sadashiv Glowalkar, *We or Our Nationhood Defined* (Nagpur: Bharat Prakashan, 1939), and V. D. Sarvarkar, "The Glories of the Hindu Nation," in *Sources of Indian Tradition*, ed. Wm. Theodore DeBary et al. (New York: Columbia University Press, 1958), 881-87. The writings on the Hindu Right are far too numerous to cite here, but see Vinay Lal, ed., *Political Hinduism: The Religious Imagination in Public Spheres* (New York: Oxford University Press, 2009).

reduces them to ghettoized targets for discrimination and violence from both state and non-state actors.

Such a hardening of religious identities presents a challenge to living in meaningful and responsible relationships with others who are different. It has resulted in a growing dysfunction in India's public life and political culture where name-calling, xenophobia, recrimination, and criminality have become common spectacles. Mutual generosity, toleration of dissent, and trust building are perhaps at their lowest ebb ever since 1947. Such trends seem to hide from view the longstanding relations of mutual accommodation and understanding that have marked the relationships between religious communities.[7] For centuries, Indian social groups have engaged in practices of daily accommodation and hospitality despite the presence of inequalities, exclusion, and conflict.[8] Today, as extremist versions of religious nationalism begin to flex their muscles, there is a real possibility that these healthy social practices are in danger of being lost. This history of daily interreligious dialogue and exchange could provide foundational materials for forging new forms of communal solidarity capable of countering the forces of extremism that foster singular visions of India and developing a humanistic ethic of pluralism. In fact, for some time now, scholars like Ashis Nandy have argued that the longstanding pluralistic religious traditions in India that have fostered social collaboration and cooperation can play a critical role in the renewal of India's political culture.[9]

---

7 I am not suggesting that conflict between religious communities was absent in precolonial South Asia, but it was certainly not as widespread as suggested by Hindu fundamentalists. See Richard Eaton, "Temple Destruction in Pre-Modern India," in *Demolishing Myths or Mosques and Temples: Readings on History and Temple Desecration in Medieval India*, ed. Sunil Kumar (Gurgaon: Three Essay's Collective, 2008), 93-139.

8 Menon, *The Blindness of Insight*. Menon argues that communalism in India is a deflection of the central issue of violence and inegalitarianism within Hindu society.

9 Ashis Nandy, "The Politics of Secularism and the Recovery of Religious Tolerance" and "Coping with the Politics of Faiths and Cultures:

So how might one understand and engage difference without succumbing to ignorance, suspicion, and even hatred? By building friendships across differences, an ethical task that we need to pursue with vigor and a sense of urgency if human communities are to build a positive future. Such ethical work is quite risky, observes Judith Butler, an American ethicist and gender theorist, in that we are called to throw ourselves into relationships with people so divergent from ourselves that we risk being personally "undone" by identifying with them.[10] Yet Butler's emphasis on a "willingness to become undone" might in fact be a way out of the cycle of ignorance, fear, suspicion, and cold indifference that continues to oppose the cultivation of a profoundly plural humanity. In doing such risky personal work, however, it surely helps to have some exemplars. One such is an Englishman, Charles Freer Andrews (1871-1940), who came to India as a missionary educator and became a pioneer in interfaith theologizing and partnerships and an advocate for Indian independence. In his day, such work bore a deep personal risk.

Charles Freer Andrews: A Synopsis

Andrews was born in Newcastle-upon-Tyne in Northeast England in 1871 in a devout Irvingite household.[11] He was educated in Birmingham

---

Between Secular State and Ecumenical Traditions in India," in Ashis Nandy, *Time Warps: Silent and Evasive Pasts in Indian Politics and Religion* (New Brunswick: Rutgers University Press, 2002), 61-88, 89-128; and "The Return of the Sacred: The Language of Religion and the Fear of Democracy in a Post-Secular World," The Mahesh Chandra Regmi Lecture 2007, December 13, 2007, Kathmandu, Nepal, 1-15.

10   Judith Butler, *Giving an Account of Oneself* (New York: Fordham University Press, 2005), 136.

11   The Irvingites were a nineteenth-century Christian sect that believed in apostolic succession, apostolic signs and wonders (e.g., speaking in tongues), and the imminent second coming of Christ. The movement declined in the latter half of that century. For a more detailed account, see C. G. Flegg, *'Gathered under Apostles': A Study of the Catholic Apostolic Church* (Oxford: Clarendon Press, 1992).

and Cambridge and then he set off to India as an Anglican missionary for the Society for the Propagation of the Gospel in 1904.[12] His subsequent life in India dramatically altered his view of the world and he became an avowed Indian nationalist who called for India's independence. Perhaps no one incarnated the risky practice of being undone in the pursuit of inter-religious dialogue and cross-cultural living better than Andrews. Also known as "Deenabandhu," or friend of the poor, Andrews remained a committed Christian whose lifelong pursuit of cross-cultural understanding allowed him to forge enduring friendships with many individuals from across the world. His friends included well-known nationalists, activists, and religious figures such as Mohandas K. Gandhi, Agatha Harrison, Gurdial Mallik, Jawaharlal Nehru, W. W. Pearson, Susil Kumar Rudra, Munshi Ram (Swami Shraddhanand), Rabindranath Tagore, and Munshi Zaka Ullah. Andrews also had close connections with government officials and multitudes of Indians, rich and poor, living in India and abroad. Andrews never failed to express his profound admiration and gratitude even while he had disagreements with these friends. It is with the help of these numerous friends that he cultivated a remarkable ability to cross boundaries formed by empire, race, class, gender, religion, theological outlook, and caste, with a unique blend of care, compassion, and humility. This openness to be undone is what allowed him to overcome his own biases, ignorance, and fear as he reached across the boundaries of difference.

---

12 A succinct autobiography can be found in C. F. Andrews, "A Pilgrim's Progress," in *Religion in Transition*, ed. Virgilius Ferm (London: George Allen & Unwin, 1937), 60-89. Biographical details about Andrews's life can be found in the following select works: Benarsidas Chaturvedi and Marjorie Sykes, *Charles Freer Andrews: A Narrative* (London: George Allen & Unwin, 1949); Marjorie Sykes, *C. F. Andrews: Representative Writings* (New Delhi: National Book Trust, 1973); and Hugh Tinker, *Ordeal of Love: C. F. Andrews and India* (Delhi: Oxford University Press, 1979).

Undoing Andrews: Becoming "Deenabandhu"

Andrews came to India in 1904 with an underdeveloped critique of race and empire. His first ten years in India as a missionary and educator at St. Stephen's College were instrumental in unpacking his paternalistic imperialism and ignorance about his racial privilege. At St. Stephen's College, where he worked from 1904 to 1914, colleagues like Susil Rudra and S. A. C. Ghose would help Andrews clarify his views and become a staunch critic of European racial attitudes.[13] In particular, his friendship with Rudra helped defamiliarize India for him.[14] Years later Andrews would gratefully acknowledge how Rudra had "weaned" him away from his arrogance, thereby breaking down the barriers that had separated him from others.[15] Andrews also began to disavow the idea of the civilizing mission of British imperialism his devout father had espoused and by 1910 had begun to entertain the idea that Britain needed to grant India complete and unconditional independence, long before such an idea was formally adopted by Indian nationalists.

This breaking of barriers of race, caste, gender, and class would remain a lifelong experience for Andrews, allowing him to be undone in numerous ways that cannot be fully explored in the short space of this chapter. He had to pay a heavy price to become "Deenabandhu," or "friend of the poor," which was more than being a friend of the poor. He had rejected high positions and careers in the fields of religious service and education, both in England and in India. He had to bear the financial, emotional, and physical toll of his work. Andrews's itinerant life brought him no regular income and he donated

---

13 See Daniel O'Connor, *A Clear Star: C. F. Andrews in India, 1904-1914*, 2nd ed. (Delhi: DC Books, 2005), 40. O'Connor's is the most detailed account, currently available, on Andrews's first ten years in India.

14 Chaturvedi and Sykes, *Charles Freer Andrews*, 38.

15 C. F. Andrews, *What I Owe to Christ* (New York: Abingdon Press, 1932), 167, 169.

his meager possessions to the Indian National Congress. His frugal lifestyle, frequent travel, and overwork were punctuated by bouts of fatigue, anxiety, nervous breakdowns, and ill health, and compounded by difficulties in hearing.[16]

The process of being undone began, however, long before Andrews came to India. Between 1895 and 1899, Andrews worked at the Pembroke College mission at Walworth, a poor urban neighborhood in South London inhabited by street vendors, some casual laborers, porters, and carriers. The work included a penny bank, rescue and preventive work among young girls, a Band of Hope, temperance meetings, soup kitchens, and so on.[17] Here, Andrews's work among the urban poor took him out of the comforts and heady intellectual environment of Cambridge and his own middle-class upbringing. He had to unlearn his privileged status to work effectively among the poor. This work gave Andrews a critical awareness of the limitations of his bourgeois roots and helped him to steer away from the common fate of his education, which, he told a friend, would have consigned him to Britain's "decadent" educated middle class.[18] His experiences at Walworth helped to prepare him for a life spent in service of the poor. In 1938, two years before his death, he reported to a correspondent that "the whole of later life which I have spent here in India among the poor received its first impulse in those years when I lived in the same manner in London. They were not only the best, but also the most formative years that I have ever spent; for they shaped the whole of my life in this one direction." What had saved him from "moral

---

16 His close friends like Tagore pointed this out to him as well and urged him to come into touch with the truth that gave inner peace. See Tinker, *Ordeal of Love*, 196. See also 129 and 198.

17 For additional details, see Alexandra M. M. Eveleigh, "Pembroke College (Cambridge) Mission, 1885-1995: An Administrative History" (unpublished MA thesis, University College London, 1997). See especially 25-27.

18 C. F. Andrews (hereafter, CFA) in a letter to his friend W. W. Pearson dated November 12, 1920, and cited in Tinker, *Ordeal of Love*, 173, 176n29.

disaster" when living in the intellectual environment of Cambridge was the time he spent with poor people. "In the slums of South-East London, among the very poorest, there was a College Settlement, where I could go down for a week end, or during the vacation, and live among those who were facing problems of suffering and poverty that were far harder to solve than mathematics. . . . I should never have understood India's poverty, if I had not lived thus as a poor man among the poor in my own country."[19] Andrews's affinity for the poor and the discriminated against would take him around the world seeking inclusion and equity for overseas indentured Indians in Fiji, British Guyana, South Africa, Australia, New Zealand, and other places.[20]

Andrews's theological unraveling began probably during his days at Cambridge under the influence of Brooke Foss Westcott (1825-1901), the charismatic biblical scholar, theologian, and bishop of Durham. Under his influence, Andrews began to look beyond European Christianity to the East for new theological resources. He once recalled Westcott reminding his pupils that "only from the East could the perfect commentary on St. John's Gospel be produced."[21] During his years at Cambridge he continued to confront this issue of reconciling his family's religious values and his own emerging ones. Andrews gradually moved away from the narrow confessional claims of his conservative Irvingite Christian roots to become part of the Anglican Church during his college years. While he was pained by the hurt it produced in his parents, he also remained true to what he

---

19 "University and Village," newspaper article, October 6, 1938, Benarsidas Das Chaturvedi Papers, Microfilm Accession No. 317, I/D-358, Private Archives, National Archives of India (hereinafter NAI), Delhi.

20 For details, see Chaturvedi and Sykes, *Charles Freer Andrews*, and Tinker, *Ordeal of Love*. See also Hugh Tinker, *A New System of Slavery: The Export of Indian Labour Overseas*, 1830-1920, 2nd ed. (London: Hansib Publications, 1993).

21 See Andrews's article on missions in *E-G, a British Weekly*, August 18, 1932, European Manuscripts, D1113/3, ff. 37-41, esp. f. 41, APAC, BL.

felt was the need to "seek *first* the kingdom of Heaven."[22] Andrews's disillusionment with the exclusivism and narrow theological outlook of Western Christianity and his own financial dependency on government and mission aid brought him to a breaking point in his relationship with the Anglican Church. In 1914, he decided to leave the Anglican Church.[23] This decision was an important marker in Andrews's story of being undone. His inner life underwent a change and he gradually grew accustomed to this new way of thinking outside the conventional paradigm of a Western missionary. Again, it was the presence of friends, and, Tagore in particular that forced him to confront this issue with greater urgency. Andrews's actions would result in the loss of most of his English friends.[24]

Andrews's experience of personal undoing was continually advanced by the diverse friendships he established in his adopted country India. He was deeply troubled by the theologically exclusivist claims of the Athanasian creed (whereby salvation was only possible through a knowledge of Jesus Christ) which left his closest friends, such as Tagore, condemned to eternal damnation. His friendship with the Arya Samajist educator Munshi Ram (later known as Swami Shraddhanand) drew him out of his confessional boundaries to undertake the study of Hindu religion and philosophy. His attractions to the Divine

---

22 These words of advice were given by his best friend Basil Westcott. Basil Westcott was the son of Brooke Foss Westcott. He worked in Delhi at the Cambridge Mission and died of cholera in 1900, an event that might have induced Andrews to move to India. Cited in Chaturvedi and Sykes, *Charles Freer Andrews*, 20.

23 Church authorities were reluctant to grant Andrews his wish, and it was never formally accepted by the then Metropolitan, George Alfred Lefroy. See Chaturvedi and Sykes, *Charles Freer Andrews*, 107-11; Tinker, *Ordeal of Love*, 95-101, 121. See also F. J. Western to Marjorie Sykes, May 30, 1946, Charles Freer Andrews Papers (hereinafter, CFA Papers), 28(i)/images 61-62, 3 pp., Rabindra Bhavana Archives, Viswa-Bharati, Santiniketan, W. Bengal.

24 See C. F. Andrews to G. K. Gokhale, August 16, 1914, from Santiniketan, File 11, no. 3, Gokhale Collection, Microfilm Accession No. 1273, Private Archives, NAI, Delhi.

Mother and Advaita (oneness) philosophy nurtured, at least for a while in the early decades of his stay in India, a quest for a broader theological understanding of God that drew on Eastern spirituality to uphold what might be called, for the lack of a better term, a Unitarian outlook. So undone and removed from the conservative Christianity he had inherited was Andrews, that he was willing to give room to other religions in their dialogue with Christianity. Therefore, in 1914 he would entertain the notion that the Hindu reform organizations such as the Brahmo Samaj and Arya Samaj would through their good work "bring in the Kingdom of Christ and might in the future, even bear some relationship to the Church."[25] Andrews had changed much since his Cambridge days where he had remained, as one contemporary described him, a "narrow-minded high Churchman."[26]

This period of doubt and theological undoing, which lasted for nearly twenty years (1904-21), caused great consternation among the English community in India and posed risks to Andrews's religious career in Christian circles.[27] It also caused him considerable anxiety. However, this painful experience of being undone also left him unfettered to broaden his friendships across religions and pursue interfaith dialogue and understanding. In 1913, he wrote to his friend Munshi Ram that "revival of the true spirit of religion not in mutually exclusive forms but rather inclusive forms, not by the revival of a zeal which makes for new and bitter rivalries but by a zeal which makes for harmony & peace." He believed that "the whole world is getting tired and wearied at heart with these ceaseless rivalries of races & creeds & with the

---

25   C. B. Young writing to Farquhar, in DMN July 1914 and also quoted in Farquhar to Mott, June 4, 1914 (New York). All cited in O'Connor, *A Clear Star*, 217-18, 266n60.

26   Canon Rev. Tissington Tatlow to Marjorie Sykes, January 6, 1947, from London, CFA Papers, 28(i)/image 188, 2 pp., esp. p. 1, Rabindra Bhavana Archives, Visva-Bharati University, Santiniketan, West Bengal. See also Tinker, *Ordeal of Love*, 24; Chaturvedi and Sykes, *Charles Freer Andrews*, 40-41.

27   Tinker, *Ordeal of Love*, 179.

sectarian spirit whether in Church or state & that the future is not with the warmakers but with the peacemakers."[28] Andrews was quick to discern the divine working in the lives of others, even if they were from other faiths, a view that was not shared by many of his Christian peers. He had a deep reverence for Dwijendranath Tagore, who was the elder brother of the poet and Nobel Laureate Rabindranath Tagore. Andrews wrote that Dwijendranath was someone "who has the face of a man who is living continually in the Presence of God."[29]

An Ordeal of Love

The process by which Andrews became undone was nothing short of what historian Hugh Tinker would call an "ordeal of love." Andrews's theological excursions allowed him to travel outside his religious roots and pursue the interfaith friendships throughout his life in India. He was able to pursue them without losing his own strong allegiance to the Christian faith, a fact noted by many of his contemporaries, drawn from a diversity of religious backgrounds. To be undone in this fashion is to allow the stranger into one's midst. In Andrews's case, the process began at home in England and it would progressively mold him to become the embracing, inclusive, and plural person he was to become. Even so, this transformation came at a considerable personal cost for Andrews as he managed the expectations of his family, peers, friends, and co-workers.

As Andrews's life testifies, the pursuit of plural friendships can be an ordeal of love. Andrews's friends, in turn, drawn as they were from other religions, would unhesitatingly testify to his Christian roots. The poet Rabindranath, himself a Universalist at heart and a

---

28 CFA to Munshi Ram, July 21 [probably 1913] from Calcutta, CFA Papers, Munshi Ram Correspondence, Microfilm Accession no. 335, reel 22, NAI, Delhi. Andrews's views here summarized a lecture he delivered in Calcutta on "International Brotherhood" at the Brahma Mandir.

29 CFA to Munshi Ram, July 30 [probably 1913] from Santiniketan, CFA Papers, Munshi Ram Correspondence, Microfilm Accession No. 335, reel 22, NAI, Delhi.

close confidant of Andrews throughout his life in India, was quick to recognize the power of the Christian faith on Andrews's life and work. A few months after Andrews's death in April 1940, Tagore recalled:

> Andrews came to India in the days of her strenuous political struggle. Once he was convinced of the justice of Indian aspirations, his Christian faith and charity led him to immediately take up the cause of the oppressed and the lowliest in the face of ridicule and active opposition from his own countrymen. We must clearly realize it is one thing to sacrifice oneself for one's own motherland, the inspiration being common and usual, it is quite another thing to sacrifice oneself to the cause of a foreign land. To recognize the common bond of the human soul, an infinite resource of love and inspiration is needed. And this he had in an ample measure. This large humanitarian spirit imbibed from Christ's religion of love made him a true Christian. In no one man have I seen such triumph of Christianity. I was fortunate in having Andrews for an intimate friend. There are people bound to us by ties of necessity whom we can replace but his is an irreparable loss to the whole country.[30]

Another contemporary and close friend, Benarsidas Chaturvedi, recalled with warmth Andrews's characteristic treatment of fellow workers at Santiniketan, an educational institution that Tagore had set up in 1921 and where Andrews worked for much of his life. Chaturvedi wrote:

> I was waiting for Mr. Andrews who had gone to see the Poet [Rabindranath Tagore] in connection with the case of the detenues, when an elderly gentleman of dark complexion, haggard face and vacant look came and asked me about him. I said that Mr. Andrews had gone to see Gurudev [as Tagore was referred to] and would be returning soon. I requested the gentleman to take a chair. He humbly declined to do so. As soon as Mr. Andrews saw him from a distance he dashed forward to meet this man. "Oh, dear dear!

---

30 Letter from Rabindranath Tagore to Secretary, St. Mira's High School, Hyderabad (Sind), August 27, 1940, typescript, CFA Papers, 26/Image 168-169, Rabindra Bhavana Archives, Visva-Bharati University, Santiniketan, West Bengal. Tagore sent this message to St. Mira's High School in Hyderabad (Sind) on the unveiling of a portrait of C. F. Andrews on September 15, 1940, by J. N. Tata, the ex-mayor of Karachi Municipality.

You are Akshay! I was anxious how I should be able to see you at Calcutta. Now you must stay with me till I go to Calcutta after three days." Mr. Andrews kept him in his embrace for a few minutes and will not leave him. There were tears of joy in the eyes of both. I never knew who this great friend of Mr. Andrews was till I was told by a teacher in Shantiniketan that Akshaya Babu was a humble and self-sacrificing worker of Shantiniketan, who had developed leprosy and had to leave the place. It was Dinabandhu Andrews who arranged for his treatment, which he was undergoing at Calcutta. The scene instantly reminded me of a passage in the Bible telling us how Christ Himself embraced a leper and truly does this C.F.A[31] move about on the face of the earth in the footsteps of his Lord.[32]

Andrews would also provide a sense of what interfaith work would look like at an educational institution such as Visva-Bharati. When the Parsee community inquired about building a Zoroastrian Institute in Visva-Bharati in 1921, Andrews wrote to Tagore about his vision of interfaith work:

> With regard to the building of a Zoroastrian Institute I am perfectly happy in my mind—just as I should welcome with all my heart an Islamic Institute. But I feel that our simple central place of worship, with its white marble pavement and its absence of all imagery and symbol—except the pure white flowers the children bring at the time of religious service—is the best expression both of our individual freedom of belief and our common worship of the One Supreme. Each of us may add what colour he likes to that pure whiteness. But if we build our separate mosques and chapels and fire-temples we stand in danger of repeating over again the religious divisions of the world.[33]

---

31 Christ's Faithful Apostle, an acronym of Andrews's initials, probably coined by Gurdial Mallik, one of Andrew's colleagues at Santiniketan.

32 B. D. Chaturvedi, "An Interview with Mr. C. F. Andrews," undated, typescript and mss., Benarsidas Das Chaturvedi Collection (hereinafter BDC), Microfilm Acc. No. 315, IC-53, Private Archives, NAI, Delhi. See also Chaturvedi and Sykes, *Charles Freer Andrews*, 135-36.

33 Chaturvedi and Sykes, *Charles Freer Andrews*, 164.

Such expressions of interfaith living made it easy for others to claim him as one of their own religionists. In 1921, the Sri Guru Singh Sabha of Kampala sent an appreciative letter to "mahatma C. F. Andrews" thanking him for visiting their Gurudwara (temple). They noted that Andrews's life of service had also made him a follower of Guru Nanak who did the same. They identified him as being a true lover of their community.[34] While Andrews clearly affirmed his commitment to Christianity, he was also successful in connecting with other religious communities.[35] In August 1929, Andrews was invited to the inauguration of the Vedic Mission School at Marabella Village in Trinidad founded by Swami Jaimini Mehta. Andrews who was dressed in Indian attire spoke at the meeting. After the hoisting the flag and closing of the ceremony, Andrews offered a prayer in Sanskrit and in the speech said he was a Christian and the Christian religion taught love and it was through love that he was participating in the ceremony. He also sang, "Lead Thou Me on, Kindly Light" (one of Mahatma Gandhi's favorite hymns).[36] Again, in 1933, when Gandhi was ill through fasting, Andrews visited his friend and offered Sanskrit prayers and sung his favorite hymns such as "Lead, Kindly Light" and "When I Survey."[37]

Andrews frequently acted as a bridge to connect individuals and organizations, state and non-state actors, who would otherwise have

---

34 Letter from Waryam Singh, President, and Saud Singh, Secretary of Kampala Siri Guru Singh Sabha, Kampala, to C. F. Andrews, November 6, 1921, BDC Collection, Microfilm Acc. No. 315, 1B-534, Private Archives, NAI, Delhi.

35 Rabindranath Tagore would assert that his life of service of the poor had taken him out of the confines of any particular religion and made him one of the world. See Rabindranath Tagore, March 22, 1924, BDC Collection, Microfilm Acc. No. 315, 1B-533, Private Archives, NAI, Delhi. The full letter is cited in the section on Tagore.

36 "Din Bandhi C. F. Andrews at the Vedic Mission School," East Indian Weekly, August 24, 1929, B. D. Chaturvedi Collection, Microfilm Acc. No. 317, 1/D-244, Private Archives, NAI, Delhi. The event took place on August 18, 1929.

37 Chaturvedi and Sykes, *Charles Freer Andrews*, 273.

remained disconnected. In 1939, when the world Christian conference was held at Tambaram (near Chennai) under the auspices of the International Missionary Council, Andrews did his utmost to get the British and American organizers to meet with as many Indian leaders as they could, both Christian and non-Christian.[38]

Andrews's interfaith pursuits did not leave him a disinterested Christian lacking in commitment to his faith. When a crude attack on the Bible appeared in the *Vedic Magazine*, the monthly journal of the Arya Samaj, he responded with a letter to Munshi Ram: "We who are struggling to maintain in the world *a living belief in God* ought not to attempt to destroy that belief in others, and to use as our weapons the accusations of atheists and agnostics. That is fighting with poisoned weapons." He also promised the editor of the journal that he would contribute some of his own writings.[39] Andrews possessed a remarkable capacity to live at the edges of his Christian faith, which he embraced fully while remaining ever willing to undo himself as he engaged with religious difference. In a letter to Gandhi in 1937, Andrews laid out his view on Christianity, religious faith, and vision of religious pluralism. He wrote about keeping his faith because he believed the message that Christ came into the world to proclaim was the most complete and the most inspiring ever given to humans. This is what had kept him a Christian. However, he expected his friends to celebrate their faiths and share them with him. He was wary of easy syncretism and overlooking of those vital distinctions that characterized different religions.

When it came to a sensitive topic such as conversion, Andrews remained generous and open ended, emphasizing the freedom of the individual. He had himself had a powerful conversion experience at the age of nineteen as had many of his own friends.[40] Munshi Ram, who had been an atheist for a long time, had undergone a conversion

---

38 Ibid., 309.

39 Ibid., 88.

40 Andrews writes about his faith journey including his conversion in a number of places. See, for instance, Andrews, "A Pilgrim's Progress," 60-89.

experience after meetings with the Arya Samaj founder Dayanand Saraswati.[41] However, he believed that all should have the freedom to convert should they decide after due consideration and without inducement and coercion. For Andrews conversion was a deeply personal invitation and expression of an individual's freedom. E. C. Dewick, a contemporary missionary and admirer of Andrews, would recall a meeting between Gandhi and Andrews where the latter advocated conversion work among aboriginals and animists while Gandhi opposed this, saying, "No; not with a view to make them Christians; only to make them better animists!"[42] Gandhi was not opposed to conversion per se, provided it came from one's heart, and often asked Christian missionaries to model the life of C. F. Andrews, whose Christian faith was displayed not through words but through his personal life, similar to the unseen but yet experienced like the fragrance of a rose.[43]

The willingness to become undone in relation to others can be a risky affair. We can never fully predict how such journeys might end. After all, how far should one go in accommodating difference? Can one continue to remain committed to one's religious beliefs, affiliations, and practices? Andrews displayed a remarkable openness that placed him at the borderlands of prevailing wisdom about religious loyalties. In a sermon delivered at the Cathedral at Lahore in 1914, he gave some insight into the kind of risky living he had begun to undertake as he stood and looked at the world from the borderlands of his Christian faith:

---

41 Munshi Ram to CFA, April 25, 1913, from Kangri, CFA Papers, Munshi Ram Correspondence, Microfilm Acc. no. 334, reel 21, NAI, Delhi. This letter is also available in BDC Collection, Microfilm Acc. No. 334, IV/B-182, Private Archives, NAI, Delhi.

42 E. C. Dewick to Marjorie Sykes, September 19, 1946, from Great Shelfford, Cambs, CFA Papers, 28(i)/images 164-170, 7 pp., esp. p. 5, Rabindra Bhavana Archives, Visva-Bharati University, Santiniketan, West Bengal. Andrews's views on conversion merit further research.

43 See M. K. Gandhi, *Collected Works of Mahatma Gandhi*, vol. 64 (Delhi: Publication Division, 1976), 421.

> This, then, is what it means to be a Christian, to follow Christ; not the expression of an outward creed, but the learning of an inner life. . . . I say this today with a new emphasis, because I myself had formerly a narrow outlook; and I have been learning at last, painfully, eagerly, wistfully learning, to look first at the life rather than the creed. And as my outlook has widened, I have found Christ in strange, unlooked-for-places, far beyond the boundary of sect or dogma, of church or chapel, far beyond the formal definition of man's devising, or of man's exclusive pride.[44]

Toward the end of his life, Andrews would do some stocktaking and conclude that over the years he had been "drifting towards a complacent and patronizing 'humanist' attitude and had left out of count the startlingly supernatural claim to absolute allegiance that Christ makes. Schweitzer's last chapter [in his book *The Quest for the Historical Jesus*] brought me sharply back to reality. It made me renew, with a fresh conviction, my faith in a supernatural Christ who commands by His moral grandeur."[45] Andrews certainly took the risky road of interfaith dialogue and communication that few, if any, were willing to undertake. It took him to places that looking back at the end of his life seemed distant from the core of his faith commitments. It undid him in ways he did not expect and yet he was willing to undertake the journey and then circle back to a place where he would reaffirm his commitment to living life as Christ did. The plurality of his inward journey took him to multiple, and sometimes risky destinations that certainly changed him from within. This journey gave him the resilience needed to continue a lifelong journey of meaningful interfaith living and communication.

Can a life like this hold any promise for the creation of a civic sensibility that secures religious freedom and dialogue in our troubled world? Can the pursuit of diverse, inclusive, and plural friendships facilitate the creation of political cultures and public spaces, give room to diverse voices, tolerate dissent, and promote cross-cultural understanding? Would such a move resist the ghettoization of identities

---

44   Cited in O'Connor, *A Clear Star*, 212.

45   Andrews, "A Pilgrim's Progress," 60-89. The quote is from p. 84.

around nation, caste, race, gender, class, and ethnicity (to name a few), by establishing the plurality of persons whose distinctive differences are simultaneously preserved? As the Nagel Institute's India program unfolded, these questions surfaced repeatedly in my mind, as did the remarkable answers offered by the life and testimony of Charles Andrews.[46]

Conclusion: Imagining a New Community

Charles Andrews's testimony speaks to us in the twenty-first century; it cues us to the fact that the friendship and partnership he experienced can only take place if we are willing to cultivate a humanity that begins with our undoing. Andrews's critical distancing of himself from his own racial, cultural, national, imperial, and religious roots gave him the freedom to extend the same moral concern for strangers he would have extended to his family, kin, and friends. He was able to cross social, cultural, and national boundaries that were otherwise hard to transgress. The large volume of writings he left behind is a testimony to his efforts to develop a new narrative imagination of the kind hinted at earlier by Martha Nussbaum. Andrews's life has become a testament to a life of friendship or what Leela Gandhi has referred to as an "affective cosmopolitanism," the "ethico-political practice of a desiring self inexorably drawn towards difference."[47]

Martha Nussbaum once wrote, "The Stoics stress that to be a citizen of the world one does not need to give up local identifications, which can be a source of great richness in life. They suggest that we think

---

46 Here, I am reminded of the promising work being undertaken the Interfaith Coalition for Peace in India and by Eboo Patel and his InterFaith Youth Core in the United States. Such organizations promise to leverage interfaith dialogue and cooperation in the area of civic engagement and higher education. See http://www.icpindia.org/index.html and https://www.ifyc.org/.

47 Leela Gandhi, *Affective Communities: Anticolonial Thought, Fin-de-Siècle Radicalism, and the Politics of Friendship* (Durham: Duke University Press, 2006), see especially p. 17.

of ourselves not as devoid of local affiliations, but as surrounded by a series of concentric circles. . . . Outside all these circles is the largest one, humanity. Our task as citizens of the world will be to draw the circles somehow toward the center."[48] Charles Freer Andrews certainly tried to draw these circles toward that shared center as he journeyed toward becoming a citizen of the world. As he became undone, he began to move outward, crossing the boundaries placed on his location by culture, power, faith, and history, in ever widening circles of inclusion and intercultural engagement. However, it will take considerable courage and imagination to seek the kind of friendships Andrews pursued as one of the vehicles for human renewal, engagement, liberation, and shared living in our world today. A few months after his death in April 1940, Andrews's close friend, the poet Rabindranath Tagore, hinted at Andrews's contribution to such an effort when he wrote, "To recognize the common bond of the human soul, an infinite resource of love and inspiration is needed. And this he had in an ample measure. This large humanitarian spirit imbibed from Christ's religion of love made him a true Christian. In no one man have I seen such triumph of Christianity. I was fortunate in having Andrews for an intimate friend."[49] The generous friendship shared by Tagore and Andrews gives us the ingredients we need to imagine what the center of a new shared circle of humanity might look like in the twenty-first century.

---

48 Martha Nussbaum, cited in Grant H. Cornwell and Eve W. Stoddard, *Globalizing Knowledge: Connecting International and Intercultural Studies* (Washington, DC: Association of American Universities and Colleges, 1999), viii.

49 Letter from Rabindranath Tagore to Secretary, St. Mira's High School, Hyderabad (Sind), August 27, 1940, typescript, CFA Papers, 26/Image 168-169, Rabindra Bhavana Archives, Visva-Bharati University, Santiniketan, West Bengal. A laudatory testimony from Mahatma Gandhi can be found in Gandhi, *Collected Works of Mahatma Gandhi*, vol. 64, 421.

Chapter 4

Christian Conversion in India

Political Exploitation or Personal Transformation?

Joshua Iyadurai

"Well, some of the untouchables (Dalits) are worse than cows in their understanding. I mean they no more distinguish the relative merits of Islam and Hinduism and Christianity than a cow. . . . I have no remorse about the propriety of the analogy."

M. K. Gandhi, *The Collected Works of Mahatma Gandhi*, 70:258.

"Conversion of an individual does not take place after a serious and comparative study of philosophies by him. It is by exploitation of poverty, illiteracy and ignorance, offering of inducements and by deceptive tactics that people are converted."

M. S. Golwalkar, *Bunch of Thoughts*, Part Two, XV, The Ways and Means: 8

In India, religious conversion has never been a purely personal or religious matter. As several of the chapters in this book make clear, anti-conversion laws have been proposed and enacted in India since colonial times, and a reaction against Christian conversions has been a driver of Hindu revivalism and nationalism over the past 130 years. Among the chief politicizers of conversion in the twentieth century were M. K. Gandhi, the highly acclaimed liberal Hindu leader who led the movement for Indian independence, and M. S. Golwalkar, the leading architect of Hindu nationalism who called conversion an anti-national activity. These two leaders portrayed all conversions as either forced or false, on the assumption that only poor, illiterates, Dalits, and Tribal people were being converted. Thus, they politicized a religious phenomenon to advance a nationalist agenda. As a result, there are many attempts in India today to restrict an individual's or a community's right to choose religious beliefs. Indians from all social ranks, however, have converted to Christianity. Indeed, by focusing on the conversion narratives of some Brahmins who have turned to Christ, this study will show that Christian converts in India are a far cry from the Hindu nationalist stereotype of them.

To a great extent, the present debate on conversion in India is still largely based on the assumptions of these two leaders, M. K. Gandhi and M. S. Golwalkar, even though they represent differing political ideologies—liberal and right-wing. Since Gandhi is held in high esteem as a liberal Hindu leader, the right-wing leaders use him today to support their anti-conversion activities. In 2017, the Bharatiya Janata Party (BJP) government in Jharkhand, a state in North India, issued an official advertisement in Hindi with a quote attributed to Gandhi on conversion of the Dalits and Tribals:

> If Christian missionaries feel that only conversion to Christianity is the path to salvation, why don't you start with me [Gandhi] or Mahadev Desai [secretary to Gandhi]? Why do you stress conversion of the simple, illiterate, poor and forest-dwellers? These people can't differentiate between Jesus and Mohammad and are not likely to understand your preachings. They are mute and simple, like cows. These simple, poor, Dalit and forest-dwellers, whom you make Christians, do so not for Jesus but for rice and their stomach.[1]

---

1 Prashant Pandey, "Jharkhand Quotes Mahatma Gandhi to Push Its Conversion Bill," *Indian Express*, August 12, 2017, http://indianexpress.

Many have denied the authenticity of this quote; however, Gandhi had made similar statements with similar views on the Dalits, such as the quote at the start of this chapter.

This politicized and caste-oriented point of view needs a response. Therefore, I present a phenomenological perspective on religious conversion to Christianity by Brahmins, the priestly caste. By using interpretative phenomenological analysis, a research tool from the social sciences, I delineate the major themes from the conversion narratives of Brahmin converts to Christianity in India who claim that conversion transformed their lives. And as a Christian theologian, I will reflect on how the agency of these individuals might be interacting with the role of God in the conversion process. This chapter is therefore a response to the politicization of religious conversion and the false assumptions of Gandhi and Golwalkar on conversion. It is simply not true that other than Dalits, Tribal people, poor, and illiterates, no one converts to Christianity. Therefore, the current debate on conversion in India badly needs to be recast.

It is fair, I think, to present the views of Gandhi and Golwalkar on conversion as a sort of baseline, and then contrast them to the themes that emerged from conversion narratives of Brahmin converts to Christianity. What we will clearly see from the data is that in the conversion process, the individuals are active and exercise agency. And what I see as a theologian is that God plays a vital role too.

Conversion, simply put, is a change in commitment regarding one's religious beliefs and practices. But in India, religious conversion is viewed as anti-national activity by both Gandhi and Golwalkar. The Western world looks at Gandhi as a Mahatma (great soul) who lived more like Christ than Christians and a liberal Hindu leader. But a closer analysis of his views on religious conversion shows that on the issue of conversion he was no better than Hindu nationalists. Gandhi saw conversion as anti-national and a threat to Hinduism, while more

com/article/india/jharkhand-quotes-mahatma-gandhi-to-push-its-conversion-bill-4792888/, accessed January 20, 2018.

concretely, Golwalkar considered religious conversion a threat to his political agenda of establishing a Hindu nation.

Gandhi on Religious Conversion

Gandhi's views on conversion seem contradictory. On the one hand, he viewed conversion as a spiritual act and said that conversion "is a highly personal matter for the individual and his God."[2] He also said that "conversion is a heart-process known only to and by God."[3] He indicated that such spiritual conversions are possible, and he was not against them. "If some people for their inward satisfaction and growth change their religion, let them do so."[4] Gandhi evidently was not against conversion for spiritual reasons, but he never accepted the need for the people in India to convert to another religion. He considered Christianity a foreign religion: "Every nation considers its own faith to be as good as that of any other. Certainly, the great faiths held by the people of India are adepuate [sic] for her people."[5] Gandhi identified Hinduism and its offshoots with the land of India itself and insisted that "India's great faiths are all-sufficing for her."[6]

Gandhi categorically stated his position in this conversation with the Anglican missionary and theologian C. F Andrews:

> C.F.A.: What would you say to a man who after considerable thought and prayer said that he could not have his peace and salvation except by becoming a Christian?
>
> GANDHI: I would say that if a non-Christian, say a Hindu, came to a Christian and made that statement, he should ask him to become a good Hindu rather than find goodness in change of faith.
>
> C.F.A.: I cannot in this go the whole length with you, though you know my own position. I discarded the position that there is no

---

2   Gandhi, *Collected Works,* 68:20.

3   Ibid., 38:16.

4   Ibid., 41:113.

5   Ibid., 51:413-14.

6   Ibid., 51:414.

salvation except through Christ long ago. But supposing the Oxford Group Movement people changed the life of your son, and he felt like being converted, what would you say?

GANDHI: I would say that the Oxford Group may change the lives of as many as they like, but not their religion. They can draw their attention to the best in their respective religions and change their lives by asking them to live according to them. There came to me a man, the son of Brahmin parents, who said his reading of your book had led him to embrace Christianity. I asked him if he thought that the religion of his forefathers was wrong. He said "No." Then I said: "Is there any difficulty about your accepting the Bible as one of the great religious books of the world and Christ as one of the great teachers?" I said to him that you had never through your books asked Indians to take up the Bible and embrace Christianity, and that he had misread your book.[7]

As his conclusion to the above conversation makes clear, he could never accept that a Brahmin could convert to Christianity.

Gandhi did not want anyone moving from one religion to another. This position suited him well as a Hindu because Hindus cannot accept anyone from outside the caste. While talking about *varnashrama* (the caste system), Gandhi made this point clear: "From time to time persons belonging to other faiths have been absorbed by Hinduism, but they were not known as Hindus during their lifetime. . . . Sister Nivedita [a Western follower of Swami Vivekananda], for instance, embraced Hinduism but we do not think of her as a Hindu."[8] Because of the caste system Hinduism cannot be a converting religion. One is born into a caste; therefore, someone who comes from another faith cannot enter a caste. Indian people can reconvert to Hinduism because they can trace their ancestral caste. Thus, Hinduism can grow only biologically. Conversion thus is a zero-sum game for Hindus, and Gandhi opposed it to block exodus from Hinduism.

Regarding the Dalits, Christianity's most numerous converts, Gandhi asked, "Where is the sense of talking of a sudden awakening

---

7 Ibid., 70:59-60.
8 Ibid., 22:315.

of spiritual hunger among the untouchables (Dalits) and then trying to exploit a particular-situation? The poor Harijans[9] [Dalits] have no mind, intelligence, no sense of difference between God and no God."[10] He further compared the Dalits to cows in a conversation with John Mott: "Well, some of the untouchables [Dalits] are worse than cows in understanding."[11] Gandhi, being a caste Hindu,[12] portrayed the Dalits as less than humans, which is a typical view shared by all the caste Hindus. To sum up Gandhi's religious concerns, he argued that India does not need another religion and that the Dalits are not capable of making a religious choice.

Gandhi's concerns about conversion were also political. He said that "conversion must not mean denationalization. . . . [It] should mean a life of greater dedication to one's country, greater surrender to God, greater self-purification."[13] But mostly it meant "denationalization and Europeanization."[14] For Gandhi, adopting Christianity was embracing the religion of the colonizers, and he implied that conversion led to losing one's greater dedication to the nation. Gandhi painted the rising conversion movements of his day as anti-national movements and began to see conversion was a threat to the nation.

Therefore, Gandhi threatened to bring anti-conversion laws into post-independence India. "If I had power and could legislate, I should

---

9   Harijan is a name Gandhi gave to the untouchables which means "children of God." This term has a derogatory connotation, referring to the children of the Devadasis (temple prostitutes). Therefore, the untouchables (Dalits) rejected this label.

10   Gandhi, *Collected Works*, 70:59.

11   Ibid., 70:77.

12   "Caste Hindu" refers to one who belongs to one of the three castes: Brahmins, Kshatriyas, or Vaisyas. Scholars and even the public these days avoid using the term "high caste" or "upper caste" to refer to the above three castes of Hinduism. Wherever there is a reference to all three or one of the castes, I use the term "caste Hindu" in this chapter.

13   Gandhi, *Collected Works*, 32:316.

14   Ibid., 39:315.

stop all proselytizing."[15] He also discredited the contribution made by Christian missionaries to India: "They (Christian missionaries) do harm to those amongst whom they work and those amongst whom they do not work, i.e. the harm is done to the whole of India."[16] Gandhi could never accept that serving humanity is the essence of Christianity. He said, "Your (Christian missionaries') duty is done with the ulterior motive of proselytizing."[17] A Christian missionary was "like any vendor of goods. He has no special spiritual merit that will distinguish him from those to whom he goes."[18]

Contrary to the secular understanding of separating religion and politics, Gandhi said that "those who say that religion has nothing to do with politics do not know what religion means."[19] On another occasion he said, "Many of my political friends despair of me because they say that even my politics are derived from my religion. And they are right. My politics and all other activities of mine are derived from my religion."[20] Even though he said that "I hold my religion dearer than my country and that therefore *I am a Hindu first* and nationalist after . . . [but] I simply thereby imply that the *interests of my country are identical with those of my religion*" (italics added).[21] For Gandhi religious interest and national interest share the same value. Having this as a backdrop, we now turn to the political context that made Gandhi politicize the issue of religious conversion.

---

15 Ibid., 67:48.

16 Ibid., 70:139.

17 Ibid., 51:178.

18 Ibid., 71:98.

19 Mohandas K. Gandhi, *An Autobiography or The Story of My Experiments with the Truth*, trans. Mahadev Desai (Ahmadabad: Navjeevan Publishing House, 1991), 608.

20 Gandhi, *Collected Works*, 63:200.

21 Ibid., 26:223.

The situation that Gandhi charged missionaries with trying to exploit was the political crisis in which B. R. Ambedkar, the Dalit leader, declared that he and his followers would leave Hinduism en masse.

The Dalits, who were one-fifth of the population, were appealing for political rights as a minority community under the British. During the 1930-32 Round Table Conference to discuss the future of independent India, Ambedkar succeeded in getting the British to recognize Dalits as a separate minority group and allow the Dalits to elect their own representatives as well as to participate along with the Hindu community in the election process. As one historian put it, "Compelled by the arithmetic of parliamentary representation, the self-styled leaders of Hinduism now woke up to the misery of their 'untouchable brethren'"[22]

Gandhi, who spoke for the Dalits all along and projected himself as their messiah, could not accept this arrangement because it reduced the dominant status of the Hindu community in the political arena. If the Dalits were not considered as Hindus, and had political rights and powers, they would be no longer under the caste Hindus, and that threatened the ability of Hinduism to prevail. Caste Hindus cannot do all the menial jobs the Dalits do for them because that would make them ceremonially unclean. The caste Hindus needed the Dalits for the servitude for the whole ritual system to survive. Gandhi rightly understood the consequences of the situation. Thus, he protested to the British prime minister: "In the establishment of separate electorate at all for the 'Depressed' classes (Dalits) I sense the injection of poison that is calculated to destroy Hinduism."[23]

But the British refused, and Gandhi declared a fast to death and projected his fast, as if it were meant for the betterment of the Dalits. He was of the view that the separate electorate would not help the Dalits and would create more tensions between the caste Hindus and

---

22   Braj Ranjan Mani, *Debrahmanising History: Dominance and Resistance in Indian Society* (New Delhi: Manohar, 2005), 345.

23   Gandhi, *Collected Works,* 57:8.

the Dalits. Gandhi assumed the role of messiah for the Dalits and took it upon himself that it was his duty to protect the welfare of the Dalits.[24]

Gandhi demanded for this provision to be revoked, or for the Dalits to give up their political rights to elect their own representatives. With the British standing by their decision, widespread public pressure grew to save Gandhi's life. Ambedkar was under tremendous pressure to save Gandhi's life by surrendering the newly gained political rights of the Dalits for a separate electorate. Eventually Ambedkar yielded to the pressure and surrendered the political rights of the Dalits to save Gandhi's life. Ambedkar, having left with no weapon in his hands to fight against the discrimination of the Dalits, picked up the weapon of religious conversion and declared that he would not die as a Hindu.

In October 1935, at a conference of the representatives of the Dalits, Ambedkar declared that he would leave Hinduism.[25] In this context, V. S Azariah, the first Indian Anglican bishop, felt it was the movement of the Holy Spirit for the liberation of the Dalits and he spearheaded the conversion of the Dalits. And conversions in South India proceeded at a rapid rate.[26] Gandhi was unhappy that missionaries were trying to turn the wind to their side and he considered V. S. Azariah the enemy number one.[27] Therefore he politicized religious conversion and projected all conversion movements, including that of Ambedkar, as anti-national and disloyal to the freedom struggle. Christianity, he insisted, was synonymous with denationalization. Thereafter, Ambedkar

---

24 Harold Coward, "Gandhi, Ambedkar, and Untouchability," in *Indian Critiques of Gandhi*, ed. Harold Coward (Albany: State University of New York Press, 2003), 47.

25 Bhim Rao Ambedkar, quoted in Bhagwan Das, *Thus Spoke Ambedkar*, vol. 4 (Bangalore: Ambedkar Sahitya Prakshan, 1980), 108.

26 Susan Billington Harper, *In the Shadow of Mahatma: Bishop V. S. Azariah and the Travails of Christianity in British India* (Grand Rapids, MI: Eerdmans, 2000), 176-220.

27 For a detailed picture on the relationship between Gandhi and Azariah, see ibid., 291-352.

observed, Gandhi became "a virulent adversary of all missionary propaganda. He particularly object[ed] to the missionaries spreading the Christian Gospel among the Untouchables."[28]

Since many of Gandhi's views on religious conversion and missionary work are no different from the Hindu nationalists' views, it is no surprise that Arun Shourie, a Bharatiya Janata Party (BJP) leader, referred to Gandhi often to justify his opposition to Christian conversion.[29] Many other right-wing Hindu nationalist leaders today also quote Gandhi to attack Christian mission.[30]

Golwalkar on Religious Conversion

M. S. Golwalkar was an early leader—in fact, the second supreme leader—of the Rashtriya Swaymsevak Sangh (RSS), meaning National Volunteer Organization, one of the parent bodies of Hindu nationalism. Golwalkar was the leading architect of Hindu nationalism. His books *Bunch of Thoughts* (1966) and *We or Our Nationhood Defined* (1939) are considered fundamental documents that shaped Hindu nationalist ideology. Hindu nationalists do not accept India as a secular state, but as a Hindu nation. The foundation for the Hindu nationalist movement is the claim that India has been a Hindu nation for ages. Said Golwalkar, "Undoubtedly . . . we—Hindus—have been in undisputed and undisturbed possession of this land for over 8 or even 10 thousand years before the land was invaded by any foreign race."[31]

For Golwalkar, the idea of nation is much more than a political entity. "National existence is entirely dependent upon the coordinated existence of the five elements constituting the Nation idea—Country,

---

28 Das, *Thus Spoke Ambedkar*, 704.

29 Arun Shourie, *Missionaries in India: Continuities, Changes, Dilemmas* (New Delhi: ASA, 1994).

30 Lalsangkima Pachuau. "A Clash of 'Mass Movements'? Christian Missions and the Gandhian Nationalist Movement in India," *Transformation* 31, no. 3 (2014): 164.

31 Madhavrao S. Golwalkar, *We or Our Nationhood Defined* (Nagpur: Bharath Publications, 1939), 42.

Race, Religion, Culture and Language."[32] Further, he argued, "Nation is a compound of five distinct factors fused into one indissoluble whole, the famous five 'Unities'—Geographical (country), Racial (Race), Religious (Religion), cultural (Culture) and linguistic (language)."[33] Hindu nationalists' ideology has the following fundamental assumptions. The religion of the land and the race is Hinduism. The culture of the country is the Hindu culture. Sanskrit is the ancient language of Hindustan,[34] and India is a Hindu nation. Hindu nationalists polarize the society as Hindus and the rest—"We and They."

This position has far-reaching consequences for religious minorities, especially for Muslims and Christians. Golwalkar was blunt in this regard:

> The foreign races (Muslims and Christians) in Hindustan must either adopt the Hindu culture and language, must learn to respect and hold in reverence Hindu religion, must entertain no idea but those of the glorification of the Hindu race and culture, i.e., of the Hindu nation and must lose their separate existence to merge in the Hindu race, or may stay in the country, wholly subordinated to the Hindu Nation, claiming nothing, deserving no privileges, far less any preferential treatment—not even citizen's rights. There is, at least should be, no other course for them to adopt.[35]

Golwalkar argued that religion was central to the nationhood of Hindustan. Separation of religion and nation was a Western creation but not true of Hindustan.

> Religion is an all-absorbing entity. . . . it has become eternally woven into the life of the Race, and forms, as it were, its very Soul. With us, every action in life, individual, social or political, is a command of Religion. We make war or pRace [*sic*], engage in arts and crafts, amass wealth and give it away, indeed we are born and we die—all in accord

---

32 Ibid., 93.

33 Ibid., 60.

34 Hindusthan means "land of Hindus." Golwalkar and other Hindu nationalists would prefer to use Hindusthan instead of India.

35 Golwalkar, *We or Our Nationhood Defined*, 104-5.

with religious injunctions. Naturally, therefore, we are what our great Religion has made us. Our Race-spirit is a child of our Religion and so with us Culture is but a product of our all-comprehensive Religion, a part of its body and not distinguishable from it.[36]

Anthropologists see religion as part of a culture; but for Golwalkar, culture is a product of religion, so with politics. The idea of nation, for him, Hindustan, is a cultural entity that emerged out of the religion, Hinduism. Therefore, politics cannot be separated from religion. "Indeed, politics itself becomes, in the case of such a Religion, a small factor, to be considered and followed solely as one of the commands of Religion and in accord with such commands."[37] Political involvement thus is a religious act for Golwalkar.

In the light of this ideology of nation, we can now understand Golwalkar's views on conversion. Golwalkar said, "If . . . they attack the national society—whether in the form of religious conversion or destruction or desecration of places of worship or insulting the memory of the great sons of this soil or in whatever other manner, such groups should be termed 'anti-national.'"[38] Religious conversion of Hindus, he argued, "is nothing but making them succumb to divided loyalty in place of having undivided and absolute loyalty to the nation. It is dangerous to the security of the nation and the country. It is therefore necessary to put a stop to it."[39]

Golwalkar's other premise is that there is no spiritual conversion, only materially interested conversion. So only the poor, Dalits, and Tribal people convert; caste Hindus, educated, and rich do not convert. Therefore, Golwalkar said, "Conversion of an individual does not take place after a serious and comparative study of philosophies by him. It is by exploitation of poverty, illiteracy and ignorance, offering of

---

36   Ibid., 22.

37   Ibid., 70.

38   Golwalkar, *Bunch of Thoughts*, Part Two, XV: 3.

39   Ibid., 8.

inducements and by deceptive tactics that people are converted. There is no question of a true change of heart involved in this."[40]

Golwalkar viewed Christian service to the poor, Dalits, and Tribal people as means to convert; he never accepted humanitarian services as the essence of Christianity. In like manner the current RSS chief Mohan Bhagwat accused the Nobel laureate and canonized Catholic saint Mother Teresa, saying that her "work had ulterior motive, which was to convert the person who was being served to Christianity."[41]

Gandhi and Golwalkar share common views on many aspects. Both considered religion and politics to be integral. Their political actions were inspired by Hinduism. They viewed Islam and Christianity as religions that were foreign to India. They considered conversion to be anti-national. They politicized religious conversion for their political gain. They considered the Dalits and Tribal people to be incapable of experiencing spiritual conversion; their conversion is either forced or enticed. Both assumed that educated or caste Hindus would never convert. On one aspect Gandhi differed from Golwalkar; Gandhi accepted co-existence of non-Hindus in India, whereas Golwalkar wanted non-Hindus either to glorify Hinduism or to leave; he left no options for them to live on an equal basis to Hindus in India. The present campaign against conversion by the RSS with the support of the government had its ideological foundation laid by both Gandhi and Golwalkar.

Today's Brahmin Converts to Christianity

So that is the ideology, but what is the reality? Contrary to the assumptions of Gandhi and Golwalkar, people in all walks of life and from all castes in India embrace Christianity. Despite the hostile situations for Christian churches in India, conversion to Christianity

---

40   Ibid.

41   Rajendra Sharma, "Conversion Was Mother Teresa's Real Aim, RSS Chief Mohan Bhagwat Says," *Times of India*, February 24, 2015, http://timesofindia.indiatimes.com/india/Conversion-was-Mother-Teresas-real-aim-RSS-chief-Mohan-Bhagwat-says/articleshow/46348555.cms.

is on the increase. Both Gandhi and Golwalkar spread the view that the Dalits and the poor convert to Christianity for material benefits. They assumed that no one from other backgrounds would convert. To counter their assumptions, I examine the conversion narratives of several contemporary Brahmin converts to Christianity by using a phenomenological approach, called interpretative phenomenological analysis (IPA). Its aim, say some leading advocates, "is to explore in detail how participants are making sense of their personal and social world, and the main currency for an IPA study is the meanings particular experiences, events, states hold for participants."[42] This approach enables us to see Brahmins' conversion from their own perspective.

For a qualitative study in general, and especially for a phenomenological study, a large sample is not required. The object is to get deep and rich reflections from one's research subjects rather than to collect broad sets of data.[43] Therefore, even though I found many more examples of Brahmin converts, I limited myself to six conversion narratives of Brahmins to Christianity.

I used a few criteria for the selection of these samples based on a purposive sampling method. One should be a Brahmin convert to Christianity and live in India or have experienced conversion while living in India. The usual method of data collection for a phenomenological study is in-depth interviews, but I chose not to use them. I did not want it to seem that I was choosing the most suitable interviewees that matched my research purpose. I took the liberty to do a Google search for my data. I searched for conversion narratives of Brahmin converts to Christianity in India. I looked for converts who were narrating their conversion experience or whose narratives were conveyed by others, but the narratives must be in the first-person account. These narratives thus were not produced for the purposes of my research, but for the converts' own reasons. The advantage of this method is

---

42 Jonathan A. Smith and Mike Osborn, "Interpretative Phenomenological Analysis," in *Qualitative Psychology: A Practical Guide to Research Methods*, ed. Jonathan A. Smith (London: Sage, 2003), 53.

43 Ibid., 56.

that the researcher has no role to play in shaping the narratives; they pre-exist. There is of course a subjective element to the narrative data irrespective of the method; converts narrating their experience are making interpretations of their experience and employing their own strategies to narrate it. This is a limitation, of course, for all qualitative study.

By using IPA, I saw the following themes emerge from the narratives. They readily corresponded to the themes that I developed within my larger study on conversion,[44] but I did not confine myself to those themes, nor did I impose those themes arbitrarily on these narratives. I have let the objective of the chapter—to make a case for converting for spiritual reasons and against the politicization of religious conversion—guide me in digging out the themes from the conversion narratives under study. I was open to pick up any new themes that emerged out of the analysis—including political ones. But there were none of those. The narrators became followers of Jesus for deeply personal reasons.

Profiles[45]

Anand Mahadevan is associate editor of *The Economic Times*. He experienced conversion at a young age while his friend was offering a prayer for him. After the prayer he felt peace and began to follow Jesus. He, his wife, and their two children follow Jesus. He narrated his conversion experience in the *Out Look* weekly in 2008 titled "I the Convert"[46] in response to all kinds of accusations against Christian conversions in India.

---

44 Joshua Iyadurai, *Transformative Religious Experience: A Phenomenological Understanding of Religious Conversion* (Eugene, OR: Pickwick Publications, 2015).

45 In order to differentiate between the converts of the study and authors, I used first names for the converts in the text and notes.

46 Anand Mahadevan, "I the Convert," *Out Look* 27 (October 2008), https://www.outlookindia.com/magazine-story-i-the-convert-238770, accessed November 27, 2017. Cited hereinafter as Anand.

Jayasudha Kapoor is a film actress from South India; she has acted in more than two hundred films. She was fond of Jesus since her school days along with other gods such as Venkateshwara and Hanuman. She is a philanthropist now and would like to emulate Mother Teresa. In an interview to a news portal, she narrated her conversion experience.[47] She miraculously escaped when she was thrown from a water scooter. Ever since she became a practicing Christian.

Mani Iyer is a traveling preacher. He was deeply involved in his religion as a teenager, when he was seeking to connect with the Supreme God. One of his classmates in school introduced Jesus to him and he found that his search ended with reading the New Testament. He was attacked, and God saved him miraculously.[48]

Rajesh Nayak is a businessman. As a boy he befriended his schoolteacher who was a Christian. That led him to attend church along with her and later he married a Catholic. He was actively involved in the church along with his family. Only after the death of his parents did he convert to Christianity. The catechism classes helped him make Jesus real in his life.[49]

Ramachandran Rajkumar is an engineer by profession who left his job to preach Jesus. He was deeply religious before encountering Jesus and believed that all religions were the same. Although his colleague told him that salvation was possible only through Jesus, he could not

---

47 Jayasudha Kapoor, "I Hated Every Minute of It," *Rediff.com*, May 13, 2000, http://www.rediff.com/movies-2000-may-13-jaya.htm, accessed November 27, 2017. Cited hereinafter as Jayasudha.

48 Mani Iyer, "Mani Iyer," *Conversions in India—Testimonies*, January 31, 2009, https://conversionsinindia.wordpress.com/2009/01/31/mani-iyer/, accessed November 27, 2017. Cited hereinafter as Mani.

49 Rajesh Nayak, "I, a Hindu Brahmin Convert to Christianity, Even Though Everyone Thought I Was Already a Catholic," *AsiaNews.it*, March 29, 2017, http://www.asianews.it/news-en/-I,-a-Hindu-Brahmin-convert-to-Christianity,-even-though-everyone-thought-I-was-already-a-Catholic-40331.html, accessed November 29, 2017. Cited hereinafter as Rajesh.

accept his claim, but he liked his colleague for his values and qualities. To prove him wrong, Ramachandran read the Bible, but that led eventually to his receiving Jesus. Now he travels around the world to preach Jesus.[50]

Susheela Ragunathan, along with her husband, is serving Jesus among the Brahmins. She was born a fifth child to her parents and that was considered as a curse. She was often considered as the cause of any mishap or crisis in the family because she was their bad luck. She studied in a Christian school, and one day she went to the chapel and cried before a crucifix. Jesus tapped her and told her that he was there for her. She was filled with joy and later led the entire family to follow Jesus.[51]

Major Themes in the Conversion Process

These narratives are rich with common themes. Eighteen of them emerged as obviously recurring motifs.

1. *Family Situation:* These converts commonly hail from Brahmin families. They are educated, and regarding economic status, they are either rich or high middle class. All had a happy childhood, except Susheela, who was considered a bad luck to the family. All the participants were religious and believed sincerely in Hinduism.

2. *Attitude toward Christianity:* India is a multi-religious society; therefore, people are aware of the basics of other religions. Jayasudha said she was "very fond of Jesus,"[52] but Mani hated Christianity. He was a member of a right-wing organization that opposed Christianity

---

50 Ramachandran Rajkumar, "Ramachandran Rajkumar," *Conversions in India—Testimonies*, January 1, 2009. https://conversionsinindia.wordpress.com/2009/01/31/ramachandran-rajkumar/, accessed November 29, 2017. Cited hereinafter as Ramachandran.

51 Susheela Ragunathan, "Jesus, Did You Really Die for Me?" *Conversions in India—Testimonies*, May 8, 2013, https://conversionsinindia.wordpress.com/2013/05/08/susheela-raghunathan/, accesssed November 29, 2017. Cited hereinafter as Susheela.

52 Jayasudha.

and called himself "a hardcore Hindu [*sic*] fanatic."[53] Not everyone in this study had a positive attitude toward Christianity to begin with, even though they embraced Christianity at a later stage.

3. *Religiously Observant:* All sincerely believed that Hinduism is a true religion and they observed religious practices. Mani, as a teen, even officiated as a priest in a local temple. "As a devotee Hindu brahmin boy," he said, "I practiced all the religious customs and rituals of my religion with great zeal."[54] Others, while practicing Hinduism, believed that all religions are the same. Ramachandran believed that "every religion was the same, all Holy Books say the same things and that there are different ways of knowing God."[55] On the one hand, these Brahmins, while sincerely believing in their religion, also believed that all religions lead to God.

4. *Exposure to Christianity:* India's multi-religious context assures that children are exposed to several religions. Jayasudha, Rajesh, and Susheela studied in a convent school and got to know about Christianity there. Even so, the conversion process frequently was initiated by a conversation or a relationship with a Christian. For Rajesh, it was his teacher. Rajesh never claimed that the teacher wanted him to follow Christianity, but he was attracted to her life and quality and was fond of her as a child. He started attending church with her. Later he married a Catholic and attended church with his wife. For Mani, his classmate told him that he would find his search for God in the Bible. For Ramachandran, it was his colleague who in effect said salvation is possible only through Jesus. Ramachandran wanted to prove him wrong from the Bible and began to read the Bible. All had someone introducing Jesus or Christianity to them, but contrary to the stereotype, it was not a pastor or a missionary.

---

53 Mani.

54 Mani.

55 Ramachandran.

5. *Disenchantment with Hinduism:* Although all of them were religious and were reasonably happy about their religious life, at one point some became disillusioned with Hinduism. They began to feel that their religion was not helping them in their life or in their spiritual search. Mani recalled, "Though I practiced all the rituals with devotion and enthusiasm, nothing realistic happened. Even after so much dedication and spending so many hours . . . [in] all kinds of Brahmanical rituals, none of the gods and goddess gave me vision. Nor were they were able to deliver me from sins and give me the peace I was longing for. . . . These happenings frustrated me, and I lost all my hope to get myself out of the sinful life."[56]

Mani was disenchanted with Hinduism because it failed to meet his spiritual needs. Sociologists John Lofland and Rodney Stark observed in a study that prior to conversion, subjects found their religion inadequate to solve personal crises.[57] This kind of disillusionment need not be everyone's experience before conversion, but it is a frequent factor.[58] Ramachandran, for example, never had disenchantment with his religion and he was happy that his prayers were answered by his gods.[59]

6. *Crunch:* Crunch, a crisis in one's life, is a personal context for many who experience conversion. In Mani's life it was a moral and spiritual crisis; he was longing for freedom from the enslavement of sin. For Jayasudha, it was an accident when she went for her honeymoon. She and her husband were on a water scooter and fell off into the water. She narrated, "I was thrown into the water and I just sank. . . . I didn't know swimming."[60] It was a matter

---

56 Mani.

57 John Lofland and Rodney Stark, "Becoming a World-Saver: A Theory of Conversion to a Deviant Perspective," *American Sociological Review* 30, no. 6 (1965): 862-75.

58 Iyadurai, *Transformative Religious Experience*, 240.

59 Ramachandran.

60 Jayasudha.

of life and death. Susheela was depressed. Her family "fell into bad times and all the misfortune was blamed on my birth. All this was too much to bear.... I was blamed for every bad thing that happened in my family."[61] When the potential converts go through such crises, some became more religious and hoped that Hinduism would help them with their predicament. When they did not find help there, they became disenchanted with their religion, and they began to look for other religious options. Conversion studies commonly observe that crisis frequently precedes conversion. Yet in a classic treatise on conversion, psychologist Lewis Rambo observes that "stress, tension, and crisis alone are not enough to explain conversion."[62] And indeed, crunch is not the personal context for every conversion. Anand, Rajesh, and Ramachandran never faced any personal crisis prior to converting.

7. *Pursuit and the Test:* Several converts in this study recalled how they became eager to know more about Christianity or to experiment with it. In most of these cases, that meant going more deeply into the Bible. Mani was challenged by what he was reading in the Bible but not willing to accept that his beliefs were wrong. "Referring to the idols the Psalmist says, 'They have mouths but cannot speak, they have eyes but cannot see' (Ps 115:5). My faith was rudely shaken by this statement.... I thought that perhaps there might be some truth in the Bible verses, yet I continued my religious practices with a detached mind."[63] He was well versed in his religious literature and that made him compare the Bible with the Vedas.

For Ramachandran, he was challenged to prove that his friend was wrong to claim that only Jesus could save him. So, he began to study

---

61 Susheela.

62 Lewis Rambo, *Understanding Religious Conversion* (New Haven: Yale University Press, 1993), 48.

63 Mani.

the Bible. Yet he also wondered whether his friend could be right: "if there was a one percent chance that what Nirmal said was true then I need to know it."[64] So he began to read the Bible.

Rajesh attended church for many years and he had Bibles at home because his wife and children were practicing Christians. However, when he received a Bible at the catechism class, he felt an urge to read it. "I started to read as and whenever I used to get time, maybe once or twice in a week."[65] Mani was fascinated with the qualities of Jesus that emanated from the Gospels. Jesus's "humility, love, honesty, truthfulness and holiness impressed me. I wanted to be like him and live a clean life."[66] Susheela found that a Bible verse written on a school chapel wall was comforting to her. She liked the serenity at the chapel, so she went often; she knew the Lord's Prayer by heart and recited it in the chapel along with other *mantras* (Hindu prayers).

In this step, the potential converts' interest to know more about Jesus or to read the Bible pushed them to explore Christianity further. There is a passion or quest to explore the Bible, to test the claims, or sometimes to pursue them further in the light of their encounter with Jesus. This phase has been identified by scholars as seekership[67] and quest.[68] This step is clear evidence that no individual accepts the gospel presented to him or her just as it is.

They exercise their individual agency to assess the suitability of the gospel and they experiment with it. The step of test is crucial in the conversion process. In my larger study on conversion, potential converts used prayer as a test and found that to their surprise Jesus answered their prayers. Some prayed to generic God, without using any

---

64 Ramachandran.
65 Rajesh.
66 Mani.
67 Lofland and Stark, "Becoming a World-Saver," 868-69.
68 Rambo, *Understanding Religious Conversion*, 56-65.

names and eventually found Jesus as the true God.[69] Ramachandran made a similar prayer: "I stopped praying to various gods by name and before reading the Bible every night would pray to the 'Living God' and ask Him if there was only one way to Him. If it was so to let me know and if not also to let me know."[70] Converts were not swayed by the claims of Christianity, but they verified the claims by reading the Bible and used prayer as a test.

Sociologist James Richardson argued that a convert is not passive but active in the conversion process. His view on conversion emphasizes that humans "assign meaning to their actions and to the actions of others within a social context."[71] Throughout the conversion process, individuals actively seek to make meaning out of what is presented to them. Although Ramachandran experienced Christ's love having an impact on him, he did not give in right away. Ramachandran expressed his struggle: "While I enjoyed this experiment with seeking the truth and the reality of Christ's love . . . I also had struggles."[72] He made up his mind later. These converts also began to see their traditional religious beliefs and practices critically in the light of their exposure to Christianity. They began to move away from a rigid religious boundary. While they were not willing to give up Hinduism altogether, they wanted to be open to see the light on the other side. Some practiced both religious practices for a time.

8. *Encounter with Jesus:* As these people moved on in their conversion process, a definite moment occurred in which they moved from learning about Jesus in the Bible to encountering Jesus in a personal experience. This encounter could be a vividly supernatural one or a milder experience. Anand, Ramachandran, Rajesh, and Mani had

---

69 Iyadurai, *Transformative Religious Experience*, 148.

70 Ramachandran.

71 James T. Richardson, "The Active vs. Passive Convert: Paradigm Conflict in Conversion/Recruitment Research," *Journal for the Scientific Study of Religion* 24, no. 2 (1985): 164.

72 Ramachandran.

mild experiences of encountering Jesus. A friend of Anand invited him to his house. His friend and his sister prayed for Anand. He said it was "a simple affair—no miracles, no angels visiting. All they did was utter a deep human cry out to the creator God and His only son Jesus Christ. When they said Amen, I felt in my heart a desire to follow Jesus. It was a faith encounter with God that I shall not even attempt to understand, rationalise or explain. I simply accept it."[73] Mani was fascinated with Jesus and wanted to be like him but thought it was impossible. His friend told him it was possible if he received Jesus in his life.

So, Mani prayed, "Dear Lord Jesus forgive all my sins and come into my heart' and accepted Jesus as my Savior and a remarkable miracle took place in my life. A new experience of freedom, joy and peace given by Jesus filled my heart." Rajesh had prayed before, but when he took the catechism classes, he began to pray to Jesus and felt his peace. He feels that this is when he became a follower of Jesus.

Ramachandran also had a quiet encounter with Jesus. He was reading the Bible secretly to find some basis to counter his friend who claimed that only Jesus could save him. He narrated:

> From the time I began to read (with the Gospel of John) I enjoyed the text particularly reading about Jesus, what He did and said. I loved the name of Jesus. As I read it seemed like God was speaking to me. I kept on enjoying the Bible reading till I came to John 14:6 where it is wrien [*sic*] that—Jesus said: "I am the way, the truth and the life. No one comes to the Father except through me." This verse hit me hard since the Lord in His own words was saying that no one ca(n) come to the Father except through Him. As I could not come to grips with this statement of Jesus and could not relate it to my preconceived notion that all ways were the same I stopped reading the Bible for almost a month and a half but every now and then this verse would come back to me and I was not able to accept the profoundness of this truth. After a month and a half, I realized I was missing the peace and joy that the reading of the Bible had

---

73 Anand.

given me and therefore decided to continue reading the scriptures even though I did not want to accept John 14:6. The more I read the Bible the more I enjoyed it and realized what an amazing person Jesus was, without sin, always forgiving, always doing good."[74]

One day an astrologer came and told Ramachandran that he would die in an accident. He was gripped with a fear of death. For the first time he prayed in the name of Jesus. He claimed, "As soon as I finished the prayer the fear went away and I had an extraordinary peace in my heart of Jesus' assurance and protection."[75] Despite this additional encounter, Ramachandran still did not became a Christian and said, "I wanted to enjoy Jesus' grace and love while at the same time continuing with my religiosity of popular Hinduism."[76] Only later in response to an altar call in a church in Germany did he commit his life to follow Jesus and became a Christian.

Jayasudha and Susheela, by contrast, had dramatic supernatural experiences. Jayasudha narrated what happened when she fell off from the water scooter:

> When I was going deep down into the sea, I cried, Jesus! And, right in front of my eyes, I saw a big face of Jesus Christ. It was such a dazzling sight that I will never forget it. Me, a person who didn't know swimming came up without even drinking a drop of water. By then, my husband took a turn and came back. He saw me coming up from the sea. . . . I survived. I don't know how I came up or who brought me up. But I know one thing, I saw the face of Jesus Christ in front of me. It was nothing but a miracle that I survived.[77]

Susheela was depressed one day when her mother told her aunt that she was the bad luck for her family. That day she went to the chapel in her school and could not control herself and cried. Then, she narrates, her encounter with Jesus began:

---

74 Ramchandran.
75 Ramchandran.
76 Ramchandran.
77 Jayasudha.

There was a caption above the crucifix that said, "I died for you." I said, "Jesus, did you really die for me? Is there anyone who loves me in the world?" At some point during my tearful prayer, I felt someone tapping me. I turned around and found none but heard a voice tell me "I am there for you." That was a real experience for me. An inexplicable sense of joy filled my heart and I thought to myself "this Jesus, the God of Christians is very nice and kind."

Jesus saved Jayasudha from drowning and assured Susheela that he was with her and for her. These personal experiences transformed their lives and made them believe and follow Jesus. Others in the study did not have any dramatic experience as mentioned above. However, they felt some connection with Jesus, while reading the Bible or in a prayer, or being filled with peace and joy, or a sense of being freed from sin, and so on.

In my larger study on conversion to Christianity, I came across several kinds of religious experience in which converts encountered Jesus. This experience happens in mystical states of consciousness, beyond the waking consciousness. "Personal religious experience," William James believed, "has its root and centre in mystical states of consciousness."[78] At the encounter with Jesus, their volition is suspended. Their salvation experience, then, is not a rational understanding of Jesus's teachings, but an experience of the person Jesus. The fact that converts suddenly realize their sins and experience a sense of being forgiven is not a rational choice.[79] Thomas the disciple of Jesus wanted empirical verification of Jesus's wounds to convince himself of his resurrection, but when Jesus appeared to him and asked to him to verify, he simply said, "My Lord and my God!" (John 20:28). When Jesus encountered Thomas, empirical verification became meaningless, but he became convinced that Jesus arose from the dead. This certainty was not merely empirical verification but a cognitive restructuring. "The conviction that Jesus was truly divine, that their sins were

---

78 William James, *The Varieties of Religious Experience* (New York: Barnes and Noble Classics, 2004 [1902]), 328.

79 Iyadurai, *Transformative Religious Experience*, 164.

forgiven, and that they were saved was given as a gift, came as they were passive and experienced a loss of volition. Some were agitated to accept Christianity before the divine-human encounter but afterward became ardent followers of Jesus."[80]

As we have seen, converts do exercise their individual agency in the conversion process. When they were exposed to Christianity, they did not blindly accept it as true religion or simply become a follower of Jesus. They took their time to decide. Despite having an encounter with Jesus, they did not convert immediately. Rajesh says it is in the hands of Jesus for one to come to him. Even though he had been associated with Christianity since his childhood, he became a real follower of Jesus only when he had a personal encounter with Jesus during the catechism classes. Ramachandran wanted to have the joy and peace offered by Jesus but was never willing to give up Hinduism.

9. *Holy Spirit Experience:* Some of the converts expressed that they had experienced the Holy Spirit. When Mani took baptism, he claimed, "god anointed me with holy spirit."[81] When Ramachandran responded to the altar call, "within a few minutes I was filled with Holy Spirit and realized I am indeed a new creation."[82] Susheela made a prayer of salvation. "No sooner had I finished the prayer than I started speaking in tongues."[83] These three distinctively identified their experience of the Holy Spirit in their conversion narratives. This comes as an associated experience of their encounter with Jesus unlike Pentecostals' experience of the Holy Spirit as a second experience.

10. *Transformative Effects:* Personal encounter with Jesus triggers personal transformation. It might even change the direction of converts'

---

80 Ibid. This book contains a detailed discussion on the divine-human encounter in conversion. See especially chapter 7, "The Mystical Turning Point," 143-68.

81 Mani.

82 Ramachandran.

83 Susheela.

lives. Converts reported that they found peace and joy as the immediate effect of experiencing Jesus. Anand found joy and hope in Jesus. Mani experienced freedom from sin: "A new experience of freedom, joy and peace given by Jesus filled my heart."[84] Rajesh felt reassured with the presence of Jesus with him. He began to see life "in a totally different way with Jesus by my side always and realized all problems have solutions if we are ready to face the truth in the God and have faith."[85] Ramachandran was surprised when someone told him that his life was transformed; others could notice the changes in his life. Personal transformation is indeed a key effect of religious experience that has been identified by several studies.[86]

Encounter with Jesus sometimes changed their vision in life. Jayasudha became more concerned about the poor and the needy and started an NGO to meet the needs for medical expenses of the poor. She also stopped acting in films. Later she prayed and decided that she would act only if the director contributed to her NGO. She said in one of the interviews, "My social service is directly connected to the God. . . . In 2001 I got a strong urge to help society and be like Jesus."[87]

---

84 Mani.

85 Rajesh.

86 See, e.g., Max Heirich, "Change of Heart: A Test of Some Widely Held Theories about Religious Conversion," *American Journal of Sociology* 83, no. 3 (1977): 653-80; Joshua Iyadurai, "Religious Experiences of College Students: The Christian Students of Chennai (Madras) City," unpublished study in the author's possession, conducted at the University of Madras, Chennai, 2003; Raymond F. Paloutzian, James T. Richardson, and Lewis R. Rambo, "Religious Conversion and Personality Change," *Journal of Personality* 67, no. 6 (1999): 1047-79; Rambo, *Understanding Religious Conversion;* Richardson, "The Active vs. Passive Convert," 163-79; David A. Snow and R. Machalek, "The Sociology of Conversion," *Annual Review of Sociology* 10 (1984): 167-90; and James, *The Varieties of Religious Experience.*

87 Jayasudha; "Chit Chat with Jayasudha," *Idlebrain.com*, March 1, 2006, http://www.idlebrain.com/news/2000march20/chitchat-jayasudha.html, accessed November 29, 2017.

Ramachandran left his job and became a traveling preacher to spread the gospel. Susheela left her computer business and started a ministry to work among Brahmins.

11. *Friendship with God/Jesus:* Converts indicate having an intimate relationship with God/Jesus who is always available to them. For Jayasudha, "He [God] is one person with whom I can share all my problems. I see Him as the only solace when I feel helpless. I believe there is a power which guides us all. I have experienced the strength of that power."[88] Rajesh found God to be "a father, a friend and a guardian."[89] For Anand, Jesus is "sinless Son of a Holy God . . . a truly amazing friend, guide, leader, saviour and God."[90] Susheela found Jesus, "the God of Christians is very nice and kind."[91] Ramachandran "enjoyed the text particularly reading about Jesus, what He did and said. I loved the name of Jesus . . . realized what an amazing person Jesus was, without sin, always forgiving, always doing good."[92] They all are fascinated with Jesus and express that they have a special kind of relationship with him. They feel an immanent presence of Jesus in their daily lives.

Finding Jesus real in converts' daily lives is something that stands out in following Jesus. In their religion, God was never a reality in their daily life. Even though they prayed and assumed that their prayers were answered, they never had a chance of experiencing their God in their lives. But with Jesus, they speak to him and he speaks back to them either through the Bible or prayer. In their narratives they have expressed that God was speaking to them. The relational aspect and conversational dimensions in the conversion process are personal, real, and unparalleled. T. Luhrmann, professor at Stanford University, did a study among the evangelical Christians at the Vineyard Church in

---

88 Jayasudha.
89 Rajesh.
90 Anand.
91 Susheela.
92 Ramachandran.

Chicago and San Francisco, on how they relate to God. She claims in her book *When God Talks Back* that the evangelical Christians relate to God as anyone would relate to a friend; the only difference here is Jesus is not a visible reality. She claims that Vineyard members were trained by to pray in this manner.[93] But converts find themselves talking to Jesus and him speaking to them is not out of any training but is spontaneous. In my larger study almost all the participants stated that this friendship with Jesus is unparalleled in their religion.[94]

12. *Prayer:* For converts, prayer is a channel of conversing with Jesus. Anand talks to Jesus daily and he talks with him about all kinds of things. Jayasudhas spends about thirty to forty-five minutes every day in prayer and claims prayer gives peace.[95] After he started praying to Jesus, Rajesh claims, "There was a vast improvement in my family life and business too."[96] Prayer, for converts, is a means of being touch with the new companion in their lives, Jesus.

13. *Bible:* The Bible plays a vital role in the conversion process, leading converts to encounter Jesus in their personal life. After conversion the Bible helps them grow in their understanding of Jesus and life. Rajesh said, "The first thing in the morning, I read the word of God and present myself to him to guard and guide me throughout the day."[97] Ramachandran said that a fellow student in German class "casually remarked to me that he had been closely watching me and that my life was constantly changing and that was because of 'THE BOOK' I was reading. I thought my Bible reading was a secret matter, but others were noticing the effect."[98] Mani says

---

93 T. M. Luhrmann. *When God Talks Back: Understanding the American Evangelical Relationship with God* (New York: Alfred A. Knopf, 2012), 6.
94 Iyadurai, *Transformative Religious Experience*, 166.
95 Jayasudha.
96 Rajesh.
97 Rajesh.
98 Ramachandran.

he gained knowledge about God.[99] Jayasudha started helping the poor after reading the Bible.

14. *Hostilities:* In India, conversion leads to problems for converts. As we have seen earlier, it is a highly politicized issue and is viewed as betrayal of one's family, community, and religion. Mani's family and friends turned against him because of his conversion. He narrated a life-threatening incident:

> One evening a group of my old friends came and caught hold of me and asked me to deny Jesus and threatened to kill me. They poured kerosene on me and were to burn me alive if I refuse to be an [*sic*] Hindu again. But with the love of Christ in my heart I smiled at them and quietly turned down their demands. I thought that it may be the last day for me in this earth. I was sure that a glorious future was awaiting me in heaven. Just then something strange and wonderful happened. I saw a glorious vision, and the sight of my friends standing near me with angry faces disappeared and I saw four young men walking in the midst of the fire. The fourth one was like Jesus and I saw Jesus standing by my side. Now I could see a change in my friends' faces and they quietly walked out of the room. I sat there alone on the floor and praised God with tears filled my eyes. After this incident my parents allowed (me) to go (to) church and have fellowship with other believers in Christ and gave me full freedom to work for Lord Jesus.[100]

Susheela mentioned an incident in her life that her dad beat her for reading *Our Daily Bread* and burned the book out of rage. Such attacks and different kinds of hostilities are common in India when someone converts to Christianity, whether they are Brahmin converts or those of other communities. All groups face hostile reactions from family, friends, and community.[101]

---

99   Mani.

100   Mani.

101   For a detailed discussion on the problems faced by converts in India, see chapter 9, "Hostilities," 198-233, in Iyadurai, *Transformative Religious Experience.*

15. *Social Pressure:* Apart from hostile reactions, converts also face tremendous social pressure to openly declare themselves as Christians. Rajesh married a Catholic and actively engaged in church activities to the extent that no one, including the priests, knew that he was not a Catholic. He wanted to convert at the time of his marriage, then at the time of baptism of his first daughter and later his second daughter, but he did not. Why? "Being the only child, I did not want to hurt my parents. . . . In the year 2006 my dad passed away and in the year 2014 my mom passed away. Now I decided it was time for me to get converted."[102]

Ramachandran, after experiencing the joy and peace in reading the Bible, was hesitant to become a Christian. He said, "My imaginations of what it meant to be a 'Christian' bothered me. I thought it is mandatory to change my name, to join with other Christians in their activities and in general have a label of Christianity attached to me. This compounded by the fear of how my friends and family would react bothered me."[103] Irrespective of one being educated or not, well settled in their profession or not, the social pressure of what others would think of being a Christian is a constant factor for converts to Christianity in India. Christianity is considered as a religion of the low caste and colonizers. Gandhi and Golwalkar were successful to some extent to create this perception that a true Indian will not adopt it. Despite such pressure, people embrace Christianity due to the encounter with Jesus.

16. *Participation:* In due course, converts overcome the pressure and hostilities and participate in a church by taking baptism—or some without it. Mani took baptism and started attending church, but his narration implied that he had attended church secretly until his family and friends came to know. They came to know of it sometime later and were enraged. Later, he could go to church after the incident in which he was miraculously saved. Rajesh took

---

102 Rajesh.
103 Ramachandran.

baptism after the death of his father and mother. Ramachandran publicly declared his faith in Jesus by responding to an altar call given by the pastor in Munich while he was posted in Germany for his job. Converts took their own time and adopted suitable strategies to participate in church and identified themselves as Christians.

17. *Sharing Their Experience:* Converts are eager to share their personal encounter with Jesus with others. Ramachandran and Susheela mentioned that their entire family accepted Jesus. Ramachandran said, "The Lord has saved many members of my family. I live in Delhi today along with my wife . . . son . . . and my mother . . . who is eighty-two years old. All of them are in the Lord and are a support to me in my Ministry."[104] Susheela said, "Today all my family members have come to Jesus Christ. My mother . . . passed away last year at the age of 59. However, she had also accepted Jesus as her Lord before she died. Both my brothers . . . along with their work, they also labour in God's Vineyard. My father . . . is in his seventies. It gives me great joy to see him grow in the Lord." Mani, Ramachandran, and Susheela are actively involved in full-time Christian ministry and are spreading the good news to others. Ramachandran wondered why other Christians were not excited about sharing such a wonderful experience. He claims, "[In the] last eighteen years it has been my privilege of being an instrument in God's hands in leading thousands to the only Savior and Lord Jesus Christ."[105]

Susheela also has similar claims: "Our organisation *Christava Brahmana Seva Samithi*, started as a mere fellowship of among believers from Brahmanical background with 52 families. Today within a span of 3 years, it has reached to 425 families."[106] Their zeal for the ministry is grounded in the personal experience of Jesus and the certainty of

---

104 Ramachandran.

105 Ramachandran.

106 Susheela.

knowing the one God. Their motive is not to increase the number of church members, for they are not primarily interested in institutionalized Christianity. But they want others to experience their joy, peace, freedom, and being connected God in Jesus. Anand explains, "If I read a good book, watch a good movie . . . or eat a good meal at a new restaurant, I would naturally tell my friends about it. In Jesus, I have discovered a truly amazing friend, guide, leader, saviour and God. How can I not tell all my friends about Him?"[107] Their motive is not about promoting a religion but helping others to find what they have found in Jesus.

18. *Identity:* Conversion gives new identity to converts and they also must deal with other identities in the light of their encounter with Jesus. All in the study identified themselves as Brahmins. Anand states at the beginning of his narrative, "I was born a Brahmin and am the grandson of a priest. . . . I am educated . . . reasonably intelligent. I am also affluent . . . [from] upper middle class . . . high-caste, rich and smart. In other words, I am not a tribal, or poor or dim-witted."[108] He gives credentials to counter the general perception that only Dalits, poor, uneducated, and Tribals convert to Christianity.

Ramachandran testifies to a new life and exclaims: "I am indeed a new creation."[109] Susheela points to a contrasting self-image: "Until then, I had considered myself a cursed being for being blamed for every misfortune. But now I was a new being; the new infilling of the Holy Spirit gave me a new identity in Christ."[110]

Regarding other identities, Anand says, "I am fiercely proud of my national identity as an Indian and I am completely at peace with my cultural identity as a Hindu. I retain the name my parents gave me."[111] For Anand, conversion does not involve a change of names

---

107 Anand.
108 Anand.
109 Ramachandran.
110 Susheela.
111 Anand.

and identities. He further reiterates, "Hinduism was my identity, not my religion. It still is."[112] Susheela's organization works toward facilitating Brahmin converts to retain their cultural identity while being a follower of Jesus. They differentiate their cultural or social identity as Hindus with their new identity gained in Jesus as a spiritual identity. For them "Christian" has more to do with the institutional church. But their experience of Jesus is something personal that they cherish and value more than their life.[113] For these converts, conversion is not a change of religious identity, but finding a new identity in Jesus who transformed their lives, who gave them peace and joy, and who delivered them from sin and curse.

Conclusion

Gandhi and Golwalkar succeeded in creating the popular perception that only the Dalits, poor people, Tribal peoples, and illiterates embrace Christianity, and that all conversion to Christianity is false because of the enticements offered by missionaries or the church. But the reality of these converts is dramatically different. They show the real core of conversion—personal encounter with Jesus—that changed their lives forever. The person Jesus, not religious ritual or affiliation is the core in Christian conversion. No one in the study came to faith because a pastor or a missionary tried to convert them. Either their own interest or situation led them to seek Jesus. Networks of relationships—a friend or teacher or wife or anyone—could be a channel of leading one to encounter Jesus. In my larger study on conversion, even strangers played a role in conversion process for some.[114] For Rajesh, his teacher was instrumental when he was small child and later his Catholic wife took him to church, but both were never after him to convert. Anand,

---

112 Anand.

113 For a detailed discussion on converts' deployment of multiple identities in India, see Joshua Iyadurai, "Multiple Identities of Converts in India: An Interdisciplinary Perspective," *Dharma Deepika* 16 (January-June 2012): 27-41.

114 Iyadurai, *Transformative Religious Experience*, 232.

Mani, and Ramachandran were introduced to Jesus through their friends. People come to Jesus through personal networks more than any other means. These converts, then, were active in pursuing their new religious option and were not forced or compelled by anyone. Individual agency drove the conversion process, then God met them at an appropriate time. Converts passive only at the encounter with Jesus; otherwise, they were actively involved in comparing, analyzing, and testing the claims made of Jesus or the Bible.

It is appropriate to conclude with the statement from Anand: "But I would never force anyone to listen to me, leave alone financially induce, coerce or con him into believing. That to me is pointless and against the very grain of my faith. But I do have a constitutional right to practice my faith and to preach it without deception, force or bribery. It pains me to see such basic rights of mankind being cruelly violated every day in this great . . . nation."[115]

---

115 Anand.

PART II
INDIAN PRAXIS, AMERICAN LEARNING

Chapter 5

American Evangelicalism, Social Action, and Christianity in India

Aminta Arrington

During our seminar in India we met Padmini, a seamstress, in Baglur, a slum area of Bangalore in South India. With great pride Padmini showed us around her home, which doubled as her shop. It was filled with an impressive assortment of sewing machines and an array of colorful saris she had made for sale. Padmini is a member of a women's micro-credit cooperative, the loans of which helped her launch her small business. Since micro-credit is of little use to someone with no skills, Padmini received tailoring training through the Divya Shanthi Christian Association, a local community development organization that has worked in Bangalore since 1967. Padmini had seen her hopes and dreams realized, and her role as an entrepreneur gave her a dignity that communicated across all linguistic or cultural barriers.

Padmini's life had changed because of the commitment of local Christians to engage the people of Baglur. Commitment to the poor and the marginalized is a responsibility set before Christians in ample scriptures in the Old Testament[1] as well as the New.[2] Christ himself

---

1 See, e.g., Deut 15:11; Prov 31:8-9; Isa 1:17.
2 See, e.g., Luke 4:18-19; Jas 2:15-16; 1 John 3:17.

equated care for the hungry, the thirsty, the naked, and the imprisoned as care for him.³

Even though the Bible supports the idea that Christian life should be characterized by concern for the poor and the suffering, American evangelical understandings of mission and social engagement remain muddled. While there is a flurry of grassroots evangelical participation in short-term missions, community development, and other forms of social action, such activities are undertaken less because of community consensus and more because of stirred individual consciences. Both evangelical theologians and mission practitioners have written much about the call to serve the poor,⁴ but the discussion has been taking place not at the center of evangelical thought, but at the margins. Unlike Catholic Social Teaching, which has an enduring place in Catholic theology and has trickled down to the parishioner level, social action is still a side issue in evangelical theology. Prominent evangelical theologian Wayne Grudem's widely used text *Systematic Theology* does not cover social action, nor does the Roger Olsen's more popular *Mosaic of Christian Belief*. In contrast to Catholic seminaries, where classes and readings on Catholic Social Teaching are common, most evangelical seminaries do not include classes on the topic. Social engagement is not part of the syllabus in the required Evangelical Theology class at my university.

So, I was struck by this contrast: in India, Christianity's concern for the poor is evident and powerful, but these commitments have

---

3 Matt 25:34-40.

4 See, e.g., the "Chicago Declaration of Evangelical Social Concern" (1973), a landmark document signed by eminent American evangelical thinkers. Quite a few evangelical scholars and activists have weighed in on the subject since then, such as Ronald J. Sider, *Rich Christians in an Age of Hunger* (Downers Grove, IL: Intervarsity Press, 1977); and more recently, Steve Corbett and Brian Fikkert, *When Helping Hurts* (Chicago: Moody, 2009); Bryant Myers, *Walking with the Poor: Principles and Practices of Transformational Development* (Maryknoll, NY: Orbis, 2011); and Richard Stearns, *The Hole in Our Gospel* (Nashville: Thomas Nelson, 2009).

not taken root as fundamental theology among American evangelicals. Despite forty years of advocacy and a flurry of grassroots evangelical action, social witness is not integral to evangelical mission. What might American evangelicals do about this? In this chapter I argue that Indian Christian thought and practice could provide powerful theological focus and guidance to American evangelicals.

New Activities, but Old Paradigms

American evangelical Christians are involved in poverty alleviation, prevention of human trafficking, social justice, and other social concerns as never before in recent memory. In fact, some are characterizing evangelical involvement in broader social concerns as a "great return" to long-neglected Christian social concern.[5] In addition to World Vision, the mammoth evangelical relief and development agency that was founded by evangelist Bob Pearce in 1950, the American evangelical social action landscape now includes World Relief, at the forefront of refugee care and advocacy; the Christian Community Development Association, which has hundreds of affiliates across urban and rural America; and Samaritan's Purse, which is involved in a plethora of activities from disaster relief to medical missions and sanitation projects. According to sociologist Robert Wuthnow, in recent years "even Christian organizations concerned mainly with evangelism became involved in a wide variety of new endeavors, including water conservation programs, sanitation efforts, health screening, vaccinations, sustainable agriculture programs, and emergency disaster relief."[6]

Rick Warren, founding pastor of Saddleback Church in Southern California and more famously the author of *The Purpose Driven Life*, exemplifies one of the more ambitious recent attempts at evangelical social action. This model is codified in his P.E.A.C.E. plan—Promote

---

5 Brian Steensland and Philip Goff, introduction to *The New Evangelical Social Engagement*, ed. Brian Steensland and Philip Goff (New York: Oxford University Press, 2014), 9.

6 Robert Wuthnow, *Boundless Faith: The Global Outreach of American Churches* (Berkeley: University of California Press, 2009), 10.

reconciliation (formerly Plant new churches), Equip leaders, Assist the poor, Care for the sick, Educate the next generation. Another aspect of Warren's plan is the primacy of the local church and lay parishioners (or "humanitarian foot soldiers" as Warren calls them) in enacting the plan: "In denominations, you pay, you pray, and you get out of the way. Let the professionals do it. The revolution I believe in and want to bring about reverses the role—the local church on the front edge."[7] The P.E.A.C.E. plan recently reached its goal of putting volunteers in every nation on the planet.[8]

But perhaps what most exemplifies American evangelical grassroots participation in missions and social engagement is the short-term mission (STM) trip. Nearly one-third of all congregations in the United States sponsor annual short-term mission trips, with a total of 1.6 million church members participating each year.[9] Trips are taken during vacations from school and work, and often involve laboring alongside long-term missionaries in Vacation Bible School, medical missions, construction projects, and evangelistic outreaches. As the movement has matured, more and more STMs involve relationships between a congregation or organization in the United States and a local congregation overseas. These relationships have tended to be direct, without the mediation of an agency or long-term missionaries, and often long-term, with STMs returning to the same location each year. In many cases, lines between senders and receivers have blurred over time, and these North-South church relationships have deepened into what Janel Kragt Bakker terms "sister church relationships."[10] According to Bakker, "these congregation-to-congregation partnerships are typically

---

7 Quoted in Timothy C. Morgan, "Purpose Driven in Rwanda: Rick Warren's Sweeping Plan to Defeat Poverty," *Christianity Today* 49, no. 10 (2005): 32.

8 Michelle Cottle, "Rick Warren's Resurrection," *Newsweek*, December 2012, 30.

9 Wuthnow, *Boundless Faith*, 168, 170.

10 Janel K. Bakker, *Sister Churches: American Congregations and Their Partners Abroad* (New York: Oxford University Press, 2013).

driven by grassroots efforts, centered around the local church as the operative unit in mission, lay led, and democratically or representatively governed."[11] Such sister church relationships certainly reflect a reframing of the original STM movement. Still, in their decentralized grassroots nature and stress on interpersonal relationships, they remain within the scope of traditional evangelical ordering of missions.

In sum, beyond the traditional evangelical emphasis on affecting society through personal spiritual transformation, American evangelicals are increasingly launching out into grassroots social engagement involving social and economic development. Yet this flurry of social action at the parishioner level is often not accompanied by paradigm-shifting reflection.[12] The very term "short-term mission" seems to preclude thinking about long-term effects of such missions.

One important reason that this flurry of social activism has not changed the overall evangelical understanding of the church's mission is that it runs head-on into two powerful old evangelical paradigms. The first is an individualistic view of transformation. According to sociologist James Hunter, evangelicals see personal evangelism not only as "a means of saving souls but of transforming individuals and, in a roundabout way, the culture."[13] Hunter quotes Bill Bright, founder of Campus Crusade for Christ and a typical proponent of this view:

> In my opinion, the only way to change the world is to change individuals. Changed people, in sufficient numbers, will produce changed campuses, changed communities, changed cities, changed states and nations—yes, in a very real sense, a changed world. Jesus

---

11 Ibid., 39.

12 Brian M. Howell, *Short-Term Mission: An Ethnography of Christian Travel Narrative and Experience* (Downers Grove, IL: Intervarsity Press Academic, 2012); Amy Reynolds and Stephen Offutt, "Global Poverty and Evangelical Action," in *The New Evangelical Social Engagement*, ed. Brian Steensland and Philip Goff (New York: Oxford University Press, 2014), 242-261.

13 James D. Hunter, *To Change the World: The Irony, Tragedy, and Possibility of Christianity in the Late Modern World* (New York: Oxford University Press, 2010), 9.

> Christ is the only One who can change people from within. We can help change the world by introducing people to Jesus Christ.[14]

This view of the social power of individual transformation is as old as evangelicalism itself and is deeply embedded in the movement's outlook. According to sociologist Christian Smith, evangelicals therefore attempt to effect social change through relational engagement, based on the belief that "the only truly effective way to change the world is one-individual-at-a-time."[15] Smith sees serious limitations to this "personal influence strategy." It constrains "evangelicals' ability to understand how the social world actually works and limits their capacity to formulate appropriate and useful responses and solutions."[16] Indeed, this individualistic focus leaves out any reckoning of the role of power in obtaining justice and the overarching influence of social structures, institutions, and systems.

A second old paradigm that tends to marginalize social action on the evangelical agenda is the primacy of evangelism in the church's mission priorities. Over the past century in the United States, this belief is usually accompanied with a suspicion that social action is a hindrance to or false substitute for evangelism. This suspicion has been implanted in the evangelical mind as a reaction against the liberal Protestant Social Gospel movement (circa 1890-1930).[17] This reaction affected foreign missions' organizations as well. Whereas missions in the nineteenth century often included such culture-making activities as building schools and hospitals, by the early twentieth century, such activities were judged diversions from what should be the primary purpose of missions: evangelism. From his experience in India,

---

14   Quoted in ibid., 10.

15   Christian Smith, *American Evangelicalism: Embattled and Thriving* (Chicago: University of Chicago Press, 1998), 187.

16   Ibid., 188.

17   George M. Marsden, *Fundamentalism and American Culture: The Shaping of Twentieth-Century Evangelicalism, 1870-1925* (New York: Oxford University Press, 1980), 85-93.

missiologist Donald McGavran wrote *The Bridges of God*, an evangelical missiological classic that is still highly influential today. He divided up missionary work into the primary activities of evangelism and discipling, and a host of secondary activities that diverted attention away from the primary activities, such as orphanages, medical clinics, schools, and agricultural work.[18]

The "Evangelism Only" mantra was clearly delineated in mission statements and appeals for funds and used to anchor their legitimacy. Many missionaries on the field, confronted daily with poverty and illiteracy, felt grieved by this approach and opened some schools and clinics "on the side." They had to justify this work and its tie to evangelism continually, and often had to use separate funds.[19] The effects of this ideological shift still linger today, with thoughts that social action is not evangelical, but only the purview of liberal mainline churches. In a Sunday school class that I taught recently on the scriptural basis for community development and caring for the poor, one of the attenders told me I "sounded like a Methodist." Social work carried on by missionaries still carries a taint in many evangelical circles.

Given these powerful inhibitors, where does the new evangelical social action come from? Rather than arising out of new theological insights or because of a paradigm shift in favor of social action, the new evangelical social engagement has come about in a largely individualistic, evangelical way. Like the old faith missionaries, today's evangelicals embrace social action because their hearts were touched. Kay Warren, the wife of megachurch pastor Rick Warren, offers a prime example. She recalls reading an article about the HIV/AIDS crisis in Africa. In the middle of the article was a quote: "12 million children orphaned in Africa due to AIDS." After wrestling with God and her conscience for months, finally, she reports, "I made a conscious choice

---

18 Donald A. McGavran, *The Bridges of God: A Study in the Strategy of Missions* (New York: Friendship Press, 1955).

19 Bill Svelmoe, "Evangelism Only? Theory versus Practice in the Early Faith Missions," *Missiology: An International Review* 31, no. 2 (2003): 195-206.

to say, 'Yes.' I had a pretty good suspicion that I was saying yes to a bucket load of pain. In that moment, God shattered my heart. He just took my heart and put it through a woodchip machine."[20] Social engagement is being propelled by the affective features of evangelical culture: opening one's heart to the Spirit's prompting, a deep desire to be willing and faithful in response to an individual call, a yearning to put faith into action, and an unquenchable optimism about being able to fulfill a call.

Often, then, missionaries are supported not because of mission agreement or vision alignment, but because of a personal connection with the missionary. Mission trips are planned based on personal vision and personal relationships. There is not a conscious consensus on the rightness or appropriateness of social action generally; rather, there are situations, relationships, senses, and callings, each of which are acted upon according to individualized commitment. Validation occurs not through evaluation based on external standards or tenets, but on the feelings of those involved in the work, the report back to the sending congregation, and the extent to which the trip participants experienced a spiritual transformation.[21] Work is often carried out with the expectation that the Holy Spirit will bless it, but with little overarching vision for how the work fits in or what the result should look like. These social ministries thus are not undertaken as the outgrowth of a new outlook or paradigm shift; rather, they are just taken. As a result, they are often piecemeal, uncoordinated, and episodic in nature.

There are obvious dangers in this approach. As theologian Vincent Bacote put it, "When intuition or 'common sense' have greater prominence than biblical knowledge, it can be easy to wind up in a situation where the most persuasive stances stem from those who tell the best personal, historical, or cultural stories."[22] Without a

---

20   Morgan, "Purpose Driven in Rwanda," 1.

21   Howell, *Short-Term Mission*.

22   Vincent Bacote, "A Perennial Moment of Opportunity," *Comment*, August 7, 2012, https://www.cardus.ca/comment/article/3395/a-perennial-moment-of-opportunity/2012.

reinforcing paradigm, evangelical social action is vulnerable to shifts in the political landscape, the eloquence of big personalities, or the capriciousness of human feeling. It nearly guarantees that evangelical social undertakings will be running behind the wider secular culture. Being guided by intuition, relationships, or persuasion seems spiritual but it is deeply subjective. It lacks the standards and guideposts that come from being rooted in biblical theology.

Evangelicals have thought biblically and theologically about the dimensions and priorities of mission. They have sponsored several high-level international consultations on the theology and mandates of world mission—such as Lausanne '74, Wheaton '83, and the Oxford Conference on Faith and Economics in 1990. These gatherings of evangelical theologians have hammered out declarations about the essential relationship between evangelism and social action, but these pronouncements have been slow to trickle down to the popular level. Despite the burst of STMs and the plethora of other evangelical social ministries since the 1990s, there have been few global meetings that have sought to bring about and convey a consensus on these issues.[23] There is much to honor in evangelical social action, but without some greater sense of mandate for all these activities, many questions remain: What is the religious worth of social concern in and of itself? How does the Christian faith infuse work on behalf of the poor and needy? How do cultures change, and what are the implications for evangelical action on behalf of culture change? What is a theology of human suffering, justice, and flourishing?

The Contribution of World Christianity

Since an evangelical understanding of social concern is such an unsettled issue, there is still room for additional voices at the table—indeed, there is a great need for them. As a number of contemporary mission scholars have insisted, doing mission in the era of world Christianity

---

23 Lausanne 2010, a major missions gathering in Cape Town, is the one notable exception.

requires listening to the voices of world Christians.[24] The great Scots historian of mission Andrew Walls stated that the expansion of Christianity in the non-Western world is "taking Christian theology into new areas of life, where Western theology has no answers, because it has no questions."[25] American evangelicals engaged in social action must not only look at what God is doing outside the West, but hear the interpretation of what God is doing from theologians from outside the West. These voices are critical. An encounter with non-Western theology can enrich the Western conversation about social ministry by way of example, showing how such engagement can in fact become integral to Christian belief and practice in the world today.

Not only has Christianity grown exponentially in the non-Western world,[26] but the rate and quality of worldwide interactivity that is possible today means that a whole world of Christian thought and action is closer and more accessible than ever before, even at the grassroots level. Having access to Christian experience and reflection across Asia, Latin America, Oceania, and Africa can be overwhelming. Therefore, in this section, I simply focus on what the theology and praxis of Christianity in India can contribute to an American evangelical understanding of social action.

Christianity has enjoyed a long history in India, beginning, according

---

24 See, e.g., Paul Borthwick, *Western Christians in Global Mission: What's the Role of the North American Church?* (Downers Grove, IL: Intervarsity Press, 2012).

25 Andrew F. Walls, *The Missionary Movement in Christian History: Studies in the Transmission of Faith* (Maryknoll, NY: Orbis, 1996), 146.

26 Philip Jenkins, *The Next Christendom: The Coming of Global Christianity*, 3rd ed. (New York: Oxford University Press, 2011); Dana L. Robert, "Shifting Southward: Global Christianity since 1945," *International Bulletin of Missionary Research* 24, no. 2 (2000): 50-58; Lamin O. Sanneh, *Disciples of All Nations: Pillars of World Christianity* (New York: Oxford University Press, 2007); Scott W. Sunquist, *The Unexpected Christian Century: The Reversal and Transformation of Global Christianity, 1900-2000* (Grand Rapids, MI: Baker Academic, 2015).

to oral tradition, with the arrival and martyrdom of the apostle Thomas, the establishment of Mar Thoma churches according to the Syrian rites, the Portuguese Roman Catholic mission at Goa beginning in the sixteenth century, followed subsequently by Protestant missions, and currently, a vibrant indigenous Christian faith that is not only locally led, propagated, and funded, but that has produced world-class theologians and thinkers.[27] Although currently only 2.3 percent of the population of India is Christian, a quarter of the nation's civil society organizations are church-sponsored. The social impact of Christianity greatly surpasses its numerical strength.[28]

Theologizing in this context is particularly rich and complex. In addition to providing a home for all the world's great religions and several that are unique to India, the nation has a long philosophical tradition, complex overlays of language, class, and ethnicity, and a still influential colonial history. Yet India is also a microcosm of world Christianity, containing storefront Pentecostal churches, Mar Thoma Christians of ancient origins, megachurches preaching the prosperity gospel, Catholics, Orthodox, Anglicans, Baptists, Methodists, various other evangelicals, Christian ashrams, and Tribal Christians, all of whom can rightly claim now to be indigenous. Indeed, while it is a tenet of world Christianity that each iteration of Christianity is a new translation,[29] it seems there is little in the history of Christian expansion that has not somehow been replicated on the Indian subcontinent.

Christianity's long history of India has produced many rivers of theology, from which I draw from only a few. While Brahmanical theology, mostly written by Christian theologians of high caste, has long presented a well-developed response to Indian philosophical and religious categories, I focus on more recent Indian theology, the

---

27 For a sweeping, magisterial account, see Robert E. Frykenberg, *Christianity in India: From Beginnings to the Present* (Oxford: Oxford University Press, 2008).

28 Lancy Lobo, *Globalization, Hindu Nationalism, and Christians in India* (Jaipur: Rawat Publications, 2002), 150.

29 Walls, *The Missionary Movement*, 26-42.

insights of Indian theologians who write specifically about caring for the poor, as well as Dalit theology, a theology arising directly from the voices of the poor, the suffering, and the oppressed.

On Holism

Whether from Asia, Latin America, or Africa, non-Western theoreticians speak of a holism that permeates life, exposing the Western dichotomous fallacy of a divide between the sacred and the secular. Likewise, Majority World evangelical theologians have challenged the Western evangelical paradigm of the primacy of evangelism. One leading voice of this critique is the Indian evangelical leader, the Rev. Canon Dr. Vinay Samuel. Samuel chaired a Lausanne Conference follow-up meeting, "Wheaton' 83," that produced the statement "Transformation—The Church in Response to Human Need." He then became founding editor of *Transformation: An International Journal of Holistic Mission*. Samuel's writings underscore the idea that neither evangelism nor social action can stand on its own; they are integrally related in mission. Evangelism alone is insufficient if it ignores social transformation; yet, social action cannot stand on its own if it does not see deep transformation coming from God in Christ. Further, because Christian conversion transforms relationships, conversion means building community. And building community is never a short-term project; it must be undertaken with long-term commitment.[30]

A holistic desire to see God's rule be proclaimed everywhere means that transformation is not just a matter of individual, personal transformation. Transformation must also happen at the societal and structural level. As Samuel and his co-author Chris Sugden put it,

> The temptation is to see God at work only in values, but he also works to transform structures to promote the values of the kingdom. While it is possible to be content with the expression of the values of the kingdom in the lives of individuals or small groups, if these

---

30 Vinay Samuel and Chris Sugden, "God's Intention for the World," in *Mission as Transformation: A Theology of the Whole Gospel*, ed. Vinay Samuel and Chris Sugden (Oxford: Regnum, 1999), 229.

values do not find structural expression they cannot bring lasting change. So, development work must also focus on structures, both to transform them and to bring to light those that already reflect the values of the kingdom.[31]

This structural approach is corroborated by Christopher Duraisingh, in an editorial in *The International Review of Mission*: "The gospel, as the good news of fuller life in all dimensions, which God offers in Christ to all, addresses the structural dimensions of culture as well."[32] The American evangelical idea has been that transformation occurs at the individual level, and if enough individuals convert and turn their hearts toward God, culture will be transformed. Indian theologians affirm personal transformation, but also state that, separate from personal transformation, some societal structures are inherently unjust or disaffirming of human dignity. These structures need to be transformed.

Indian theologians are not debating about evangelism only, for that is a Western question based on individualistic views of relationship with God and dichotomistic, body-spirit assumptions about being human. Indian theology assumes holism and the transformative power of the gospel over every aspect of life. Regarding the Indian subcontinent, it is best to avoid generalizations, particularly about history or theology. Yet I will take the risk and say that, generally, the foundation of Christianity in India is that faith is much more than an inner, individual experience. Faith extends outward into the world, permeating every facet, every structure, every relationship, every organization. The corollary this has for Christian mission, then, is that "it is necessary that the rule of the one true God be proclaimed in all areas and levels of life."[33] There is much to be learned from world Christianity, specifically Christianity in India, about a theology of holism.

---

31 Ibid., 194.

32 Christopher Duraisingh, "Gospel and Identity in Community," *International Review of Mission* 85, no. 336 (1996): 4.

33 Samuel and Sugden, "God's Intention for the World," 186.

On Suffering

Bollywood movies show an India of pristine homes, new cars, and beautiful university campuses. However, the slums where I met Padmini belied a thoroughly different reality. India is a land of staggering economic inequalities, with huge gaps between the haves and the have-nots. According to the Human Development Index (a composite statistic of life expectancy, GNP per capita, years of schooling, fertility, and inflation), India ranks 130th of 188 countries measured.[34]

For Indian philosophers and theologians, then, a prime question, going back many centuries has been "Why is there so much suffering in the world?" Although India is a land of joy and deep cultural richness, it has also been a land of profound suffering, oppression, and injustice. Suffering is at the core of newer reflections as well as the ancient schools of thought. Dalit theology, a Christian theology of resistance dating from the 1980s, arose specifically from the broken, crushed nature of Dalit existence, at the bottom of the caste system. Dalit theology has a well-developed Christology, finding in Christ, the Suffering Servant, one who shared in the Dalit experience of suffering, and one who resisted the social norms of his own day. According to A. P. Nirmal, "Jesus as the Son of Man had to encounter rejection, mockery, contempt, suffering and finally death. All this was from the dominant religious tradition and the established religion. He underwent these Dalit experiences as the Prototype of all Dalits."[35] Jesus is not the one who pities the poor; Jesus is one who bears injustice and oppression *alongside* the poor. Jesus is "co-sufferer."[36] As Prachi Patil

---

[34] United Nations Development Programme, "Human Development Reports—India," http://hdr.undp.org/en/countries/profiles/IND.

[35] A. P. Nirmal, "Towards a Christian Dalit Theology," in *Indigenous People: Dalits: Dalit Issues in Today's Theological Debate*, ed. James Massey (New Delhi: ISPCK, 1998), 227.

[36] Sathianathan Clarke, "Dalit Theology: An Introductory and Interpretive Theological Exposition," in *Dalit Theology in the Twenty-First Century: Discordant Voices, Discerning Pathways*, ed. Sathianathan Clarke, Deenabandhu Manchala, and Philip Peacock (New Delhi: Oxford University Press, 2010), 32.

states, "The Dalit Jesus is one who openly sides with the suffering lot, a Jesus who breaks social norms for the emancipation of the oppressed and a Jesus who is crucified for transgressing social norms."[37]

In Dalit theology, many basic categories become reordered. Those on the margins, the suffering and the oppressed, minorities and indigenous peoples, move to the center. The local takes priority over the universal. Dalit theology, according to an address given by A. P. Nirmal, "will be based on their own Dalit experiences, their own sufferings, their own aspirations and their own hope. It will narrate the story of their pathos and protest the socio-economic injustices they have been subjected to through history. It will anticipate liberation which is meaningful to them."[38] Dalit theology makes suffering, injustice, and oppression the focal point of theological inquiry. According to M. J. Melanchthon, "a commitment to the oppressed and taking sides with them along with their allies should be the basis and starting point of theologic al reflection and theological education."[39]

Dalit theology emphasizes the systemic nature of injustice and believes that "the biblical God is the God of the oppressed."[40] Suffering is not just at the hands of evil individuals; suffering is the result of evil systems and institutions. Therefore, it is the duty of Christians to work toward justice. Suffering is not, according to Dalit theology, to be merely borne, tolerated, or endured. Quite the contrary. The reality of systemic suffering at the hands of oppressive structures demands that Christians work for justice. As Y. T. Vinayaraj states, "Dalits read the Bible for change."[41]

---

37 Prachi Patil, "Jesus's Two Great Commandments: Analysing Indian Theology through Caste and Gender," *Feminist Theology* 25, no. 1 (2006): 59.

38 Quoted in Clarke, "Dalit Theology," 20.

39 M. J. Melanchthon, "Theological Education for Transformation: India," *Colloquium* 47, no. 2 (2015): 241.

40 M. Gnanavaram, "'Dalit Theology' and the Parable of the Good Samaritan," *Journal for the Study of the New Testament* 15, no. 50 (1993): 59.

41 Y. T. Vinayaraj, "Envisioning a Postmodern Method of Doing Dalit Theology," in *Dalit Theology in the Twenty-First Century: Discordant Voices,*

Many Indian theologians echo Dalit theology's emphasis on suffering but add further dimensions. According to Samuel and Sugden, "the clear Christian option set forth in the Scriptures demands a life of suffering." Suffering is itself witness, an anti-prosperity gospel, a reminder that the kingdom of God is not yet in its fullness. Suffering is also a result of righteous conflict with unjust structures. "Jesus changed history through his suffering—much more than through his miracles."[42] Samuel also emphasizes the need for victory over suffering, for resilience. In his own work with the poor in the slums of Bangalore, Samuel noted that the impoverished carried with them a sense of defeat. While the poor have aspiration and enterprise, that is not enough. They need resilience, which is an essential quality for transformation.[43]

On Personhood

Indian theology also focuses on human nature, departing from caste and outcaste status to identifying all as image-bearers of God. This doctrine has a practical implication for Dalit believers. Christianity has given them a full humanity they have never had before. According to Duraisingh:

> The powerful symbol of table fellowship that Jesus exercises in his ministry comes to mind. Jesus calls and names those who have been systematically excluded from their dominant culture and yet they are not left to themselves. Diverse and different as they are, they are drawn together, in their freedom, around a table to share a meal as a token of a new paradigm of liberated identities in community.[44]

This liberated identity is what I noticed in Padmini and others like her. At a meeting of members of women's cooperatives at the Divya Shanthi Christian Association compound, the low-caste women spoke

---

Discerning Pathways, ed. Sathianathan Clarke, Deenabandhu Manchala, and Philip Peacock (New Delhi: Oxford University Press, 2010), 98.

42 Samuel and Sugden, "God's Intention for the World," 190.

43 Vinay Samuel, remarks at Nagel Institute seminar, Bangalore, India, June 23, 2015.

44 Duraisingh, "Gospel and Identity," 6.

confidently to the large assembled group. Padmini and the other women entrepreneurs demonstrated liberation not just as a theological category, but as a lived experience.

This theological identity and lived experience as a liberated person, is however, still firmly rooted in community. In the West the basic unit is the individual, but in India, as in much of the non-Western world, it is the family. According to Vinay Samuel, the poor have no other way of interacting with people except as family.[45] Indeed, in much of Indian theological reflection, the subject of inquiry is not the individual, but the individual embedded in community. "The individual is an individual only as a part of the community."[46] Paul J. Bhakiaraj, after mentioning Abraham's call to be a blessing to the nations (Gen 12:3) and St. Paul's declaration that this theme is still relevant to the church (Gal 3:14), concludes that "it becomes clear that our identity includes being involved in the communities in which we live. We should both contribute to them and critique them. Our faith as Christians should lead us to challenge unjust elements of our local communities, whether these take the form of unjust systems of labour or discrimination based on caste or ethnicity."[47]

A theology of individual-embedded-in-community affects programming. At the Christian Medical Center in Vellore, Tamil Nadu, our seminar saw medical ministry applied to whole families, not just individual patients. Even if there were no remaining medical options for the patient, the family was still a ministry focus. Likewise, the women's micro-credit cooperatives we saw in Bangalore operated on

---

45 Samuel, remarks at Nagel Institute seminar, Bangalore, India, June 23, 2015.

46 Roja Singh, "Bama's Critical-Constructive Narratives," in *Dalit Theology in the Twenty-First Century: Discordant Voices, Discerning Pathways*, ed. Sathianathan Clarke, Deenabandhu Manchala, and Philip Peacock (New Delhi: Oxford University Press, 2010), 218.

47 Paul J. Bhakiaraj, "Identity and Community," in *South Asia Bible Commentary*, ed. Brian Wintle (Grand Rapids, MI: Zondervan, 2015), 101.

a communal concept, which built in support and accountability. So, community and family resonate deeply throughout Indian theology. Rebecca Samuel Shah put it this way: "Are we autonomous individuals with untrammeled freedom of choice who live an atomized existence or are we persons created to live and serve each other in community?"[48] At the core of this idea of personhood is that the Christian faith is much more than an inner, individualistic experience.

Conclusion

The past few decades have seen a rise in American evangelical social action and the rise of world Christianity. These two dynamic trends are intersecting on a variety of fronts, but perhaps one of the most important ways they should relate to one another is that world Christians can contribute to American evangelicals' understanding of the deeper Christian dimensions of social action. Indian theology is a theology of a local experience, yet it can deepen the global Christian faith.

Indian theology, like much of the theology of the non-Western world, is rooted in the experience of the poor and the suffering, the marginalized and the oppressed. It speaks from the inside about realms that American evangelical social action is trying to address from the outside. Indian theology is as much about being as American Christianity is about doing. Out of Indian theology comes a faith that is more than a personal relationship with Christ, or even salvation in the life to come. Rather, it is about upholding human dignity, striving for justice, stewarding the creation, resisting evil, and creating community. Ultimately, it is about the coming of the kingdom of God, on earth, as it is in heaven.

---

48 Rebecca Samuel Shah, email message to author, December 1, 2016.

Chapter 6

What God Has Joined Together Let No One Separate

Local Church and Development Agencies in God's Mission

Darren Duerksen

As our group of Christian educators listened to church and agency leaders in various parts of India we learned about the recent surge of religious tensions and pressure. In some cases, churches had been burned and Christian pastors had been attacked and killed. Was this volatile religious climate also affecting Christian Development Organizations (CDOs), I wondered, and, if so, how did it impact their relationship with the Christian community and church?

One day our group had the privilege of meeting with leaders from one of the largest CDOs in India. This organization had done much to alleviate poverty in various parts of India and had developed a stellar reputation for professionalism among other development organizations. But these leaders quickly confided that they were not immune from the scrutiny and pressure that churches and other Christian agencies were experiencing from the Hindu nationalist organizations and their followers in government. These were perilous times for any organization with a Christian identity in India, no matter its size. How then was this CDO navigating the tensions?

Like any good organization, its leaders said, they adapted to new realities. Though they desired to work with local churches they assured the government and donors that they would not use their resources for proselytism or church-planting. They positioned themselves first and foremost as a development organization that prioritized and worked with districts with a low human development index (HDI). And from one standpoint, the strategy seemed to be working. They were able to work with and appeal to a wide range of political and religious communities, allowing them to continue operations while other CDOs were being closed. A little over one year after we met with this group, the Indian government forced the closure of another large CDO, Compassion International, amid accusations that it was using its funds and resources to proselytize children.

But while the strategy of emphasizing human development more than religion seemed important, if not necessary, for CDOs to continue their work in India, we wondered about the impact of this approach on their relationship with local churches. Local churches had once been strong and primary partners for the CDO we visited but working closely with local churches had proven to be a difficult relationship for its staff to navigate. Though the CDO maintained a department for church relations, local churches were no longer the central agents or focus of development projects. Churches were invited to participate in projects, but the CDO no longer expected projects to begin with local church involvement. Local churches were welcome partners, but not necessary ones.

As our conversation made clear, the relationship between CDOs and local churches in India is complex. This chapter will reckon with this complexity and argue that CDOs should recommit themselves to working with and through local churches. The rich missiological concept of *missio Dei* (mission of God) makes the church primary to God's mission. It points especially to the local church as the central agency of God's mission. This framework should prompt CDOs and churches to form deep, collaborative relationships that recover and better understand the role of local churches in God's mission program and their ability to be agents of healing and shalom in their immediate contexts.

Christian Development Organizations and Local Churches in India: Select Challenges

A Case Study

Unfortunately, the experience of the large CDO we visited is not unique; many CDOs struggle with how they relate to local churches. I saw a practical example of this several years ago with a South Indian church denomination and its CDO. At that time the CDO sought to help several remote, rural villages that had little health care available to them. Government-paid doctors rarely came to these villages, though they were hired to do so. To get to the nearest hospital or major clinics villagers would have to travel quite a distance, costing them much money in transportation and lost work wages. Because of this situation, some villagers would instead go to local healers who would sell to them various prayer mantras, herbs, and other remedies. However, locals also complained that these healers often took advantage of them, charging high prices for remedies that did not work. As a result, villagers often suffered from health conditions that could easily have been cured by basic medical care. Several of these villages also had small, local churches with which the CDO sought to work. How could the CDO address the local health issues, and what might its relationship to the local churches look like?

As the denominational CDO officers in this case study considered how to engage local churches to help address health care issues, they encountered several challenges.

Political Pressure

First, the officers encountered a charged political climate regarding religious conversions. Although India's Constitution allows the freedom for individuals to change religions, public policy, cultural traditions, and Hindu fundamentalist groups often exert pressure to dissuade people from converting away from Hinduism. Concern over conversion does not simply focus on the change of an individual's beliefs. Conversion often seems a threat to social and political power. That is, the Hindu community and structures lose influence when people turn to other religions. The Hindu majority also loses power when minority religions gain material, social, and political resources through education, development, jobs, and rising social status. In such a context, a Christian organization may incur scrutiny, criticism, and even vigilante action when it is seen to proselytize or give special preference to the Christian community.

One of the results of such pressure is that CDOs may stay distant from or only tangentially related to local churches to avoid the accusation of conversion. The leader of the South Indian CDO in our case was aware that local village and district governments could stop their work if health care was seen to be a front for evangelism. Political forces could also restrain or stop the CDOs work if it were seen as giving too much preference to the Christians. Thus, the identity and goals of a CDO can be shaped not only by its own sense of mission but also by external pressures.[1]

Professional versus Nonprofessional Skill and Approaches

In recent decades, development organizations in South Asia have become more and more professionalized.[2] As Anloor Ebrahim

---

1 Gerard Clarke, "Faith Matters: Faith-Based Organisations, Civil Society and International Development," *Journal of International Development* 18 (2006); Tamsin Bradley, "A Call for Clarification and Critical Analysis of the Work of Faith-Based Development Organizations (FBDO)," *Progress in Development Studies* 9, no. 2 (2009).

2 Anloor Ebrahim, "NGO Behavior and Development Discourse: Cases from Western India," *Voluntas: International Journal of Voluntary and Nonprofit Organizations* 12, no. 2 (2001); Sangeeta Kamat, "The NGO Phenomenon and Political Culture in the Third World," *Society for International Development*

describes it, "Throughout the 1970s and 1980s, India as well as many other countries of the South witnessed an unprecedented growth in NGOs, particularly in the form of young, educated, and professional individuals joining and creating development organizations."[3] This continued into the 1990s and was motivated increasingly by interactions with foreign funders, "which made it necessary that NGO staff be sufficiently trained to manage substantial funding, reporting, and monitoring requirements."[4]

This training and hiring of professionalized staff has transformed the cultures of development organizations and has created gaps of knowledge and power between the NGOs and local communities.[5] Because local church members are usually poor and untrained in socioeconomic development, CDOs can often view churches as traditional, slow, and a hindrance to progressive work.[6] In the case of the South Indian CDO, the local pastors had basic Bible college or seminary training and few, if any, had health or medical training.

46, no. 1 (2003); Neema Kudva, "Uneasy Partnerships?: Government-NGO Relations in India" (Berkeley: University of California, Institute of Urban and Regional Development, 1996); Padmaja Nair, "Historical Analysis of Relationships between the State and the Non-Governmental Sector in India" (University of Birmingham, 2007); Lester M. Salamon, Leslie C. Hems, and Kathryn Chinnock, "The Nonprofit Sector: For What and for Whom?" in *Working Papers of the John Hopkins Comparative Nonprofit Sector Project* (John Hopkins University, 2000); Celayne Heaton Shrestha, "'They Can't Mix Like We Can': Bracketing Differences and the Professionalization of NGOs in Nepal," in *Development Brokers and Translators: The Ethnography of Aid and Agencies*, ed. David Lewis and David Mosse (Bloomfield, CT: Kumarian Press, 2006); Eric Werker and Faisal Z. Ahmed, "What Do Nongovernmental Organizations Do?" *Journal of Economic Perspectives* 22, no. 2 (2008).

3   Ebrahim, "NGO Behavior and Development Discourse," 88.

4   Ibid., 89.

5   Shrestha, "'They Can't Mix Like We Can.'"

6   David Bussau and Russell Mask, *Christian Microenterprise Development: An Introduction* (Costa Mesa, CA: Regnum Books, 2003).

The CDO leader, on the other hand, was professionally trained in development theory and practice. Sometimes he struggled to gain the involvement of local pastors. Pastors who did get involved sometimes insisted on controlling the finances and planning of a project, though they lacked skills for doing so. In such circumstances, the chances were greatly increased that resources would be mismanaged or diverted, that projects would ultimately fail, and that relationships between local churches and CDOs would be badly damaged or ruined.

Limited Vision

Some local churches place little, if any, emphasis on socioeconomic development. These churches prioritize the "spiritual" ministry of the church over social engagement. Many CDOs, moreover, do not value or prioritize the importance of worship, discipleship, and other aspects of church life. In the South Indian example, the church pastors learned in Bible college to prioritize evangelism and discipleship ministries. "Church" for these pastors was where spiritual needs were addressed and members helped each other as best they could. In contrast, the CDO desired to address the wider systems and engage the broader community in alleviating poverty and bringing development. Both understood the primary interest of the other, but the vision for their own work remained limited to what they saw as their primary calling.

In summary, political pressures, professionalization of development, and conflicting visions often cause tension and misunderstandings between CDOs and churches. Because of this many CDOs prefer to operate independent of local churches.[7] Bryant Myers, a former executive at World Vision International, speaks for many development professionals when he confesses that they often have "deeply ambiguous feelings" about the church.[8]

---

7   Ibid.

8   Bryant L. Myers, *Walking with the Poor: Principles and Practices of Transformational Development* (Maryknoll, NY: Orbis, 2011), 78.

The church represents a special challenge to many involved in Christian development, since much of the work in the last quarter-century has been done by the so-called para-church agencies. Made up of Christians, these agencies go directly to Christians in the pews to solicit funds and then directly to poor communities to help the poor. The local church on both ends is too frequently ignored, or worse, seen as part of the problem.[9]

These are the realities of church-CDO relationships, but could things be different? What might this relationship look like if shaped from a theological and missiological perspective? How might Christian workers and scholars reflect differently on this relationship? To begin answering these questions we can turn to recent discussions in missiology about the mission of the local church.

Missiology: Local Church and the *Missio Dei*

As church historians will tell us, tensions between churches and Christian agencies, such as CDOs, are not new. Catholic orders have had both congenial and contentious relationships with Catholic bishops and parish churches throughout their histories. On the Protestant side, Christian para-church agencies have proliferated to move out on a mission when churches hesitated. Such "fortunate subversions" of the church, as Andrew Walls has observed, allowed Christianity to spread beyond its European context.[10] Yet churches and mission societies still shared the main goal of evangelization and church building.[11]

Starting in the 1960s, however, and particularly through the work of the World Council of Churches (WCC), missiologists started to critique this church-centered view of mission. Mission begins with God, not the church, they argued, and it is directed first and foremost to the world. The concept became encapsulated in the phrase the *missio*

---

9 Ibid., 79.

10 Andrew F. Walls, "Missionary Societies and the Fortunate Subversion of the Church," in *The Missionary Movement in Christian History*, ed. Andrew F. Walls (Maryknoll, NY: Orbis, 1996).

11 Ibid., 253.

Dei.¹² God's missional work was no longer bound to church institutions, and the church was not the goal of mission. The church, though one component of mission, was no longer central to this mission, and in some cases could even be a hindrance.¹³

Strengths and Challenges of *Missio Dei* Missiology

The implications of this shift were substantial. Most missiologists lauded the theological richness and post-colonial openness of the *missio Dei*. Since God and not the church is the initiator and sustainer of mission, Western churches had no mandate to exercise control over mission.¹⁴ The new missiology critiqued colonial and Christendom notions of mission as a one-directional movement from the West to the rest of the world.¹⁵ Christian activists and visionaries found in this language the encouragement to start new organizations that addressed God's call to ecological stewardship, social justice, and human flourishing, particularly when churches were slow to embrace or critical of these causes.¹⁶ Here was prime justification for independent CDOs.

However, some missiologists grew concerned that some interpretations of the *missio Dei* and the shift from "church" to "world" simply perpetuated a church/world dichotomy.¹⁷ Lamenting the early

---

12 David J. Bosch, *Transforming Mission: Paradigm Shifts in Theology of Mission* (Maryknoll, NY: Orbis, 1991), 391.

13 James Scherer, "Church, Kingdom, and *Missio Dei*: Lutheran and Orthodox Correctives to Recent Ecumenical Mission Theology," in *The Good News of the Kingdom: Mission Theology for the Third Millennia*, ed. C. Van Engen, D. S. Gilliland, and P. Pierson (Maryknoll, NY: Orbis, 1993), 85.

14 Mark Laing, "Missio Dei: Some Implications for the Church," *Missiology* 37, no. 1 (2009): 92.

15 Ibid., 94.

16 Craig Van Gelder and Dwight J. Zscheile, *The Missional Church in Perspective: Mapping Trends and Shaping the Conversation* (Grand Rapids, MI: Baker Academic, 2011), 30.

17 John G. Flett, *The Witness of God: The Trinity, Missio Dei, Karl Barth, and the Nature of Christian Community* (Grand Rapids, MI: Eerdmans, 2010), 71.

turns of this missiology Lesslie Newbigin wryly noted: "An unchurchly mission is as much a monstrosity as an un-missionary church."[18] In addition, Newbigin and others were concerned that this new emphasis marginalized the church and its role in God's mission.[19] With this concern in mind missiologist L. A. Hoedemaker concluded that the term *missio Dei*, while making possible "a liberation from obsolete conceptual models and a deepening reflection on the world-relatedness of the church,"[20] has more weaknesses than strengths. It easily led to a view of the church as a secondary player in the movement of God's mission.[21]

Reformulating *Missio Dei*: Integrating Church and Mission

Over the past thirty years many mission theologians have attempted to create a synthesis between a church-centric and world-centric view of mission. Most continue to agree that the church can never contain or exemplify the totality of God's work in the world. However, they have also responded to the marginalization of the local church and affirmed that the church has a central role in God's mission.[22]

While some WCC members had in earlier years presented the wider and less church-inclusive understandings of *missio Dei*, the WCC itself published in 2013 a statement that affirmed the central role of the

---

18   Lesslie Newbigin, *The Household of God* (Eugene, OR: Wipf and Stock, 1954), 169.

19   Bosch, *Transforming Mission*, 392.

20   L. A. Hoedemaker, "The People of God and the Ends of the Earth," in *Missiology: An Ecumenical Introduction*, ed. A. Camps, L. A. Hoedemaker, and M. R. Spindler (Grand Rapids, MI: Eerdmans, 1995), 162.

21   Ibid., 171.

22   Bosch, *Transforming Mission*; Brian Fikkert and Russell Mask, *From Dependence to Dignity: How to Alleviate Poverty through Church-Centered Microfinance* (Grand Rapids, MI: Zondervan, 2015); Lesslie Newbigin, *The Open Secret: An Introduction to the Theology of Mission*, rev. ed. (Grand Rapids, MI: Eerdmans, 1995).

church in the *missio Dei*: "The church is a gift of God to the world for its transformation towards the kingdom of God. Its mission is to bring new life and announce the loving presence of God in our world"[23] and "it is not possible to separate church and mission in terms of their origin or purpose."[24] In fact, holding them together clarifies the true nature of the church as a primary agency of mission.[25] The WCC thus challenged CDOs and other para-church organizations to remain connected to churches: "While para-church movements can find accountability and direction through ecclesial mooring, para-church structures can help churches not to forget their dynamic apostolic character."[26]

Thinking back on the health care work in rural South India, could a CDO-led health care project that bypassed the local churches or failed to engage them in meaningful ways still be considered an expression of the *missio Dei*? Mission starts with God and occurs in part beyond the confines of local churches. However, no matter how imperfect churches were and are, the church is the "primary agent of mission"[27] and serves the *missio Dei* by "representing God in and over against the world, pointing to God."[28] Para-church agencies and CDOs thus need to reckon with that reality more closely than they now do.

The Local Church in God's Kingdom

Before this matter is settled, however, we still need to ask, what exactly do we mean by "church"? How should we understand the relationship of the South Indian CDO to the village churches? The CDO was certainly "Christian" in that it was run and staffed by Christians

---

23 Jooseop Keum, ed., *Together towards Life: Mission and Evangelism in Changing Landscapes* (Geneva: WCC Publications, 2013), 7.

24 Ibid., 21.

25 Ibid., 27.

26 Ibid., 24.

27 Bosch, *Transforming Mission*, 380.

28 Ibid., 391.

who attended churches and its director aligned its work with biblical mandates. Indeed, the CDO was under the legal structure of a church denomination. Was the CDO itself thus a "church," a part of "the church," or a "para-church"? And what was its relationship to the local village "churches"?

The New Testament provides various metaphors and examples for church. Many of these primarily refer to the assembly of believers in specific locales, or the local church.[29] However, various passages in Colossians and Ephesians, and other terms/concepts such as the kingdom of God, suggest that the "church" may have a wider and more expansive identity as well. The various images suggest that the church is a local community, a collection of communities (like a denomination), and/or a wider, unseen collection and movement of people of God. Is the church an equal combination of all three? Or does it have an essence that also relates to other entities?

Throughout church history theologians have debated these notions of church and attempted to reconcile them. The Reformer John Calvin, for example, distinguished between the visible church as the institution in each locale and the invisible church as the community of all God's elect, including those who were at work throughout society.[30] In the early twentieth century, the Dutch Reformed theologian Abraham Kuyper developed notions of "sphere-sovereignty." Like Calvin, Kuyper saw society as composed of multiple spheres of activity, including the arts, politics, church, education, and others, each with its own unique, God-given role.[31] Where is the church in all of this? Kuyper suggested

---

29 Miroslav Volf, *After Our Likeness: The Church as the Image of the Trinity* (Grand Rapids, MI: Eerdmans, 1998), 137-38.

30 Yosep Kim, *The Identity and the Life of the Church: John Calvin's Ecclesiology in the Perspective of His Anthropology* (Eugene, OR: Pickwick Publications, 2014), 156.

31 Michael Brautigam, "A Queen with a Throne? Harnack, Schlatter, and Kuyper on Theology in the University," in *The Kuyper Center Review*, vol. 5, *Church and Academy*, ed. Gordon Graham (Grand Rapids, MI: Eerdmans, 2015), 113.

that the church exists throughout, but in two different forms: as an institution and an organism. As an institution the church serves society's religious sphere and is characterized by worship, the sacraments, and the spiritual edification of its members. As an organism, however, the church moves beyond the bounds of the religious sphere and becomes involved in all other spheres, even creating organizations to influence those spheres.[32] Thus Christians participate in the institutional church as they gather for worship and sacraments and in the organic church as they work in and engage the other spheres of society.

The Reformed tradition, including Kuyper's more recent framework, has been influential and provides certain strengths for Christians who seek to affirm the work of Christian organizations and CDOs as expressions of the church-in-mission. For example, pastor and author Timothy Keller shows that it is not realistic to expect local churches to give attention and leadership to the many issues facing society while also tending to ministries of worship and discipleship. As institutions, local churches are limited.[33] Therefore, Christians form such agencies as the CDO, which becomes part of the church-as-an-organism, focusing on larger policy or social issues and allowing the leader of a local church-as-an-institution to remain free to "build up the church through evangelism and discipleship."[34] Regarding our South Indian case study, Keller might suggest that the Indian CDO and local churches are each "church," but have particular spheres of expertise and calling. Thus, while it might be advantageous for the two to partner together, the CDO is participating in the *missio Dei* in its own way and through its calling.

---

32 Ad de Bruijne, "Not without the Church as Institute," in *The Kuyper Center Review*, vol. 5, *Church and Academy*, ed. Gordon Graham (Grand Rapids, MI: Eerdmans, 2015), 78.

33 Timothy Keller, *Generous Justice: How God's Grace Makes Us Just* (New York: Riverhead Books, 2010), 144.

34 Ibid., 145.

While this framework addresses the limitations of local churches, it also has weaknesses. One of particular relevance to our discussion is that it can lead to a bounded view of the identity and role of the church that may keep the (institutional) church from witnessing to the wider world and from challenging social injustices.[35] Whereas it could be argued that the institutional church informs the organic church on other spheres of society, it is not always clear where the institutional church ends and the organic church begins, or when the institutional church has inappropriately extended beyond its supposed sphere. In the South Indian example, this framework might excuse local village churches from engaging in their community's social and health issues since their sphere of responsibility is more on the spiritual care of their members. Mission then runs the risk of being dichotomized (spiritual versus social) and parceled out according to perceived areas of expertise and responsibility.

Countering this, theologians as diverse as Jürgen Moltmann, Stanley Hauerwas, and Miroslav Volf insist that the local church, while not seeking to control or dominate other spheres, is called to speak prophetically to and be at work within them. For Moltmann, churches as Christian communities should show the wider society what it means to be formed and shaped by the lordship of Christ.[36] For Hauerwas and William Willimon, the church does not simply have a social ethic, but is a social ethic—a witness and model to the wider world. They reject a limited sphere of influence while delineating the manner of the church's influence.[37] For Volf, quoting Otto Weber, the church is a "visible assembly of visible persons at a specific place for specific

---

35 J. Vorster, "Kingdom, Church and Civil Society: A Theological Paradigm for Civil Action," *HTS Teologiese Studies/Theological Studies* 71, no. 3 (2015).

36 Jürgen Moltmann, *Ethics of Hope*, trans. Margaret Kohl (Minneapolis, MN: Fortress Press, 2012), 22.

37 Stanley Hauerwas and William H. Willimon, *Resident Aliens: Life in the Christian Colony* (Nashville, TN: Abingdon, 1989), 81.

action."[38] The "action" includes preaching, sacraments, and obeying Christ's commands[39] which are important for the church's internal life but also shape and contrast it from the wider world, allowing it to be a model and witness to that world.[40]

Must we make a separation at all between types or forms of church? Volf, reflecting a Believers Church perspective, provides what I think is a helpful way forward. Though Volf, as we saw above, sees the church as "the visible assembly" he also notes that the church does not cease to exist when it disperses. As Daniel Strange summarizes, "Whatever this (non-gathered) aspect is and is called, it is inextricably tethered to the visible gathered local church, and it is this visible gathered and local church which is most natural and normative, in terms of biblical usage."[41]

Following on these insights, I would suggest that, rather than defining and distinguishing between different forms of church, whether as institution and organism or local church and CDO, it is more helpful to see the church as a locally rooted assembly whose life moves out into society through its people. CDOs and other Christian para-church organizations are thus not churches, or a part of a universal church as organizations. Development workers as Christians need to embrace the fact that their local community of faith is the local church wherever they work among the poor.[42]

---

38 Otto Weber, *Versammelte Gemeinde: Beitrage zum Gesprach die Kirche und Gottesdienst* (Neukirchen, Austria: Buchhandlung des Erziehungsvereins, 1949), 32; as quoted in Volf, *After Our Likeness*, 137.

39 Volf, *After Our Likeness*, 130-31.

40 "Soft Difference: Theological Reflections on the Relation Between Church and Culture in 1 Peter," *Ex Auditu* 10 (1994).

41 Daniel Strange, "Rooted and Grounded? The Legitimacy of Abraham Kuyper's Distinction between Church as *Institute* and Church as *Organism*, and Its Usefulness in Constructing an Evangelical Public Theology," *Themelios* 40, no. 3 (2015): 440.

42 Myers, *Walking with the Poor*, 77.

In sum, CDOs have an important place in God's mission, and their role may indeed extend beyond the local church even as God's mission does. However, where possible CDOs should have a renewed understanding of the primacy of local churches in God's mission and seek to help local churches fulfill their role in that mission. For the villages and churches in South India, a prominent question during our discussions was, was it enough for the CDO to simply implement its own health program, even if using local Christians? Or was there a way for the CDO to empower and work through the local church as a group? In other words, was there a way the CDO could help the local church fulfill its part in the *missio Dei* by helping to facilitate health care for its community? And might the local church help the CDO implement some of the "best practices" of development, such as sustainable development that empowers local structures?

Development in and through Ecclesial Communities: The Cultivation of Deep Collaboration

In recent decades CDOs have become well-acquainted with the skills needed for working with local communities in identifying and addressing development concerns.[43] I would suggest, however, that while such skills are indispensable for a deep collaboration between a CDO and a church, a more fundamental shift may be needed, particularly on behalf of CDOs, if they are to prioritize the mission of local churches and help development work to be truly "rooted in and lead back to a believing community."[44] The shift regards distinguishing between two types of challenges.

Technical and Adaptive Challenges

In considering the way in which CDOs and churches may together address local challenges I have found helpful the distinction that Ronald A. Heifetz and Marty Linsky make between technical and adaptive

---

43 See, for example, a summary of helpful practices and principles for healthy community engagement in ibid., 205-38.

44 Lesslie Newbigin, *The Gospel in a Pluralistic Society* (Grand Rapids, MI: Eerdmans, 1989), 227.

challenges.⁴⁵ A technical challenge is one that can be addressed by using clear and familiar skills, roles, and sequence of steps. Many of the problems that churches, and organizations encounter are assessed and easily solved through technical solutions, and CDOs and other development organizations are well-trained at solving technical challenges. For example, a CDO may assess the poverty of an area, determine certain needs (such as water, education, health care, etc.), and implement known and tested plans using its skills in community organizing, technical expertise, financial accounting, and the like to bring about a solution.

These skills, while readily available to CDOs, are often not found within local churches, and this disparity creates a potential tension. For example, in our case of the South Indian health care project, the CDO director saw the situation as a technical problem to be solved with the application of a health care program and curriculum that he had successfully implemented in other locations. Since local churches did not have the expertise to implement such a program, the project director took clear and direct leadership. He engaged the input of local village leaders beyond the church and brought in health professionals to hire and train local women in basic health care skills. The project was successful in several ways: some local women, including some

---

45 Ronald A. Heifetz and Marty Linsky, *Leadership on the Line: Staying Alive Through the Dangers of Leading* (Boston: Harvard Business Review Press, 2002); Ronald A. Heifetz, *Leadership Without Easy Answers* (Boston: Harvard University Press, 1994). See also application of this theory to local churches by Mark Lau Branson and Juan F. Martinez, *Churches, Cultures, and Leadership: A Practical Theology of Congregations and Ethnicities* (Downers Grove, IL: Intervarsity Press Academic, 2011). The following also closely relates to and complements the work of development theorist David Korten, who cautioned development agencies against following the "blueprint model" and to instead embrace a "learning process approach." David C. Korten, "Community Organization and Rural Development: A Learning Process Approach," *Public Administration Review* 40, no. 5 (1980); David C. Korten and Rudi Klauss, eds., *People-Centered Development: Contributions Toward Theory and Planning Frameworks* (West Hartford, CT: Kumarian Press, 1984).

from local churches, received needed employment, and the villages received more consistent health care.

However, because most local church leaders and members had little to no involvement in the visioning and implementation of the program, the churches' sense of vision and mission remained unengaged and untouched. The church was not empowered. The problem with technical assessments alone is that they rely solely on the expertise of the CDO, and local people and groups do not feel fully empowered to address their challenge. The way the CDO conducted its technical assessment and solutions did not further the *missio Dei* by enhancing the local church's participation in its God-given mission.

An alternative way of assessing this South Indian case is to see it as adaptive challenge.[46] In many if not most development situations, the goals and the pathway forward are not completely clear. There may be some vague sense of what the outcome may look like, but it is not well-defined and cannot be solved solely by using pre-existing techniques and plans. Adaptive challenges require those involved to engage deeply and change their values and actions.[47] The focus becomes not just the local people (churches and villages), but the values, attitudes, or habits of all involved (including the CDO). See table 6.1 for a summary of differences between technical and adaptive challenges.[48]

---

46 Richard Pascale, Mark Millemann, and Linda Gioja, *Surfing the Edge of Chaos: The Laws of Nature and the New Laws of Business* (New York: Three Rivers Press, 2000).

47 Heifetz, *Leadership Without Easy Answers*, 87.

48 From Branson and Martinez, *Churches, Cultures, and Leadership*, as adapted from Heifetz, *Leadership Without Easy Answers*, 73-88, and Heifetz and Linsky, *Leadership on the Line*, 13-30.

Table 6.1

Technical Challenges	Adaptive Challenges
Clear goals	Murky future
Known methods	Unknown road
Current knowledge	New learning
Available resources	Resources not identifiable
Familiar roles	Unfamiliar roles
Adequate competencies	Competencies not developed
Predictable and manageable change	Unpredictable and uncontrollable change
"We are who we need to be"	"We need to become different"

An adaptive challenge may look, at least at the outset, like a familiar problem. On deeper inspection, the situation may be less clear. What might it take to not only provide health care to remote villages, but to also engage local churches such that they are empowered, and they participate in God's mission? And how might the churches' embrace of such projects help promote lasting change? Such are questions that may not have clear answers right away. In addition, such questions suggest more patience and a much slower process, one that many CDOs may be unused to. Most difficult, however, is the recognition that the emerging vision and pathway forward, when eventually and together discerned, may require both the church and the CDO to change in some ways.

Components of the Adaptive Change Process

What might it look like for churches and CDOs to engage in mutually adaptive change? The following are some components of an adaptive change process that might be relevant for such a collaboration.[49]

---

49 The following are drawn from *Leadership on the Line* and Branson and Martinez, *Churches, Cultures, and Leadership*.

Get on the Balcony

A crucial first step is for leaders to come together and gain a "big picture" of what is going on. As an outsider to a context, the CDO may have a particularly helpful role at this stage it has not been immersed in all the detail of the local context. However, the church is important here as well, because it has important insider knowledge. In the case of the South Indian villages, is health care the primary need? Perhaps other issues need to first be addressed to help prevent health problems, such as malnutrition, sanitation, the status and roles of women, or education. Perhaps significant work needs to be done within the churches to help them value, embrace, and engage work on behalf of their communities. The CDO and church inquire together about the bigger picture of the situation.

Identify the Adaptive Challenge and Change

It is after gaining a bigger picture of the situation that a CDO would be able to offer its skills and programs to bring a technical solution to the problem. However, if engaging the situation as an adaptive challenge, a CDO will need to avoid plunging ahead with a technical fix to the problems and instead continue to listen to its church partner. To return to Heifetz's question, both the CDO and church consider, what changes in values, attitudes, or habits of behavior will be needed to move forward and conserve any progress? To frame this step missiologically, in what ways does the church need to grow or change to fulfill what God may be calling it to? What changes might be required of the CDO? On a basic level, members of a local rural church may never have seen themselves as able to address a local issue. Perhaps the church is newly established and the relational bonds between the members are relatively fresh. Perhaps the emphasis and teaching has been on addressing the spiritual issues of individuals. Perhaps the pastor has been trained to devote his time to spiritual conversations and to stay out of community problems. The goal is to not necessarily devalue the values and habits that exist, but to consider what it might take to add or reshape these to address the "balcony" issues identified.

It is also at this stage that the CDO and church begin to develop steps to address the challenges they have identified. However, rather than create and follow a full plan with all the resulting steps, it is important to identify the next steps and anticipate that they will need to "learn their way" into the future. In adaptive situations organizations cannot simply implement linear, mechanical (technical) solutions to the problem. Rather, solutions in these cases often develop over time and through experimentation and reflection.[50]

Even though CDOs should be cautious about quickly bringing their technical expertise to a solution, this does not mean such skills are unimportant. Such organizations obviously have important and needed resources for development. And, empowering the local church in its mission does not mean that the CDO should try to make local churches experts in all the skills needed for a development project. Rather, after taking time to develop a close collaboration, the CDO and the church discuss how each can bring their own gifts for a common vision,[51] even setting up separate structures parallel but related to the church to run finances separately and independently from the church.[52] There is a multitude of creative ways that CDOs can partner with local churches, bringing their expertise to the service of God's mission and the church's role in it.

Regulate the Stress

After taking time to assess the problem and the types of changes that may be needed, there are several components that leaders should keep

---

[50] Myers, *Walking with the Poor*, 246. Myers draws on David Mosse, "Process-Oriented Approaches to Development Practice and Social Research," in *Develoment as Process: Concepts and Methods for Working with Complexity*, ed. David Mosse et al. (New Delhi: India Research Press, 2001), 6.

[51] Megan C. Boucher, "Ten Talents: The Role of Church-Based Programs in the Microfinance Industry," *Missiology* 40, no. 2 (2012).

[52] David Befus, "Discovering a Role in God's Provision," in *The Local Church in a Global Era: Reflections for a New Century*, ed. Max L. Stackhouse, Tim Dearborn, and Scott Paeth (Grand Rapids, MI: Eerdmans, 2000), 55.

in mind. The first is to recognize that change creates stress. Within the church, the discussion of new ideas and possibilities may bring conflict and disagreement that need to be continually processed. Externally, there can be huge tensions and barriers as well. An Indian church that becomes more confident and assertive in its work may upset the religious equilibrium of a community. The Hindu majority may be uncomfortable with the increased empowerment of a lower-caste Christian minority. An adaptive change process recognizes that there will be stress that needs to be monitored by the church and CDO leaders and regulated with slow, patient work. As Myers summarizes, "because unintended consequences are the norm in adaptive social systems, we need to make monitoring much more frequent and pay much more attention to anything that changes, not focus only on the indicators we set early on. The program plan needs frequent assessment, but so does the social environment of the program."[53]

Focus Attention

There are many things upon which a church and a CDO can focus as they engage a development issue adaptively. One natural tension, however, based on the church's mission to minister holistically across a broad front, is prioritizing and maintaining attention on the agreed upon issues. This is not to devalue other interests and foci of the church, but to make sure the church remains committed to addressing the identified issues. Once again, this will take patience on the part of the CDO and a willingness to think about the issue's broader dimensions, not just its more narrowly instrumental aims.

Even so, churches will need to move development issues from being peripheral activities and announcements and toward being integrated into the very life and worship of the church. For example, the Divya Shanthi Christian Association (DSCA) and Trust began in the 1970s as an outreach and extension of a church to poor children and families in north Bangalore, India. Over the ensuing years its founders, Vinay and Colleen Samuel, and staff have successfully developed numerous

---

53 Myers, *Walking with the Poor*, 247.

development programs, including schools, day care services, health centers, vocational training for youth, cooperatives, and women self-help groups. These programs, however, are also integrally connected to local Divya Shanthi churches. In many cases the pastors of the churches have a dual role—pastor of a church as well as staff in one of the development initiatives of DSCA. These integrated roles provide the pastors with training and skills to care for people in the community in holistic ways, such as negotiating with local hospitals to lower a bill, gathering and counseling men who want to deal with alcohol addiction, or praying for families who request it. At the same time the pastors also bring the concerns of the neighborhood families into the life and worship of the church community through corporate prayer, sermons, and church initiatives, allowing liturgy and church life to be shaped in unique ways.

This example illustrates how an adaptive task may challenge all involved to change their normal practices and roles to meet the new demands. CDOs do not often consider themselves experts in church liturgy, but they may be called to adjust their roles, modify their normal modus operandi, and attain new knowledge to help with the process of integrating focus and concerns into the life and worship of the local church.

The Uneasy but Divine Marriage—CDOs and Churches as Co-Agents of Missional Transformation.

CDOs and churches in places like India operate in a challenging context, and their relationship is often scrutinized and strained by a host of social, political, and other factors. Considering this, it is understandable that each would settle into and accept an uneasy and sometimes distant marriage. However, I have argued that CDOs and churches in India and elsewhere should not allow their mission to be controlled by the social and political challenges they face. Rather, some may need to rediscover the importance of the local church for God's mission in the world today and recapture a strong theological conviction that God means and has always meant for the local church to be a central agent in his mission. That, as Newbigin has said, the church is meant to be a sign, instrument, and foretaste of God's healing, shalom-bringing kingdom.[54]

Therefore, CDOs need to more fully consider the implication that their primary mission may not be to the poor directly, but rather to help local churches fulfill their call and primary role in God's mission to the poor. They also need to be reminded that the mark of their success is not the immediate impact of projects. Rather it is enduring and progressive change, sustained by people who have been empowered to build their lives. CDOs may come and go with their projects, but the church, as God's ongoing mission agent in a place, will, by God's grace, remain.

Second, it does not help to divide the church into different categories; doing so risks creating dichotomies between the spiritual/pastoral work of a local church and the development work of a CDO. What God has joined together, let not theologians, local churches, or CDOs separate. Lasting change only comes via such vital, longstanding partnerships in mission.

Third, it is important for CDOs and churches to recognize that this type of close collaboration is an adaptive challenge for which pre-planned, technical solutions may be inadequate. Instead, each will need to learn and adapt to meet the more fully orbed needs of the community. This is, no doubt, a tricky and perilous process, but the potential outcome, from both a theological and a development perspective, can be enormously beneficial. If and when churches partner with CDOs; when churches allow the development ideas and concerns brought by a CDO to permeate, mix, and help shape their sense of mission; when the CDO values and honors the church's primacy as mission agent in that place; when the church draws on the CDO's expertise; when the members of the churches are empowered to be a part of transformation and to find their own role in their communities as conduits for hope, healing, health, wealth, and learning—in such cases it is probable that the calling of the Christian development organization will contribute to God's mission in ways not otherwise possible.

---

54 Newbigin, *The Open Secret*, 110.

PART III

NATIONALISM, VIOLENCE AND FREEDOM

Chapter 7

Bollywood and the BJP

An Analysis of Indian Identity in Karan Johar's Films

Samuel Thambusamy

The Bharatiya Janata Party (BJP) led by Narendra Modi won the 2014 General Elections held in India. Modi embodied the BJP's political message—Governance, Development, and Decisive Leadership—albeit with the Hindutva[1] subtext. Modi's credibility, charisma, and charm had a phenomenal connect with people across India and more importantly with the Indian diaspora around the world. Interestingly, the large Hindu segment of the Indian diaspora, particularly in the United States and the United Kingdom, played a supportive role with funding, volunteer force, and social media technical support in the BJP campaign.[2] The

---

1 Hindutva is an ideology that seeks to define Indian culture in terms of Hindu values. While "Hindu" is a religious term, "Hindutva" is a political expression of Hindu-ness. For a detailed description of Hindutva, see Jyotirmaya Sharma, *Hindutva: Exploring the Idea of Hindu Nationalism* (New Delhi: Penguin Books, 2011).

2 The Overseas Friends of the BJP (OFBJP) conducted a two-day national convention that was attended by more than 100 delegates from

"Modi wave" was real and the resultant "saffron surge" helped the BJP to make huge political gains across India and to form the first ever non-Congress Party majority government since Independence. Modi, who had been a controversial and polarizing politician until then, emerged as the preferred choice of a new India. Modi's victory was simultaneously Hindutva's victory for mainstream acceptance.

After the historic win, Prime Minister Modi undertook visits to Japan, the United States, the United Kingdom, Dubai, and Australia to seek support for his diplomatic and economic objectives. Earlier in his career, the United Kingdom, the United States, and some European nations had imposed a travel ban, holding him responsible for the 2002 anti-Muslim carnage in the state of Gujarat while he served there as governor.[3] Modi's election victory and more importantly his official visits to the United States and the United Kingdom were also deemed a victory for the Hindutva-leaning diaspora organizations that lobbied hard for Modi's cause for almost a decade. They organized grandiose public receptions for Modi, and his rock star-like performances at these events evoked deafening applause and raucous cheers from the audience. These public rallies were akin to a well-scripted Bollywood blockbuster; they were full of dance, color, lights, and fanfare. Such public receptions were unprecedented and unparalleled for any foreign leader, let alone the Indian prime minister.

Modi's connection with the diaspora was not merely a function of his personal charisma. It is reflective of a Hindu revivalism, and it shows that the resurgence of Hindu nationalism within India has had an impact on the Hindu diaspora worldwide. The destruction in 1992 of the Babri Masjid, a centuries-old Muslim mosque, and

---

22 states in America and a few die-hard Modi supporters from Canada as well. The convention resolved to work toward getting 272 seats for the BJP and called it Mission 2014. Many BJP leaders, including Modi, addressed the convention. Modi urged his Indian-American supporters to play a meaningful role in the victory of the BJP.

3 See James Mann, "Why Narendara Modi Was Banned from the US," *The Wall Street Journal*, May 2, 2014.

the subsequent violence marked a new phase in Hindu Nationalism both at home and across the Indian diaspora. Since then the BJP has been working actively with the Indian diaspora in the United States, the United Kingdom, and elsewhere. The Hindu diaspora is an important part of the BJP's political strategy. Since the 1990s, large sections of the Hindu diaspora have been huge supporters of Hindutva and have contributed to the growth of the BJP. In fact, the BJP's earlier government (1999-2004) led by A. B. Vajpayee launched an annual event called the Overseas Indian Day in 2003 to galvanize the Indian diaspora to play a supportive role in India's development. As a result, the 2004 elections saw a significant political engagement by the Hindutva supporters across the diaspora. While several factors might have contributed to the growth of Hindu revivalism among the diaspora, this chapter explores the role of Bollywood films of the 1990s in the construction of a Hindu identity, both at home and among the Indian diaspora.

Cinema is an integral part of contemporary Indian society and its influence is all pervasive.[4] Indian commercial cinema (re)shapes both public culture and the political space by capturing the collective national imagination. Bollywood cinema, the film industry that is based in and around Bombay (now Mumbai), has gained a "national" character,[5] this despite a robust regional cinema based in Chennai (formerly Madras), Kolkata (formerly Calcutta), and Hyderabad. The lure of Bollywood is its stardom, music, and thematic components that unify diverse people groups/communities across India. Patriotism and pleasure are two major dimensions of Bollywood. Nasreen Munni Kabir, a British-based Indian producer and critic, contends that every Bollywood film

---

4   India is the largest film-producing country in the world; about 800 films are shown in 13,000 cinemas each year. The International Indian Film Academy (IIFA) estimates about 23 million Indians go to see a film every day.

5   See M. Madhava Prasad, *Ideology of Hindi Film* (New Delhi: Oxford University Press, 2000).

"must address the theme of what it means to be Indian or reflect on Indian thinking."[6]

Bollywood's fascination with Indian-ness is as old as Indian cinema itself.[7] Since its earliest days (circa 1913), every filmmaker has recast the patriotism motif across different genres and times. Bollywood, in its representation of Indian-ness, has portrayed a close relationship between religious identity and nationalistic fervor, and this linkage was particularly evident during the anticolonial Freedom Movement. Historically, Bollywood has privileged the Hindu perspective to the question of Indian-ness/identity. Studies by Melanie Wright and Rachel Dwyer have shown that Bollywood is "primarily informed by Hinduism" and even when it is less obvious, Hinduism still "remains its invisible norm."[8] In the past two decades, Bollywood's appeal and influence have spread across Europe, North America, and the Pacific. These new cultural viewing contexts and changing consumption patterns have forced Bollywood to re-invent itself. Popular filmmakers such as Yash Chopra,[9] Sooraj R. Barjatya,[10] and Yash Johar and his

---

6 Nasreen Munni Kabhir in the foreword to Jonathan Torgovnik, *Bollywood Dreams: An Exploration of the Motion Picture Industry and Its Culture in India* (London: Phaidon Press, 2003).

7 Indian-ness is the cultural identity that informs the activities and concerns of daily life for vast number of Indians. See Sudhir Kakar, "Indian-ness: So What Really Makes Us Indians?" *Little India*, http://www.w3c.org/TR/1999/REC-html401-19991224/loose.dtd.

8 Melanie J. Wright, *Religion and Film: An Introduction* (London: IB Tauris, 2007), 149; for a detailed discussion on Hinduism and Hindi cinema, see Rachel Dwyer, *Filming the Gods: Religion and Indian Cinema* (New York: Routledge, 2006).

9 Yash Chopra is a popular filmmaker who is known for filming romantic tales in exotic locales, particularly Switzerland. His efforts have been recognized by the Swiss government, which has even presented him with a special award. For a glimpse into his films and film company Yash Raj films, see his official website http://www.yashrajfilms.com.

10 Sooraj Barjatya directed the film *Hum Aapke Hain Koun* (Who Am I to You? 1994), which showcased Indian culture and celebrated elaborate

son Karan Johar have repackaged Bollywood (with multi-star casts, extravagant sets, designer costumes, and exotic locales).[11] However, the re-invention of Bollywood as a global brand has not changed its basic conventions. "Pleasure-patriotism" dimensions, a key ingredient of the Bollywood flavor, have been retained to meet spectators' demands and contextual needs. In fact, the unprecedented success of Bollywood cinema beyond India, particularly in recent times, is due to its representation of Indian-ness.[12]

In this chapter, I will take a closer and more critical look at this Indian-ness as conveyed in commercial Hindi cinema by focusing on four of Karan Johar's popular films: *Kuch Kuch Hota Hai* (Something, Something Happens, 1998), *Kabhie Khushie Kabhie Gham* (Sometimes Happy, Sometimes Sad, 2001), *Kal Ho Na Ho* (Tomorrow May Never Be, 2003), and *Kabhi Alvida Na Kehna* (Never Say Goodbye, 2006). I have chosen Johar's films because they were extremely popular, both in India and abroad. Also, these four films best represent the strand within Bollywood that seeks to cater to the changing needs/contexts of urban India, immigrant Indian communities, and the larger South Asian diaspora. Through a textual and visual analysis of these films, I will argue that these films achieved unprecedented success, particularly

---

wedding ceremonies. The film became a huge commercial success and set a new trend in Bollywood. The film is said to have inspired a new breed of younger filmmakers such as Aditya Chopra (Yash Raj Films) and Karan Johar (Dharma Productions).

11 For a discussion of the prolific work of Yash Johar, see Dharma Productions' official website http://www3.dharma-production.com/ourprofile.html.

12 The International Indian Film Academy estimates Bollywood's overseas income between 15 and 20 percent and projects the Indian film industry to grow at a compounded annual growth rate of 18 percent (gross $2,244 million) by 2008. See IIFA website, http://www.iifa.com/web07/cntnt/theindianfilmindustry.htm. For a list of overseas earnings of Bollywood films since the mid-1990s, see Box Office India's website, http://www.boxofficeindia.com/cpages.php?pageName=overseas_earners&PHPSESSID=ab98ee3d811c54cf3978c14600bf6208.

among the diaspora, because they represent Indian-ness as Hindu religious identity. Thus, they provide powerful, mass-mediated support for Hindu nationalism. For this analysis, I propose to use a critical reading that looks for things that either seem not overtly intended or are not always obvious in the films. It is my belief that such a critical reading of Bollywood unmasks its ideological underpinnings, whether fully intentional or not.

But first we need to locate this reading within Bollywood's own story. Bollywood has a longtime fascination with the patriotism motif, particularly through the interplay of religion and Indian identity. Then we will be able to see how these representations of Indian-ness progress in Johar's films and how he privileges the Hindu perspective by using a variety of devices. Before closing this discussion, I also want to inject a note of hope. Bollywood is not bound to this approach. New visual narratives, vocabulary, and composition make possible a more inclusive understanding of what it means to be Indian.

Understanding the Dynamics of Bollywood

The history of Indian cinema began with the screening of *Harichandra* (King Harichandra, dir. Phalke, 1913) at Coronation Cinema, Bombay.[13] The initial impulse, particularly in the era of silent films, was to re-tell Indian mythology in film. However, the political usefulness of films (particularly during the movement for national independence) eclipsed the religious impulse. With the advent of new technologies (such as sound) and the changing political context, filmmakers explored other genres such as historical, social, and realist films. Since the 1950s golden age of Hindi cinema, it has evolved into a more commercial music-drama form popularly known as "Bollywood."[14]

---

13 Dadasaheb Phalke, the father of Indian cinema, was inspired by the film *The Life of Christ* and wanted to bring images of revered Indian deities to the screen, just as Christ's image had been presented in the West. See Ravi Vasudevan, "Dadasaheb Phalke," Film Reference available at http://www.filmreference.com/Directors-Pe-Ri/Phalke-Dadasaheb.html.

14 Although the Indian film industry has objected to the use of the word "Bollywood," it has now been included in the new edition of the

Bollywood: A *Masala* Twist to Hollywood Tales

The evolution of Hindi cinema to Bollywood, particularly its *masala* formula,[15] is a fascinating story. No filmmaker can afford to disregard its formulaic conventions, especially its distinctive music-drama format. This format is an ingenious mix of varied elements within traditional theater (Parsi), Indian mythology (particularly the two great epics Ramayana and Mahabharata), and Indian aesthetics, emotions, and sentiments. A Bollywood film must necessarily have a loose narrative structure dealing with familiar themes marinated with a "*masala*-mix" of spectacle, emotions, comic subplots, mythological resonances, and social obligations to cater to Indian audiences. The spectators' demand and need for heroism, emotions, romance, social obligations, cultural negotiation, and song-and-dance sequence dictates the logic of Bollywood's "mix-and-match" approach.

Bollywood is not entirely insulated from Hollywood influences. It continues to draw inspiration for its plot line, filming techniques, and cinematic technology from Hollywood.[16] However, even Hollywood inspirations are subjected to such cultural re-locations and given a *masala* twist. Thus, despite Hollywood traces, Bollywood remains distinctively Indian in its form.

Bollywood and Patriotism: Indian-ness Explored

Patriotism is one among the many recurrent themes of Bollywood. Interestingly, Phalke's pioneering attempt to make cinema was deemed as a "swadeshi" effort and subsequently seen as an alternative to

---

Oxford English Dictionary (OED). See *The Hindu*, June 10, 2003, http://www.hinduonnet.com/thehindu/menue.css" type= text/css.

15 *Masala*, a flavorful mix of Indian spices, is a term used by film critics to evoke the Bollywood formula of celebrating lively, colorful India.

16 See Ally Ostrowski, "Found in Translation: From Hollywood Hits to Bollywood Blockbusters," *Journal of Religion and Film* 11, no. 2 (October 2007).

Hollywood.[17] Not surprisingly, Bollywood reflects strong patriotic sentiments in its visual narrative and style. Bollywood studies have pointed to nationalistic intent as its underlying theme since the early films readily reflected the growing spirit of nationalism. In fact, the mythological, historical, and social films acted as subtle metaphors for the struggle for national independence. The nationalist project was further intensified in the post-independence era, as Bollywood arose, and its narratives addressed the experience of urbanization.[18] India's partition with the creation of Pakistan provided an occasion for popular Hindi cinema to be put to political use in the cultural integration of the newly less Muslim nation.

In the 1960s, popular Hindi cinema developed the themes of migration and settlement as films represented the West as a corrupting influence and counter referent to Indian values. The "angry young man" of the 1970s cinema appropriated the political movements of the peasants and the working classes that led to the Emergency of 1975-77, in which the Indian government suspended many civil liberties and outlawed opposition leaders and parties. In the 1980s, connection to film stars, Hindi music, and nostalgia for the homeland established Bollywood's transnational networks. Films of this period celebrated Indian culture by featuring arranged marriages and wedding ceremonies. In the 1990s, a new series of films were made that held up the Non-Resident Indian (NRI) as a hero testifying to the liberalized economy of the 1990s.[19]

Bollywood as a Global Brand: The Reinvention of Indian-ness

Bollywood cinema underwent a marked shift in the 1990s. The liberalization of the Indian economy and the new cultural contexts

---

17 The "swadeshi" movement during the Indian quest for independence was an attempt to boycott foreign goods and to enhance Indian production.

18 Prasad, *Ideology of Hindi Film*.

19 Sudhanva Deshpande, "The Consumable Hero of Globalised India," in *Bollyworld: Popular Cinema Through Transnational Lens*, ed. Raminder Kaur and Ajay J. Sinha (New Delhi: Sage Publications, 2005), 186-206.

of both urban India and the diaspora forced Bollywood to re-invent itself. Bollywood films began to cater increasingly to the Indian middle class, by featuring aspirations for social mobility and diasporic displays of affluence. The main protagonist of popular films was no longer the farmer or factory worker but rather was either living in or visiting Western Europe or America. The NRI became a cultural placard for India's emergence as a key player in global economics. However, the glaring portrayals of Western lifestyle invited a new kind of conservatism in favor of celebrating age-old Indian traditions—family ties, arranged marriages, and lavish wedding ceremonies. Two films—*Hum Aapke Hain Kaun* (Who Am I to You? dir. Sooraj Barjatya, 1994) and *Dilwaale Dulhaniya Le Jayenge* (The Big Hearted Will Take the Bride, dir. Aditya Chopra, 1995)—were instrumental in setting the trend of NRI-based films and have been a great inspiration to new-age filmmakers.

The film *Who Am I to You?* is a love story of Prem (played by Salman Khan) and Nisha (played by Madhuri Dixit) who were willing to sacrifice their love for the sake of their family. This drama celebrated the extravagant Indian wedding and family traditions like never before. In fact, the film had an unusually large number of songs—fourteen—that are popular even today. *Who Am I to You?* had all the classic ingredients of Bollywood but its celebration of traditional Indian values made an especially strong emotional connect with audiences, particularly among the Indian diaspora. The grand celebration of the Indian family values in the film contributed to its huge success at the box office. The film premiered at Mumbai's Liberty Cinema and ran continuously for more than one hundred weeks. *Who Am I to You?* is easily one of the biggest blockbusters of the modern era.[20] Culturally, it made a lasting impact as its songs are replayed at weddings even today.

Similarly, *The Big Hearted Will Take the Bride* was a story of two young NRIs Raj (Shah Rukh Khan) and Simran (Kajol) falling in love during a vacation through Europe. Both Raj and Simran decide to hide their love and get married only with the blessing of the elders.

---

20   http://www.boxofficeindia.com/movie.php?movieid=11.

This drama dealt with an Indian family's problems of transnational location but celebrated the conservative agenda within courtship and marriage. Moreover, the film presented Baldev Singh (Simran's father) as one who feels lonely and lost in a foreign land and one who keeps "Indian culture" even in a foreign land. *The Big Hearted Will Take the Bride* is also one of the highest-grossing Bollywood films. In fact, it is the longest-running film in the history of Indian cinema. Even after more than twenty years after its first release, it is still being shown at the Maratha Mandir theater in Mumbai. The success of *Who Am I to You?* and *The Big Hearted Will Take the Bride* led other filmmakers to focus on the diaspora for commercial success. Specific ideologies, symbols, and cultural markers to celebrate Indian identity (read Hindu) were employed within the narrative to connect with the diaspora. In both *Who Am I to You?* and *The Big Hearted Will Take the Bride*, Indian-ness is a conflation of Hindu religious identity and Indian national identity.

Subsequently, two trends emerged. First, there was a celebration of the grit and valor of the Indian soldier or the heroes of the independence struggle. *Border* (dir. J. P. Dutta, 1997), *LOC Kargil* (dir. J. P. Dutta, 2003), and *Deewar* (dir. Milan Luthria, 2004) celebrated the grit and valor of the Indian soldiers. Moreover, there was a flurry of films on the freedom fighters and nation founders: *The Making of the Mahatma* (dir. Shyam Benegal, 1996), *Dr. Babasaheb Ambedkar* (dir. Jabbar Patel, 2000), *Veer Sarvarkar* (dir. Ved Rahi, 2001), *The Legend of Bhagat Singh* (dir. Raj Kumar Santoshi, 2002), *Shaheed- E-Hasam* (dir. Sukumar Nair, 2002), and *23rd March 1931: Shaheed* (dir. Guddu Dhanoa, 2002). Film critic Aarti Wanni observes that "the strange revival of interest in Freedom struggle is due to liberalization on the one hand and the rise of Hindu majoritarian politics on the other."[21] Surprisingly, these films failed to do well at the box office, both at home and abroad, despite rising patriotic fervor across the nation.

---

21 Aarti Wani, "Three Films and a Nation," *MR Zine*, October 22, 2005, http://mronline.org/2005/10/22/three-films-and-a-nation/.

Another emerging theme was a celebration of the "uncompromising" or "unbeatable" Indian who either fights (Pakistan-sponsored) terrorism or remains unvanquished against all odds. Bollywood films employed this theme and unconsciously appealed to the Hindu sensibilities by portraying political solidarity consolidating around Indian (read Hindu) identity. The blockbuster film *Gadar: Ek Prem Katha* (Revolt: A Love Story, dir. Anil Sharma, 2001) portrayed the classic Bollywood obsession with Pakistan. *Revolt* tells the story of Tara Singh, a Sikh truck driver bringing back his Muslim wife after successfully decimating the Pakistani forces through a violent battle. The backdrop of partition sets the aggressive tone and tenor of *Revolt*. The people of Pakistan are presumably proven weak as they lose out to the unstoppable Tara Singh. Worse, much of Tara Singh's anti-Pakistan rhetoric is directed against Indian Muslims. Revolt, as Ziya Us Salam puts its, moves "inexorably first towards pulp patriotism, then jingoism and climaxes very near xenophobia."[22] Wanni rightly concludes that the rise of Hindutva ideology with its virulent militarism that saw the Pakistani and Indian Muslims as its enemies created an atmosphere conducive to the reception of these films.[23]

Similarly, *Lagaan* (Taxation—Once Upon a Time in India, dir. Aushutosh Gowariker, 2001) presented the unbeatable Indian theme through a historical drama based on a game of cricket. *Taxation* was set in the nineteenth century and told the story of Bhuvan'saccepting a challenge to play cricket against the British, said to be masters of the game. Taxation thus resurrected the stereotypical white villains of the 1980s films. The victory of the Indians against the British resonated strongly within the diaspora. As the Lithuanian scholar of Indian film Deimantas Valančiūnas points out, "*Lagaan* has clearly pronounced mythological and myth-religious symbolism and underlines

---

22 Ziya Us Salam, "Peddling Patriotism," *The Hindu*, March 15, 2002, http://www.thehindu.com/thehindu/fr/2002/03/15/stories/2002031500070100.htm.

23 Wani, "Three Films and a Nation."

its function as a useful tool in transferring ideas related to national identity, nationalism, and anti-colonialism to the viewer."[24]

Not surprisingly, both *Revolt* and *Taxation* were runaway commercial hits. *Taxation* was nominated for the best foreign-language film at the Academy Award nominations ceremony.

Mediating the Other: Bollywood and Religious Identity

In the earlier years of Indian cinema, the euphoria surrounding the Freedom Movement was used to communicate Indian-ness. The West/East binary was often used to demarcate the boundary between "us" (moral Indians) and "them" (immoral Westerners). With the changing contexts, Bollywood began to employ religion to reinforce notions of Indian-ness. Since Partition, religion has been used to create a sense of solidarity and worse, to drive a wedge between faith communities. Rachael Dwyer details the conflation of the "Hindu" and "Indian" in her book *Filming the Gods*. Not surprisingly, Bollywood films represent the upper-caste, North Indian, Hindu male as the norm for Indian-ness.[25] In fact, popular Muslim lead actors had to conceal their religious identities and even adopt Hindu names when portraying these characters.

Moreover, non-Hindus (particularly Muslim men and Christian women) are represented as outsiders to Indian-ness. The viewer in the theater is made to identify and name the Other through markers such as names, slang, appearances, costumes, characters, religious images, beliefs, faith communities, and sociocultural practices. For example, the Christian/Anglo Indian woman with short skirts and loose morals is represented as the Other of the sari-clad Hindu middle-class woman. The Hindu woman, in contrast, is a chaste woman, a good wife, and a loving mother. Christian men are usually comics, portraying drunks

---

24 Deimantas Valančiūnas, "Myth in Constructing Contemporary Indian Identity in Popular Hindi Film: The Case of Ashutosh Gowariker" *Acta Orientalia Vilnensia*, 9.2 (2010).

25 Dwyer, *Filming the Gods*, 140.

and criminals, while the Hindu grand patriarch is in control of an undivided and happy family. By contrast, the Muslim has been cast in complex depictions through the years as friend, alien, terrorist (an agent of Pakistan), gangster, and evil politician. The Hindu, by contrast, is shown to be a fervent nationalist. Pakistan and surprisingly not the Middle East or Malaysia is identified and named as the enemy, ostensibly as a veiled attack against Indian Muslims.

The Representation of Indian-ness in Karan Johar's Films
Bollywood and the "K factor"

During the mid-1990s, Bollywood was recasting its magic, albeit with a global appeal and gloss. *The Big Hearted Will Take the Bride* and *Kuch Kuch Hota Hai* (Something, Something Happens, dir. Karan Johar, 1998) have been landmark film projects in re-packaging the old Bollywood formula. Johar has been part of the "re-invention" project (having been part of *Big Hearted* as well) and is undeniably one of Bollywood's most successful filmmakers in the past decade. His visual craft, storytelling style, and creativity have changed Bollywood. I will briefly describe what is popularly known as the "K factor."

The "K factor"—with its trademark Shah Rukh Khan thrills,[26] Kandy floss romantic tales, and K-worded titles—in Bollywood began with Karan Johar's directorial debut venture *Kuch Kuch Hota Hai* (Something, Something Happens, 1998). Johar, like many new

---

26 Shah Rukh Khan is one of India's most celebrated and prolific movie and television actors and also a major philanthropist. He has played leading roles in many blockbuster ventures. SRK's films *Dilwale Dulhaniya Le Jayenge* (1995), *Kuch Kuch Hota Hai* (1998), *Chak De India* (2007), *Om Shanti Om* (2007), *Kabhi Khushi Kabhie Gham* (2001), *Kal Ho Naa Ho* (2003), *Veer-Zaara* (2004), and *Kabhi Alvida Naa Kehna* (2006) remain the biggest Bollywood hits, both in India and abroad. SRK has featured in all of Karan Johar's films. SRK's greatest ability is to provide "thrills" for audiences playing Raj/Rahul with his histrionics, teary eyes, feel-good-look-good yuppie appeal.

entrants[27] to Bollywood in the mid-1990s, is the son of a celebrity, the popular filmmaker Yash Johar, who made popular films such as *Dostana* (Friendship, 1980), *Agneepath* (Fire Path, 1990), and *Duplicate* (1998). Yash Johar's, Dharma Productions is known for producing films with lavish sets and in exotic locations while upholding Indian traditions and family values.[28] Karan Johar has continued the family tradition and as a product of the emerging India has brought a more globalized gloss to Bollywood. The overwhelming success of his films is in part due to an entry that coincided with the Bollywood's re-invention to reach out to urban India and the overseas market and in part due to his creative genius and personal branding.[29]

Karan Johar's films represent the core of Dharma Productions with their exquisiteness, grandeur, and touching storylines.[30] Underlying these traits are the discernable patterns such as the stardom of Shah Rukh Khan., on-screen romance, an ensemble of big stars in supporting roles, heightened emotions (over conflicts, discord, separation, and renunciation), religious images (explicit Hindu rites and social rituals), enviable mother-son relationships, designer clothes, revamped heroines (who look good in both Indian and Western attire), traditional cultural markers (undivided Hindu family, grandma, homeland links), Nationalist

---

27 The mid-1990s also saw the entry of "star-kids" into Bollywood cinema and these progenies of popular film stars and filmmakers (Karishma Kapoor, Kareena Kapoor, Abhishek Bachan, Hritik Roshan, Kajol, and Ajay Devgan, to name a few) have become an integral part of the "new look" cinema.

28 See Dharma Productions profile, http://www3.dharma-production.com/ourprofile.html.

29 Besides hosting many popular television shows, he has become a brand ambassador for Bollywood cinema. He has been invited to speak at leading universities such as Harvard Business School and Wharton School at the University of Pennsylvania. He has also been listed as one of the 250 Global Young Leaders by the World Economic Forum.

30 See Dharma Productions profile, http://www3.dharma-production.com/ourprofile.html.

symbols (Indian flag, National Anthem, nationalistic slogans), and wholesome family entertainment (occasions for tears and laughter).

Karan Johar and His Films

Karan Johar's directorial debut *Kuch Kuch Hota Hai* (Something, Something Happens, 1998) explores romance and friendship through the lives of Rahul (played by Shah Rukh Khan), Tina (played by Rani Mukherji), and Anjali (played by Kajol Devgan) set within Bollywood's triangular love formula. The simple storyline is expanded with comic subplot (set at a summer camp in Simla), tragic event (death of Tina), and Anjali's tryst with failed love. *Something, Something Happens* became one of the biggest commercial hits of that year, both in India and abroad.[31]

Johar's second film was a multi-star family drama *Kabhi Kushie Kabhie Gham* (Sometimes Happy, Sometimes Sad, 2001), which was also a big blockbuster and broke all box office records at the time.[32] The film explores the theme of familial relationships in the context of new cultural (dis)locations. The film deals with conflictual situations that arise when the younger generation is exposed to the global economy. It also points to how these conflicts may be resolved with resources within Indian cultural traditions.

Johar's next directorial film *Kabhi Alvida Na Kehna* (Never Say Goodbye, 2006) was infamous for its controversial subject for Indian sensibilities: unhappy marriages and marital infidelity. The film betrays a subtle shift in the "K formula" in that it does not use customary names for characters, or national symbols, cultural markers, and religious images. The theme of unhappy marriages and extra-marital affairs is

---

31 *Kuch Kuch Hota Hai* was the highest-grossing Indian movie of 1998; it made Rs.500,000,000 (approx. US$7,880,000). For more details about the film's production, see its entry in The Internet Movie Database, http://www.imdb.com/title/tt0172684/.

32 *Kabhi Khushi Kabhie Gham* was the highest-grossing Indian film overseas until 2006. For more details about the film's production, see its entry in The Internet Movie Database, http://www.imdb.com/title/tt0248126/.

not a welcome subject in India and not surprisingly the film received only a moderate box office reception in India. However, it was popular in the United States and in the United Kingdom.[33]

Meanwhile, Karan Johar has also been involved as a script writer in the film *Kal Ho Na Ho* (Tomorrow May or May Not Be, dir. Nikhil Advani, 2003). I have included this film since it explores the theme of a mixed marriage (Hindu-Christian) and offers a stark contrast to the religious images in earlier films.

Encountering Indian-ness in "Kandy Floss" Films

So, what do we find by way of Indian-ness in Karan Johar's films? They offer an illustrative case for continuity in Bollywood conventions, but with experiments with redefining acceptable boundaries, and perhaps even some evolution toward a new kind of cinema, which Christiane Brosius prefers to call "Bollyworld."[34] We find four main devices used in Johar's films to inform Indian-ness: the homeland link, safeguarding Indian culture, celebrating achievements, and mediating the Other.

The Homeland Link

Bollywood has played a significant role in shaping the cultural lives of the Indian diaspora. Through its stories, DVDs, music, star shows, and award ceremonies, Bollywood brings the homeland into the social and cultural (dis)locations of the diaspora and presents an imaginary link back to India. Bollywood thus creates "a culture of imaginary

---

33 *Never Say Goodbye* was a success internationally and in the United States it became the highest-grossing Indian film of all time, beating *Sometimes Happy, Sometimes Sad*'s five-year-old record. In the United States it grossed more than $1.3 million and $1.4 million in the United Kingdom on its opening weekend and was screened in more than 1,200 cinemas worldwide.

34 Christiane Brosius, "The Scattered Homelands of the Migrant: Bollyworld through the Diasporic Lens," in *Bollyworld: Popular Cinema Through Transnational Lens*, ed. Raminder Kaur and Ajay J. Sinha (New Delhi: Sage Publications, 2005), 209.

solidarity across heterogeneous linguistic and national groups that make up the diaspora."[35]

In *Something, Something Happens*, the protagonist Rahul asks the Oxford-educated Tina, "Have you forgotten to speak Hindi in London?" She replies, "Living in London and studying and growing up there has not made me forget my roots." Mr. Malhotra, Tina's father, explains his return to India: "We used to live there but when my wife died, I couldn't live there. So, I came back to my home country." Interestingly, Rahul initially rejects Tina as undesirable because "she's not Indian enough." She becomes wife-material only after she establishes her homeland links: visits the temple, sings a Hindi bhajan, and wears more traditional attire. Territorial belonging and cultural rootedness become signs of Indian-ness.

Similarly, in *Sometimes Happy, Sometimes Sad* Johar resorts to sloganeering (particularly through the character Anjali, the protagonist's wife) to appeal to the homeland link. Anjali represents one who is firmly rooted in the homeland, in contrast to her husband Rahul and her sister Pooja who carry traces of Western influences. Anjali is proud of her connections with India and constantly says, "My India is the greatest country in the world" and is uncomfortable with life in England: her English neighbor, his British accent, and her son's Englishness. She longs to return to India: "Wouldn't it be better to have lived in Chandini Chowk (a locality in Delhi)?" "This is not our country, let's go back."

The young are taught Indian-ness by re-rooting them in cultural traditions. Anjali says, "I don't sing for them [English neighbors], do I? I sing so that my son learns about our country. He knows nothing about our country, our religion and our traditions, our heritage. He's already half Englishman." The lack of Indian-ness in children recurs as a theme in three of these films as a matter of concern and is resolved through the words of mothers and grandmothers who provide the

---

35 Vijay Mishra, *Bollywood Cinema; Temples of Desire* (London: Routledge, 2002), 237.

homeland link. Says one in *Something, Something Happens*, "If you don't pay attention to prayer, what will you teach your children, the way we think and the things we say have a deep impact on our children?"

The diasporas connect with Bollywood is not merely longing for Indian culture. These films also treat factors such as workplace discrimination and/or alienation within the Western mainstream's cultural space. Viewing these films can be a way of coping with social and cultural marginalization that Indians experience as minorities.[36] In contrast, Bollywood provides, as Vijay Mishra, notes, a "secure spectacle" for immigrant communities to both belong and connect when they experience social and cultural dislocations. These same factors also add to the appeal and popularity of the Karan Johar films in India. Johar's mythic construction of the diaspora (as those longing for return) also captures the collective imagination of Indians within India while for the diaspora Indians it satisfies their nostalgia.

Safeguarding Indian Traditions

Apart from providing homeland links, Karan Johar's films become a teaching tool to mediate acceptable attitudes toward tradition, behavior, and clothing. Johar uses a tradition/modernity binary to uphold family values and cultural traditions. Like other Bollywood counterparts, Karan represents Indian culture as replete with Hindu images, music, and ritual celebration and makes it the norm. The younger generation growing up outside India are perceived as "not Indian enough." What constitutes Indian-ness emerges through a generational perspective, usually mouthed by Grandma or Grandpa the Patriarch. Significant features of Indian culture such as family relationships, kinship ties, and family-arranged marriages are cast against the background of increased conflicts within the family due to Western influence. Johar's celebration of the Hindu divided family is an attempt to dissolve such conflicts, if any, by an appeal to tradition (*Parampara*). A caution is sounded to

---

36 Mary Gilespie, *Television, Ethnicity and Cultural Change* (London: Routledge, 1995) quoted in Mishra, *Bollywood Cinema*, 246.

those wishing to marry non-Indian brides (in the words of Yash, the grand patriarch in *Sometimes Happy, Sometimes Sad*:

> You didn't even think once about the background of the girl, her status, her breeding, you didn't give a thought to whether the girl will be able to understand our culture . . . our traditions. Will she understand our rites and rituals? Will she understand our ethics and principles? Will she adhere to the values of the family? Will she? How did you ever dare to think that she can be part of the family?

Even so, Johar provides cultural allowances for changing times. The invention of the new love triangle, with revamped heroines, divorce, re-marriage, and even taboo themes such as marital infidelity is explored. The earlier rigid emphasis articulated in *Something, Something Happens*—"We live once, die once, and marry once"—is let go in *Never Say Goodbye* where the question raised is, "What happens if you find true love after your marriage?" Similarly, despite explicit Hindu religious images, Karan hints in *Something, Something Happens* at the case for secular life, when Aman Mehra says: "I can't handle this religious thing. I can't listen to this anymore . . . even God gets fed up with so many hymns." Johar is also open to multi-faith reality as in *Tomorrow May Never Be*, where he explores the theme of a mixed marriage. He makes allowances for urban subcultures' pastimes such as partying, flirtations, and alternate sexuality, as in *Tomorrow May Never Be* and *Never Say Goodbye*. Yet the old ways repeatedly receive fond recognition in these films.

Celebrating the Global Indian Achievement

Johar's films also make a point of celebrating Indian achievement, particularly in the context of the globalized economy. The Indian presence on the global stage gets admiring recognition in *Tomorrow May Never Be*, where one character exclaims, "In New York, one in every four is an Indian!" These films crow about Indian prowess and achievement in business education and highly skilled labor: "India can do anything, anywhere . . . anytime!" The film *Something, Something Happens* an American anthropologist, Thomas Blom Hansen, notes, "served to make the Indian community visible and recognized on the basis of its distinct cultural heritage, suitably modernized, de-ethnicized and packaged to suit the tastes of the so called cosmopolitan audiences."[37] Indeed, the confident images and messages in all these films project the changing stature of India on the global stage.

The India presented in Johar's films is far removed from the older stereotypical images of India—as a land of snake charmers, elephants, malnourished children, and abject poverty. In fact, he turns away from the larger social-cultural reality of poverty in India and draws attention to a "Shining India"—the India of the rising upper middle class. Not surprisingly, the pivotal characters are all English or otherwise Western-educated, social elites, and employed in senior positions if not successful entrepreneurs. Deshpande traces this change to "the demise of the *chavanni* (quarter rupee) audience," and the need for more "consumable" actors in the context of economic liberalization and the changing economics of film production.[38]

As we look closer at this new portrayal of characters we see that the leads are alumni/ae of prestigious schools and/or universities. In *Sometimes Happy, Sometimes Sad*, Rohan and Rahul study at Woodstock International School; in *Something, Something Happens*, Rahul, Anjali, and Tina study in St. Xavier's College and Tina returns from Oxford University to complete her studies in St. Xavier's. In *Sometimes Happy, Sometimes Sad*, Rahul, Rohan, and Pooja study at British universities, while in *Tomorrow May Never Be*, Rohit and Naina are enrolled in a business school. The celebration of Indian students as fit to study in the West is made in the context of a steady flow of students to universities, particularly in United States, the United Kingdom, Germany, Australia, and New Zealand. In fact, Indian students form the fastest-growing

---

37 Thomas Blom Hansen, "In Search of the Diasporic Self: Bollywood in South Africa," in *Bollyworld: Popular Cinema Through Transnational Lens*, ed. Raminder Kaur and Ajay J. Sinha (New Delhi: Sage Publications, 2005), 251.

38 For a detailed description of the contrast of the new liberalized hero of the 1990s with the earlier "angry young man," see Deshpande, "The Consumable Hero of Globalised India," 186f.

and second largest cohort of international students (186,267) in the United States.[39] Johar's two earlier films equate Indian universities as being equal, if not better than Western universities: "After all we are no less than Oxford" (*Something, Something Happens*) and "Why England? Why can't you study here? There are many Universities here" (*Sometimes Happy, Sometimes Sad*). Such "swadeshi" slogans are toned down in the latter two films (*Tomorrow May Never Be* and *Never Say Goodbye*), which are in New York.

In these films, the pivotal characters are also elites (Yashvardhan Raichand in *Sometimes Happy, Sometimes Sad*, Karsanbhai Patel in *Tomorrow May Never Be*, and Samarajit Singh Talwar [a.k.a. Sexy Sam] in *Never Say Goodbye*), own large corporations, and enjoy opulent lifestyles with their own helicopters, palatial houses, and frequent visits to Europe. The children, as heirs to such wealth, reflect the life of the super-rich in their choice of cars, clothes, and pastimes. This is a deliberate turning away from the usual Bollywood conventions, which identify with the poor. The characters in the movies hold senior positions in big corporations or are self-made entrepreneurs. Perhaps Johar's characters are tributes to growing numbers of Indian billionaires among the world's richest men and Indians in senior positions within global corporations, such as Citigroup and Pepsi. This is a complete reversal of the stereotypical Hollywood representations of Indians as taxi drivers, religious saints, and maharajas and a turn away from the earlier Bollywood casting of the lead actors as wage earners, lower middle class, rustics, slum dwellers, and alcoholics. In fact, in *Tomorrow May Never Be*, the popular "unbeatable Indian" motif of *Lagaan*, an earlier film where a group of rustic Indians beat the British in a cricket match, is reformulated as establishing businesses abroad and boldly competing with the Chinese.

Johar's films also lavishly celebrate Indian national symbols such as the Indian flag, the Indian national anthem, and nationalistic slogans

---

39 Leading Places of Origin, Open Doors 2017, https://www.iie.org/Research-and-Insights/Open-Doors/Data/International-Students/Places-of-Origin.

such as *Vande Mataram* (Salute the Mother) and "*Sāre jahān se acchā hindostān hamārā* (Better than the entire world, is our Hindustan). These signs of Indian-ness evoke a transnational sense of solidarity among the diaspora.

The Other-ed Indians

These celebrations of Indian achievements remain exclusive. They appear in these films as the sole preserve of the Punjabi (North Indian), rich and upper caste. Johar's characters named Rahul, Rohan, and Naina also bear caste names such as Khanna, Kapoor, Raichand, Sharma, and Pate. The earlier Bollywood films did not explicitly name the characters' caste and made no attempts, according to Deshpande, to "locate the hero in specific social and/or temporal terms."[40] Moreover, religious images, bhajans, music, and social practices in excess privilege Hindu-shaped Indian-ness.

There is a near absence of Muslims in Karan's films and this despite his film crew being largely Muslim, as is his greatest male lead Shah Rukh Khan. The diversity of the film crew and cast, let alone the diversity of India, is not represented in his stories. Muslim culture and history is accorded little or no space. Johar, unlike other Bollywood filmmakers, does not name the demonic as Muslim but fosters the idea of Hindu India by the absence of Muslim culture and history. The influence of these films thus assumes greater significance against the background of the resurgence of Hindu fundamentalism in the 1990s and the promotion of the Hindutva ideal.

Karan's caricature of Indian-Christians is also disturbing. Colonel Almeida in *Something, Something Happens* has a strong admiration for the British Empire and he feeds comic subplots in the film with his desire to hoist the British flag, discomfiture with the Indian flag, and unfamiliarity with Indian cultural and religious traditions. These are in fact the same allegations raised against the Indian-Christian community. Colonel Almeida's apparent disloyalty to India is countered by the

---

40 Deshpande, "The Consumable Hero of Globalised India," 194.

patriotism of the filmic mother, Mrs. Khanna, who reminds him that the "British went away and left you behind. You fool, you should teach the kids. . . . My Bharat (India) is the best." Colonel Almeida is thus forcibly re-converted. Jenny in *Sometimes Happy, Sometimes Sad* is repeatedly named as the cause for the breakdown and unhappiness of the divided Hindu family. However, *Tomorrow May Never Be* does present or mention Christian religious symbols such as church, Jesus, prayer, and angels as never before and in stark contrast to the earlier films' excessively Hindu religious images. Shah Rukh Khans Aman Mathur in the film, is a Jesus figure/messiah to the Kapoor family, but he remains a Hindu man who will eventually meet Naina in subsequent lives.[41] Similarly, Naina, who was raised by a Christian mother in a Hindu home, prefers a traditional Punjabi engagement ceremony and is presented as a Hindu bride with cultural markers such as *mehendi* (decorated) hands and a festive *bindi* (red dot) on the forehead.

Johar's characters, in the final analysis, are entirely "Hinglish"-speaking and represent the Hindu upper middle class. Interestingly, the laboring classes and lower-caste people are nearly absent in these films and even eclipsed by the opulence of the lead characters. Such portrayals appear to alienate the poor who live in the other India, which may explain the rise of films in Bhojpuri (a dialect spoken in Bihar and Uttar Pradesh) as a parallel industry.[42]

The Need for a New Visual Narrative

We have seen that Johar's films are not just innocent romantic tales or family melodramas, but they come loaded with markers of Indian-ness. A version of Indian-ness is presented, promoted, and almost normalized. The markers of Indian-ness in the films may not have been intentionally planned and self-consciously projected in any overt attempt to restate the Indian reality in Hindutva terms. However,

---

41 Ostrowski, "Found in Translation."

42 Bhojpuri cinema as a parallel industry is worth an estimated billion rupees (http://timesofindia.indiatimes.com/India/Bhojpuri_cinema_heads_to_Berlin_/rssarticleshow/2764728.cms).

films play a significant role in meaning-making, pattern-forming, and significance giving. Cinema does more than reflect existing values in society. It plays a vital role in creating and legitimizing views and values. Film experience provides a surplus of meanings negotiated within a specific sociocultural and political context. In a time of increasing communal violence against Muslims and Christians, these melodramatic films can be read to privilege an exclusivist view that can feed the hate. So, I hope that this critical reading of these familiar and the popular film texts may challenge the wider tendencies to define Indian-ness as being Hindu. Perhaps, it may even help give rise to a new visual culture and vocabulary that breaks down the walls of separation and alienation between religious communities.

Indeed, there are three films worth considering here that have presented an alternative to jingoistic or exclusivist notions of Indian-ness.

Veer Zara (dir. Yash Chopra, 2004) is a story of Veer, an Indian army officer and pilot (played by Shah Rukh Khan) who falls in love with Zara, a Pakistani girl (played by Preity Zinta) who comes to India to scatter the ashes of one of her family's loyal servants, surprisingly an Indian. When Veer visits Pakistan to marry Zara, he is falsely implicated as an Indian spy by the Pakistani military establishment and left languishing in a secret prison. Saamiya Siddiqui (played by Rani Mukherji), a Pakistani human rights lawyer, fights for Veer's release much to the dismay of the Pakistani political establishment. The film also has Zara serving the cause of women's education in Veer's native village in India all the while Veer is imprisoned in Pakistan. The film shows religion and ethnic borders as a source of conflict and sorrow and yet steers clear of the nationalistic jingoism that is usually part of the film that features Pakistan. The film also presents Pakistan as a separate legal entity, and its citizen is neither despised nor questioned but rather, welcomed as a guest.

Veer Zaara has successfully overcome the phobia of Pakistan and thus stands distinctly different from *Gadar* (2001). *Veer Zara's* positive presentation of Pakistan assumes greater significance as the film was released in the aftermath of the nuclear weapons test (1999) conducted by the two countries and the Kargil War (1999).

Ashutosh Gowrikar's *Swades* (2004) also adopted a liberal approach in presenting its brand of patriotism. *Swades* narrated the story of Mohan Bhargava (played by Shah Rukh Khan), an idealistic NASA engineer, whose journey back to India becomes a journey of self-discovery. Mohan leads the village into the act of creating electricity from the nearby stream. In fact, *Swades* was inspired by a true-life story of Aravinda Pillalamarri and Ravi Kuchimanchi, who returned to India and worked to establish schools in remote villages. The film also dealt with issues of caste, gender, primary education, and development. Unfortunately, the film failed to do well at the box office despite winning critical acclaim and the hearts of urban India. Perhaps, Mohan's abandonment of Western materialism and his embracing of social responsibility for nation building was much ahead of its time.

Road to Sangam (dir. Amit Rai, 2009) was a bold film about Hasmat Ullah (played by Paresh Rawal), a devout Muslim mechanic entrusted restoring the truck, a Ford V8 engine for carrying the recently unearthed Mahatma Gandhi's urn. Hasmat Ullah is caught between his passion and a protest by prominent leaders of the Muslim community against police atrocities on Muslim youth in the aftermath of a bomb blast. The film captures the struggle of a patriotic Muslim caught between a call toward responsibilities and the demand for rights. The film's worldwide critical acclaim illustrates the possibility of presenting Hindu-Muslim communal tensions with a touch of sensitivity. Bollywood stars, filmmakers, and production houses should take notice. They must reject all the veiled attacks on Indian Muslims by resorting to either Pakistan-bashing or through negative portrayals in films.

The commercial success and critical acclaim of these films stand as testimony to the spirit of inclusion that is part of Indian ethos and culture.

Conclusion

Karan Johar illustrates the new look of Bollywood and its family melodramatic formula. However, Johar's films are not just innocent romantic tales or family melodramas but they come loaded with signs of Indian-ness. A version of acceptable Indian-ness is presented and promoted—and worse, almost made a norm.

Johar's films provide both the homeland link and the imaginary solidarity. First, the films cater to the need for the globalized and Westernized Indians to be culturally rooted and attempts to resolve the cultural dilution by re-rooting those living outside in the homeland culture through Hindu religious images and messages. Second, the films and actors become cultural texts that teach the second generation of globalized Indians to safeguard Hindu traditions to retain their Indian-ness. Third, Indian-ness in these films is about achievements in the realm of education and economics which in the film version remains the preserve of the Punjabi, the upper caste, and the Hindu. Fourth, there is a subtle suggestion that one becomes truly Indian only under the observance of Hindu ritual. By comparison, the viewer learns that his Indian-ness creates a boundary between "us" and "them," the less truly Indian.

It is not difficult to see that Johar privileges the Hindu perspective and gives credence to the thesis that Bollywood undergirds Hinduism and therefore is vital for understanding Hinduism.[43] It is important that we ask the question: What images and stories are being presented and more importantly, why are these characters/stories (re)played for public consumption in Indian and the South Asian diaspora? Johar's films are family melodrama replete with Hindu images that construct an exclusivist notion of Indian-ness as Hindu. While most popular films use "Pakistan bashing" and "the terrorist as the imagined enemy" devices, Karan Johar circumvents it. He privileges the film texts with Hindu perspective through his melodramatic storytelling mode.

---

43 Wright, *Religion and Film*, and Dwyer, *Filming the Gods*.

The conclusions I draw from the critical reading may be unintentional on the part of Karan Johar. However, film texts are involved in meaning-making, pattern-forming, and significance giving. Cinema does more than reflect existing values in society. It plays a vital role in creating and legitimizing views and values. Film experience provides for a surplus of meanings negotiated within specific sociocultural and political context/s. The increasing communal violence against Muslims and Christians provides a context of hate wherein these melodramatic films can be read to privilege an exclusivist view. I hope that this critical reading of some familiar and the popular film texts (as undertaken in this chapter) may challenge the wider tendencies (both in India and beyond) to describe Indian-ness as being Hindu and worse, conflating the two.

Bollywood contributes to the consolidation of the Indian diaspora around an Indian (read Hindu) identity. Bollywood has learned to weave patriotism through a shrill assertion of Indian-ness and wrap it within a song-and-dance cultural foil. Films with an anti-Pakistan and anti-Muslim slant have done extremely well at the box office. Such portrayals prepare the viewer to anticipate, accept, and legitimate violence against minorities. Such narratives of blatant jingoism and exclusivist notions necessitate a new visual vocabulary and narrative to help correct Indian cinema. Bollywood plotlines could be inclusive and welcome stories about Muslims, Christians, Sikhs, Jains, and Buddhists.

We need a new visual culture and vocabulary that breaks down the walls of separation between the once harmonious religious communities. There are already signs of hope. Johar's message in *My Name Is Khan* (dir. Karan Johar, 2010) is a welcome change to the messages in his earlier films. *My Name is Khan* is a story of Rizwan Khan, an Indian Muslim man in the United States who embarks on a cross-country journey to tell the president that his name is Khan and he is not a terrorist. The film presents the many hostilities that the Khan family had to face in the aftermath of the 9/11 attacks. Interestingly, *My Name Is Khan* is the only movie in defense of Muslims post 9/11. *Rangoon*'s (dir. Vishal Bhardwaj, 2017) lead characters are Christian, Parsi, and

Muslim and interestingly, the religious identities of these characters are not explicitly established and even its appeal to love the nation is not "constricted by a restraining ideology." Saibal Chatterjee contends, "In a diversity deficient Bollywood, which predominantly subscribes to the set, immutable notions of heroism and nationalistic fervor, *Rangoon* presents a full-fledged revolt."[44] One hopes that *Rangoon* will set the trend and inspire young filmmakers through the next decade just as *Who I Am to You?* and *The Big Hearted Will Take the Bride* set the trend for the 1990s.

New age filmmakers must desist from jingoistic notions and exclusivist visions of Indian-ness. Rather, they must celebrate the diversity of India and thereby rewrite the Bollywood formula. The dialogue at the end of *Veer Zara* (in the words of Zakir, the senior advocate who defends the Constitution and the rights of the Pakistan state) is a perceptive comment: "But now, I understand that the future of these countries is in the hands of youngsters like you, who do not measure humans as big or small, man or woman, Hindu or Muslim, who do not rake up memories of the wars of 1947, 1965, 1999 at every pretext, who wish to address the future with truth and only the truth. And there is no stopping a country where truth prevails."

---

44 Saibal Chatterjee, Rangoon Movie Review, NDTV.com, February 24, 2017, http://movies.ndtv.com/movie-reviews/rangoon-movie-review-kangana-ranaut-shahid-kapoor-saif-ali-khan-are-first-rate-in-this-sweeping-film-3019.

Chapter 8

Human Rights and Freedom of Religion—The Ground Experience

Interviews with Dr. John Dayal and Rev. Vijayesh Lal

Karuna M. John

John Dayal and Vijayesh Lal are authors of the last two Civil Society Reports about freedom of faith in India for the Universal Periodic Review (UPR) of human rights in India, held every four years by the United Nations Human Rights Council (UNHRC) in Geneva. The last one was in 2016.[1] Human rights have taken a beating in the country, beset as it has been with political confrontations and disquiet in various states. Freedom of faith, then, must be seen within the matrix of a variety of contexts: of violent conflicts between population groups defined by religion, caste, and ethnicity; of the peace enforced aggressively by armed police; and in regions such as predominantly Muslim Kashmir and the northeastern region, where Christians are in

---

1 United Nations Office of the High Commissioner for Human Rights, "Universal Periodic Review—India," http://www.ohchr.org/EN/HRBodies/UPR/Pages/INIndex.aspx, accessed February 12, 2018.

a majority in three states. And in the most general terms, the context is a nation where Hinduism is the faith professed by 79.8 percent of the population, according to the Census of 2011. Authentic data on communal strife, human casualties, and "collateral damage" of properties, places of worship, and institutions such as hospitals, schools, and colleges are difficult to come by, with police loath to admit to the gravity of tensions between groups and the frequency of the violence that often results. India was ranked fourth in the world in 2015—after Syria, Nigeria, and Iraq—for the highest social hostilities involving religion, the *Huffington Post* reported on April 14, 2017.[2]

The election campaign of 2013 leading up to the elections of 2014 that brought the Hindu nationalist Bharatiya Janata Party (BJP) to power saw invective and hate raised to unprecedented levels, with both Muslims and Christians as special targets, but other groups not untouched. Old wounds, dating back to the bloody Partition of India in 1947 (that gave birth to a Muslim majority Pakistan), and the 1992 demolition of the five hundred-year-old Babri Mosque in the state of Uttar Pradesh were opened, and cut deeper. In responses given to questions in Parliament, the government admitted that "communal violence," the term used to define clashes between religious groups, had increased 28 percent over three years to 2017. Uttar Pradesh—the most populous state in the country—reported most incidents (1,488) over the past decade. As many as 7,484 communal incidents have been reported over the past decade—between 2008 and 2017—or 2 every day, killing more than 1,100 people.

But as the UPR reports show, while direct physical clashes, murderous violence, and police action may be the visible evidence, the persecution, especially of Christians, is rooted in structural issues: nuances in common understanding that are biased against the

---

2 "On Religious Hostilities, India Ranked Just Slightly Better Than Syria: Pew Study. Animosity between Hindus and Muslims Drove India's Poor Ranking in 2015," *Huffington Post*, April 14, 2017, http://www.huffingtonpost.in/2017/04/13/on-religious-hostilities-india-ranked-just-slightly-better-than_a_22037994/, accessed February 12, 2018.

faith community and regulations that target clergy as much as the common believer. A case in point is the situation of indigenous Tribal communities that have been adversely affected by mining policies. Tribal Christians have faced further violations due to their intersecting identities of religion and ethnicity. Field researchers and activists have noted that Tribal Christians have been ruthlessly alienated from forests where they have lived in and depend on for their livelihood. The Tribals have been deemed "anti-development" as they resist violations of their fundamental right to life and livelihood. A government-appointed High-Level Committee on Socio-economic, Health and Educational Status of Tribal Communities of India, in its 2014 report, observed: "Laws and rules that provide protection to tribes are being routinely manipulated and subverted to accommodate corporate interests. Tribal protests are being met with violence by the State's paramilitary forces and the private security staff of corporations involved."[3]

Far more pernicious is the Constitution (Scheduled Castes) Order of 1950, which arguably works as the most powerful law against religious conversions, impacting perhaps as many as 200 million Dalits, or members of former untouchable castes. Uncounted numbers of them profess in private that Christianity is their faith but remain Hindus in the Census and their identity records. This has been called the largest "underground church" in the world. Its impact is not fully understood in the rest of the world, which is more familiar with the Freedom of Religion Acts, unlike anti-conversion laws, prevalent in six of the states of the nation.

Article 341(1) of the Indian Constitution empowers the president of India to specify, through a public notification, the castes, races, or tribes (or parts of or groups within castes, races, or tribes) which are deemed to be Scheduled Castes. These groups then are eligible

---

3 Ministry of Tribal Affairs, *Report of the High Level Committee on Socioeconomic, Health and Educational Status of Tribal Communities of Indi,*(Delhi: Government of India, 2014), 31, http://www.kractivist.org/wp-content/uploads/2014/12/Tribal-Committee-Report-May-June-2014.pdf, accessed February 12, 2018.

for affirmative action, including reservations in Parliament and state legislatures, scholarships for education, and jobs in government agencies. The 1950 Order, now incorporated as Part 3 of Article 341, however, limits this status to those professing Hinduism, or Sikhism and Buddhism, which have been labeled "Indic religions," born of Hinduism. Conversion to Islam or Christianity means an end to these privileges, and in brutal reality, it may mean unemployment, if not starvation. Because of the 1950 Order, Muslim and Christian Dalits are excluded from the purview of Scheduled Castes, denied reservations in jobs and elected bodies that are available to their Hindu, Buddhist, and Sikh counterparts, and are also excluded from protection from and redress for caste-based atrocities through the law, such as the Scheduled Castes and Scheduled Tribes (Prevention of Atrocities) Act of 1986.

Further, Hindu Dalits are deterred from converting to Christianity or Islam due to fear of losing such benefits from the government. This situation is violative of their freedom of religion or belief, and Dalit Christians have appealed to the Supreme Court to end this religion-based discrimination. The UN Special Rapporteur on Freedom of Religion or Belief also has called for an end to such a law. Yet these basic structures and conditions are all still in force in India, and in recent times, with the BJP in power and local Hindu radical groups feeling empowered, human rights investigators report a scaling up of violence.

Recent times have seen, for example, the Christian and Muslim communities targeted by Cow Protection Groups, arch Hindu nationalists who now roam the countryside trying to enforce the newly enforced ban on the slaughter of cows and other cattle deemed to be holy to the Hindus. Beef is commonly consumed by Christians, Muslims, Dalits of all religions, Tribals, and others. Several states now prohibit the slaughter of cows or the possession, transport, and consumption of beef through state legislation. Hindu vigilante groups "implement" this law by publicly humiliating, brutally attacking, and sometimes killing those suspected of possessing or consuming beef. Dalit communities have rebelled in recent times, but the police seem to be abetting the lynch mobs, as the Karawan e Mohabbat, a peace movement, found in 2017 in a journey across the nation.[4]

So, we join two veteran Christian human rights advocates, John Dayal and Vijayesh Lal, in a discussion of the situation they have experienced and analyzed in recent years for Indian Christians at the grassroots. Here are their responses, in a free-ranging interview.

Q: How has religious freedom of Christian citizens in India been threatened? Which incident (or incidents) was a glaring example of such a threat?

John Dayal: Kandhamal[5] was the single largest incident of targeted violence against Christians in recent Indian history, comparable in intensity with much bigger episodes of violence against Muslims, Sikhs, and Dalits where the count of the dead was much larger, but the impunity, the complicity of the state, and the ruling ideology were of a similar intensity. No discussion of persecution in India can take

---

4 Sanjukta Basu, "Karwan e Mohabbat: Uncovering How Violence Against Minorities Has Been Normalised," *First Post*, December 21, 2017, http://www.firstpost.com/india/karwan-e-mohabbat-uncovering-how-violence-against-minorities-has-been-normalised-4098127.html, accessed February 12, 2018.

5 "Kandhamal is a district of the eastern Indian state of Odisha, formerly known as Orissa, where an orgy of violence descended on the impoverished Christian minority in August 2008. A series of riots led by radical Hindus left roughly 100 people dead, thousands injured, 300 churches and 6,000 homes destroyed, and 50,000 people displaced, many forced to hide in nearby forests where more died of hunger and snakebites. The violence was carried out by mobs adorned with saffron headbands, a sign of right-wing Hindu militancy, and shouting slogans such as *Jai shri ram!*—victory to the Hindu god Ram—and *Jai bajrang bali!*—a tribute to another Hindu deity. Attackers wielded rods, tridents, swords, firearms, kerosene, and even acid." John L. Allen Jr., "'Kandhamal' tells the whole story of anti-Christian persecution," *Crux*, July 28, 2015, https://cruxnow.com/faith/2015/07/28/kandhamal-tells-the-whole-story-of-anti-christian-persecution/, accessed February 12, 2018.

place without constant references to Kandhamal, the human tragedy, the state crime, and the political complicity.

But Christmas 2017 is as good a point to begin as any other: Advent in 2017 saw the beginning of a mob frenzy and political aggression with members of the *Sangh parivar*[6] announcing they would not allow public display of Christmas festivities, calling them alien influences that were sullying classical Indian culture. The Catholic Church, which does not always react when individual Pentecostal or charismatic pastors are beaten up, was forced to call out the government when a priest and several of his seminarians were attacked as they sang carols in a village in Satna in Madhya Pradesh. They were beaten up, their jeep burned in a harrowing recall of the way in January 1999 Australian missionary Graham Stuart Staines's jeep was set afire by a Bajrang Dal activist, Dara Singh, leading a mob in a forest in the state of Orissa. Staines and his two sons sleeping in the vehicle were burned alive.

In Madhya Pradesh, the priest and his students were not in the jeep when they were attacked. But if they thought they were lucky to escape death at the hands of the violent mob, they were to find that they faced further problems. The police arrested them for trying to fraudulently convert the local Hindus and put them in jail.

It took a week-long legal struggle to get them released, and that too on bail. They may face an arduous legal battle ahead of them, as indeed hundreds of Christians are facing in various parts of the country under the same insidious anti-conversion laws. No one will eventually be convicted because all these cases are false, with political activists making fictitious accusations and paid witnesses drumming up what they call evidence.

How can any pastor or Catholic priest forcibly or by fraud convert a poor Hindu villager in a social situation where the entire village is Hindu, its local panchayat, the local self-government unit, is headed by Hindus, the police officer is a Hindu, and the administrator is a

---

6 *Sangh parivar* refers to a broad federation of Hindu nationalist organizations.

Hindu? The cases fall flat before a good judge. But in the meantime, everyone has been put through a harrowing trial.

It does not help that often the state prosecution officer also belongs to the RSS.[7] I have seen often how the lawyers and bar associations, all swearing loyalty to the RSS, make any effort at a sane justice delivery system so difficult. I have faced them myself in the state of Orissa.

The other Christmas season case was in Uttar Pradesh, where the Hindu Jagran Manch[8] warned Christian-run schools in the town of Aligarh not to celebrate Christmas at all, or else they would face "consequences," as they call violent action. And in distant Maharashtra, Chief Minister Devendra Fadnavis's wife Amruta Fadnavis was attacked on social media for simply supporting a Christmas-themed charity event. She was accused of encouraging Christians in their alleged efforts at "harvesting souls." As newspapers reported, Amruta Fadnavis had to counter this charge by reaffirming that she was a "proud Hindu" and celebrated "every festival in my country."

The leading web media Scroll.in reported the peculiar case in Mumbai where Ashish Shelar, a BJP MLA who heads the party's city unit, was trolled in social media for inviting Mumbai residents to attend a Christmas festival in the city. Among Shelar's detractors was the chief strategy officer of the right-wing magazine *Swarajya*, who criticized the event—which features a music competition, food stalls, and sand football on Mumbai's Chowpatty Beach—as "a cultural war against Hindus."

This was just during the Christmas season when perhaps three or four dozen cases of coercion or violence took place in major states of the country. I think there is a reason why violence has peaked this time, and sometimes in the past, during the Christmas season. This is when there is a sustained community festivity, visible and audible.

---

7 RSS: Rashtriya Swayamsevak Sangh. The RSS is a Hindu nationalist paramilitary agency.

8 Jagran Manch: an affiliate of the RSS.

Even nominal Christians profess their faith, if only by participating in the community festivities.

I would say it is the prime minister, Mr. Narendra Modi, who has sought to diminish, even trivialize, Christmas and shear its religious sanctity. Within six months of taking office, the Modi government declared that December 25 would henceforth be celebrated as "Good Governance Day," with schools, colleges, and government offices forgoing the traditional holiday and replacing festivities with essay competitions and other "nation-building activities," as they chose to define them. The church has, collectively, not challenged this in a court of law, perhaps because the orders are couched in words that are not directly confrontational. Mr. Modi tweets his greetings to the citizens with a tepid Happy Christmas, but the people are wary.

Since December 2007 in Kandhamal, Christmas celebrations have not been the same carefree joyous festive community occasions we had seen until the turn of the century. The government has in effect given up any pretense of protecting the Christian community during its most important faith season. Most churches now have barbed wire atop their boundary walls, closed circuit television cameras inside and along the perimeter, and private guards at the gates. In Delhi, this was in fact done on the advice of the city police force, which said it could not provide security on a long-term basis. But armed policemen are posted at major churches on Christmas eve. In Kandhamal and other "trouble spots," Christmas continues to be under police protection. It takes the zest out of the celebrations, but the brave community even in forest areas has decided it will not be cowed, and turns up in numbers even for the evening Mass.

Vijayesh Lal: The threat to religious freedom of Indian Christian citizens in an organized way, and in a much visible manner, is almost twenty to twenty-five years old. The late 1990s was a time when the names of Christian victims started getting noticeable among the victims of communal violence and hate crimes that were so far focused mainly on the Muslims. Starting from the rape and killing of nuns in Jhabua to the burning of churches in 1998 in South Gujarat, to the killing of Graham Staines and Fr. Arul Dass, the 1990s, especially the latter part, set up the stage for what we see all around us today.

The threat to religious freedom of Indian Christian citizens has two dimensions: the physical and the structural. The physical part of it is evident in acts of hate crimes, physical violence, and gender violence; in acts of stopping worship services and attacking pastors, priests, and nuns; and in vandalism of church buildings and Christian structures. The Evangelical Fellowship of India (EFI) compiled more than 350 incidents of hate crimes that were perpetrated against Christians in 2017. Every year the list has remained between 100 to 200, from 1999 to 2014 or even 2015. It was in 2016 that the number exceeded the 200 mark, and in 2017 it breached the 300 mark. The EFI includes in its list only the incidents we have been able to verify.

There are a lot of incidents that have not even been reported, and then there were many incidents that were reported but we were not able to verify them. Only verified incidents are added to the list, so it is really the tip of the iceberg. We have seen increased impunity, an increase in the number of church worship services and private worships being targeted, even in the sanctity of the worshipers' own homes. The law enforcement agencies are being used, it seems, as tools of the non-state actors. An invasion of the private space where an individual or his family and extended family are targeted and beaten up because they gather to worship is a blot on the freedom of faith guaranteed by the Constitution of India.

Recent incidents include children being detained in the police station, kept away from their parents, and even beaten up all on the pretext of keeping them safe from forcible conversions and kidnapping. There have been at least four such incidents that I can recall where Christian children going to Christian camps with the approval of their parents were apprehended and were kept inside the jail, then sent to government children's home. Custody was not given to their parents for days. In one instance a parent taking his child to a Christian camp along with others was also detained along with the child and today faces a charge of kidnapping. In another incident the court had to intervene before the parents could take custody of their own children who were "rescued" by the law enforcement agencies. Both these incidents are from Madhya Pradesh which has been ruled by the BJP now for more than fifteen years.

What in your opinion has been most disturbing about these incidents and their aftermath? Is the local reaction a matter of apathy and restrictions asked for, or is it the rules and law and order conditions asked for by the government authorities? Or are there other, less obvious reasons?

JD: The Christmas violence and threats are dangerous portents. These make the state complicit in many ways. The prime minister's choosing the day as Good Governance Day is a deliberate and sly message that he does not care about our feelings or our sense of insecurity that his actions generate. We are dispensable, in his scheme of things. The enthusiastic support of the officials too is a signal. The open aggression of the non-state actors who work as enforcers are a clear signal that the *Sangh* cadres enjoy protection. This set of connected actions and messages are seen in just about every act of violence against members of the Christian community in most of the states.

The government restrictions are far more dangerous than would be thought because the anti-conversion law operates only in six states of the Union of India. This law does not have the sort of pan-India force that marks the law barring Christians, and Muslims of Dalit origin, from the affirmative action benefits in education, employment, and political participation guaranteed to members of former untouchable castes by the Parliament of India through its Article 341. That law was enacted in 1950 when the Constitution of India was adopted. But within months of that event, the law was amended to bar non-Hindu Dalits from seeking benefits of the law. This not only entirely disempowered them, but, in retrospect, has acted as a more vicious anti-conversion law than the six state laws.

This has had the effect of creating a large body of people who follow Christ but remain Hindus on government records to take benefit of the laws. They live a double life, so to speak. I have in the past called it an underground church, Christians who cannot publicly profess their faith. They remain open to blackmail and prey to violence. They are also vulnerable to action by the government. At various times, local administrations and police have sought to identify them, and then punish them by various methods, including denying them public facilities and natural resources such as water from the community pond. Those who have government jobs live in perpetual fear of being found out. They are being put to the test, and daily.

Collectively, this law and the perception that the anti-conversion laws are operational in the entire landmass of India sort of empowers the police and cadres of the Hindutva group to take the law into their own hands and enforce a "Hindu Rashtra" regime, especially in rural areas and small towns.

There is another reason not entirely connected with the government or with the *Sangh*. It flows out of the concept of caste and its further subdivisions. In a local community, members of sub-castes have a common identity, a common social capital, and, to some extent, even common shared resources such as grazing grounds, common cemeteries, or cremation areas. The most basic manifestation is in community celebrations of traditional festivals, some rooted in agricultural cycles or season changes.

Communities fear that converts to Christianity no longer participate in such activity, thereby reducing its impact, displeasing the gods, or reducing the funds, grain, animals for sacrifice, or whatever was essential in the group celebrating or observing the festival, such as the plowing of the first furrow in a field in the sowing season. This is a serious and complex matter, especially in Tribal areas, and a major cause of tension, conflict, and violence. The *Sangh* cadres and the government have often exploited this and fomented fissures, divisions, and violent clashes that leave long-lasting cultural and social wounds. Christian pastors have not been able to adopt any workable enculturation stratagem to tide over this situation.

VL: We see new groups coming up every year. These groups are often local, not national, are indirectly connected to the *Sangh Parivar* and are more violent than the RSS. They often enjoy the patronage of the BJP and of the state government if it is a BJP-ruled state. They act with impunity and expect to get away with whatever they do.

But one must realize that this violence is not only directed against Christians. Anyone or any group that Hindutva perceives as the Other will always be treated with the same disdain, same hatred, and same intensity. If Muslims are not safe in India, Christians and other minorities can never be either.

The structural threat to the freedom of religion of Indian Christian citizens is even more interesting because it is not as stark as physical violence and it does not show up too often, but it is a potent weapon. When laws are used against a community or people, there is little that one can do. The anti-conversion laws are an example. Not only this, in denying reservations and affirmative action for Christian and Muslim Dalits, the state itself offers an incentive favoring the majority religion and encourages conversion to Hinduism. Provisions in the laws are often used to harass Christians, and other minority, institutions. The Juvenile Justice Act is a case in point and has been used effectively to close so many Christian orphanages that were serving and helping the poorest of the poor.

What is perhaps the most disturbing is that Hindutva has become generic. What was until recently considered the "fringe" now seems to be the "mood of the nation" reflective of the way that common people of India think. The church and the average Christian today are viewed with suspicion. This did not happen overnight. It has taken a propaganda effort that has lasted more than twenty years. The RSS and its affiliates seem to have been successful in brainwashing the Indian people. While I would hesitate to say that the church has lost its goodwill, I can certainly say that the image of the church has taken a beating. We are now looked upon as fanatical converters and are increasingly counted as the Other. This is not because of what we have done but what we have failed to do, to counter the propaganda.

The restrictions on Christians, for example, the anti-conversion laws, are not a new thing. Non-right-wing governments in the past, including those led by the Congress Party, have had such rules as well. Your thoughts?

JD: Some of the anti-conversion laws are from the colonial period, when some of the rajas ruling principalities, especially in central India, tried to stop their people from converting, especially to Christianity. It is a matter of some speculation why the British, who were ruling India at that time, did not put pressure on the rajas who were their vassals, or suffragans. Many would argue that despite the British banning such terrible social aberrations as sati,[9] they did not want to interfere too much in the Hindu religion, which could make for a rebellious kingdom difficult to rule by the small numbers of British officers in the country.

Colonial interest was paramount. India provided soldiery for the European theaters of war, and India provided manpower for the cane fields of the Americas. Both required the cooperation of the local satraps ruling their tiny fiefdoms. This is also one reason why a large group of people, now called the Other Backward Castes/Classes, were left almost untouched by British evangelists, Catholic and Protestant, who worked either with the Dalits, or with the Brahmin and other upper-caste groups. The farming and land-owning castes and classes were not touched, not disturbed.

The Congress inherited the ground situation as India gained Independence. The Congress of the Freedom struggle, led by Mahatma Gandhi, was a motley coalition of all sorts of groups, ranging from the enlightened political thought of Jawaharlal Nehru to every Hindu, almost fundamentalist, section led by people including the first president, Rajendra Prasad, the home ministers of the early years, including Vallabhbhai Patel and Govind Ballabh Pant, and chief ministers such as Ravi Shankar Shukla. Perhaps its hand was forced by the extreme Hindu group within its own ranks.

---

9   The custom of widows being immolated on their husbands' funeral pyres.

But it must be said that while the anti-conversion laws in the states were enacted either by the Congress government in the provinces or while the Congress was in control of the national government, the administration did not invoke these laws or enforce them with any zeal. There was little violence as, until about the mid-1980s, the Congress had kept the Hindu extremists in check. The Congress seemed to lose its moral compass during the Emergency of 1975-77 when the Constitution was all but suspended, and especially following the rise in Sikh militancy, the confrontation at the Golden Temple, and the terrible mass killing of the Sikhs in the aftermath of Mrs. Indira Gandhi's assassination on October 31, 1984. An estimated eight hundred Sikh men were killed, many of them burned alive. That gave the space for the rise of Hindu fundamentalism in all its fury. There was no looking back after 1992 when they demolished the five hundred-year-old Babri Mosque in Ayodhya to build a temple to Lord Rama.

The BJP has been in power in two stints, the National Democratic Alliance of Prime Minister Atal Bihari Vajpayee from 1998 to 2004 and Mr. Modi's government from 2014. Both these periods have seen blatant government support of the *Sangh* and a criminal level of impunity. The *Sangh* is active with great ferocity whenever the BJP is in power.

Together with the late Fr. John Vallamattom, who was secretary in the Catholic Bishops Conference of India offices, I had monitored anti-Christian violence in various parts of the country. The violence started increasing from 1997 when the *Sangh*, under Mr. Vajpayee and Mr. L. K. Advani, was making a thrust for power in New Delhi.

In our last presentation to the United Nations Human Rights Council's Universal Periodic Review for India, we noted that in 2014 there were more than 147 incidents where Christians were targeted, with many more going unrecorded. The states of Karnataka, Madhya Pradesh, and Chhattisgarh recorded the most number of attacks in the past 2 years. The Evangelical Fellowship of India has recorded as many as 177 such cases in 2015. This includes physical violence, stopping of worship in churches, attacks on churches, arrests of pastors and their companions, and rapes of nuns. There were more than 100 incidents across the country in the period of January-July 2016.

Another common phenomenon is the social boycott being experienced by Christians in several parts of the country; local panchayats are also known to have imposed fines on Christians for practicing their faith. I would like to particularly mark the frightening escalation in hate campaigns by senior BJP leaders, including members of Parliament and some who have gone on to become ministers and chief ministers. This provided fodder to the cadres coercing the Christian community.

VL: Personally speaking, I think that there has been no non-right-wing government in independent India. Even during Jawaharlal Nehru's time there were always elements of the right-wing in the government. The Congress is no beacon of secularism, certainly not the party that we see today. It has moved far away from the ideals of its founders.

Restrictions on Christians are not new. Before India became independent, the princely states in India wanted to pass laws to restrict the freedom of religion of Indian Christians. One only must look at the Constituent Assembly debates to see how the word "propagate" was included as part of Article 25.

The question goes much deeper: does India share the values of our founding fathers who strove to put a secular Constitution in place and give minorities their space and freedom without imposing majoritarianism on them? The question is whether India is truly secular in spirit as it is in the law. I think it is. But our commitment to secularism and fundamental freedoms for all is being severely tested and the way we respond will determine the kind of nation that we will leave to our children.

In the end it is the people of India, and not just political parties, that will determine our future as a nation.

How have Christians worked to strengthen religious freedom in India? How has the church responded to the restrictions on the community? Do mainstream churches and church groups work in tandem with independent pastors?

JD: The Christian church, especially the Catholic Bishops Conference and some Congregations who run schools and colleges, have taken recourse to the legal processes by challenging in the Supreme Court any government move to dilute the fundamental right to profess, practice, or propagate faith. But for many reasons—political and the lack of unity and cohesiveness of purpose in various denominations of the faith in India—the government could make inroads and has chipped away at the constitutional guarantee of freedom of faith. The community is politically quite disempowered and has not been able to mount the sort of challenge required to win back the pristine rights under the 1950 Constitution.

Perhaps all is not lost despite the darkness we see in the sky this 2018 spring. But this will require a concerted campaign not by the church alone, but in conjunction with the equally beleaguered Muslim community and a strong core of what we call the secular Hindu. This is still a tepid campaign. The Christian community is still to come out of its shell. And, unfortunately, there is a selfish group, small but high profile, which seeks to make peace with the *Sangh*, and in fact, supports its aggressive campaign against the Muslims.

It is a sad reflection on the community, but unity eludes us. The ritualized ecumenical movement is mere tokenism, and prominent Christian groups are quite ready, perhaps even willing, to betray each other to win momentary peace for themselves and their institutions. The independent pastors live a risky life, and when in trouble, find themselves entirely alone, at the mercy of the wolves. Recent efforts by the newly resuscitated United Christian Forum, with its helpline and support of such groups as the Evangelical Fellowship and the Alliance Defending Freedom India group of lawyers, is an insufficient move to extend some semblance of protection.

Community leadership across denominations must wake up to the emerging crisis and harness resources to create structures for advocacy, legal training, and judicial defense.

VL: Christians in India have always upheld religious freedom for everybody. Time to time, the Christian community has used legal means to challenge threats to fundamental freedoms. Sometimes, our efforts have not been united and that has resulted in some erosion of freedoms. The church in India is politically naive and we have a long way to go as far as this is concerned. Our failure to successfully fight for the rights of Dalit Christians is a big example of this.

When the community started being targeted in the late 1990s the initial reaction was that the community responded as various denominations rather than one unit. However, in the years following that, the Christian community has come together at least at the leadership level, and today we have the national United Christian Forum (UCF) composed of the Catholic Bishops Conference of India (CBCI), the National Council of Churches in India (NCCI), and the Evangelical Fellowship of India (EFI). This forum has spoken with one voice on many matters important to the community. We as a community still must filter this unity down to the grassroots for it is there that visible unity is needed.

There has been a great improvement in the relationship between mainstream churches and independent congregations but there is always room for more improvement. When Pastor Sultan Masih was killed in Punjab, all the churches came together irrespective of their denomination and condemned it and asked for justice.

Pooling of resources is going to be a key in our response to organized persecution.

In your opinion what does the future hold for Christians in India, and of Christian-run educational, health, and social welfare institutions?

JD: We have survived two thousand years. But we need to reflect if we have flourished as we should have, or that we could have taken advantage of the freedoms given us by the Constitution. The fault must lie with the community and the church leadership. As a community poor in material resources, we remain dependent on the West. This also makes us vulnerable.

Our training programs, legal aid, and even welfare schemes are dependent on Western resources, Catholic or Protestant and evangelical. This makes the community's social action and institutions prone to government pressure. The government's making foreign funding so difficult is a case in point. In effect, the government will crack down on any church or its agency suspected of doing anything that empowers people. The action on compassion is a case in point. The government and the *Sangh* would want the church to work in providing education and health as a service agency, but not as a faith leader, much less as an empowering group or a spiritually liberating force.

VL: Christians in India have a bright future not because of the current scenario but because God wants to bless this nation through his people. I am confident that God will continue to lift his people and through them bless the nation of India. Even though today there is an effort to push Christians to the margins, the church will continue to contribute to the nation and its people driven by love, compassion, and a God-given mandate. The service that the Indian church provides must be Indian in terms of funding as well. Sometimes foreign funding can keep us vulnerable to various undesirable interventions by both government and non-state actors.

The last government and this government view the social sector with suspicion. The current finance minister has even gone on record making his suspicion plain. The current atmosphere is favorable for bodies that want to act as service providers but is not favorable for bodies who are into empowerment work or rights-based activism.

The RSS with its social services is giving a formidable challenge to church-run institutions, but there is one thing that sets us apart, which is that we are people of God, called by him to be partners in his mission, and are driven by his love, for his glory. We need to keep this greater reality always before us.

How do we deal with this scenario? Do we have a strategic response ready?

JD: As an activist, I think that the international Christian community, the governments, and the international human rights organizations have betrayed us, or have exposed their own inability, even impotency, in helping vulnerable communities. India is a vast market, and international governments and their business communities and agencies want to be in the good books of the government of India.

The Christian community in India is essentially left to its own devices. It must come together and create structures to fight its battle, which indeed is a battle for existence, and to fight it in peace and without any violence. This will require revolutionary thinking in all three segments of the church, the Catholics including the oriental churches, the Protestant or Reformed churches, and the evangelical and Pentecostal churches whose independent pastors are the most vulnerable, and whose members are not even on the radar of our consciousness.

I hope and pray it will find the native genius to do so in the next five or ten years before there comes a cusp that will make it impossible, as has happened in several countries in the Middle East and the Far East.

VL: I believe the church is not ready yet. We have been doing perhaps the best we could, but we need to do better. Creating awareness within the community on issues of importance to the community, creating awareness within the nation in partnership with like-minded groups, and creating structures in partnership to defend fundamental freedoms and constitutional values is something that the church, as a whole, must start doing as soon as possible.

The strategic response cannot emerge in a vacuum. Partnership within the community and outside the community with people of other faiths and with people of secular persuasion and those who cherish the constitutional values of India is a must.

Chapter 9

Christian Response to Violence in India

Vikas Ram
and
Kay Higuera Smith

Through this whole experience, I understood that being a Christian and persecution are one and the same things. Sometime there is persecution from outside, while other times, there can be persecution from inside. Then there is also inward persecution. We are strengthened by the fact that God is present with us, even at the time when we are going through suffering and persecution. I and my family's journey through persecution has helped us to know that Jesus is for real. We can trust upon him. He is always there and never leaves us, no matter what happens.

Shaurya[1]

Background Information

The Indian subcontinent has been home to people with distinct racial, ethnic, linguistic, and cultural peculiarities since the pre-historic era, millennia before India as a nation was formed in 1947.[2] These distinct people groups have existed side by side in a context of considerable

---

1 Shaurya [pseudonym], interview with the author, April 2015.

2 K. S. Singh, "A Note on the Series, Peoples of India—Anthropological Survey of India," http://www.ansi.gov.in/people_india.htm, accessed on September 22, 2015, identified 4,635 distinct groups in India.

peace for centuries.³ However, during the pre-Independence era, divisive ideologies, which have focused on religion, began to surface. One of the manifestations of this is the growing violence that Hindu nationalists are committing against other religious groups. In this chapter, we discuss violence against Christian minorities in India, and we examine the Christian theological responses that are emerging out of this violence.

Ram Puniyani explains how this phenomenon of divisive religious ideologies developed. First, during the colonial era, the more progressive thinking sectors of society, made up of rising classes of industrialists, businesspeople, workers, and educated people, came together to form regional political bodies, such as Madras Mahajan Sabha, Pune Sarvajanik Sabha, and the Bombay Association. These regional organizations then began to work for an over-arching political identity, which eventually resulted, in 1885, in the formation of the Indian National Congress (INC), aimed at the creation of a secular and democratic nation-state that would ensure development for all classes and religious groups on the subcontinent.⁴ The Hindu and Muslim landlords and the local kings of the era did not support this move. They had enjoyed a privileged social status in a highly stratified and hierarchical society before this time, and the INC threatened to challenge that status. Puniyani concludes that, due to their declining social influence, these groups of lords and landlords resorted to a politics that sought to harness the power of religion to shore up their waning power in the wake of these progressive social and political changes.⁵

---

3 This was argued by Ashis Nandy, address to the Nagel Institute Scholars, YMCA International Guest House, New Delhi, July 1, 2015.

4 Ram Puniyani, *Hindu Nationalism versus Indian Nationalism*, http://www.countercurrents.org/puniyani240713.html, accessed January 23, 2016.

5 See Ram Puniyani, *Communal Politics: Facts versus Myths* (New Delhi: Sage Publications, 2003), 73. The term "communalism" is referred in the Western world as a "theory or system of government in which virtually autonomous local communities are loosely in federation." But in the Indian subcontinent context, communalism has come to be associated with tensions

In this way, traditional religions gained new power. As a result, organizations such as the Muslim League and the Hindu Mahasabha came into existence in the early twentieth century and quickly began to argue for Muslim and Hindu nationalisms respectively. Their concerns were not merely economic, however. The Hindu Mahasabha and the Indian Muslim League had different motivations for disagreeing with Congress. The former's opposition to the INC was primarily based on ideological disagreements about whether India should be a "Hindu" country. The Muslim League disagreed with the INC because it wanted more legislative representation in states where there were significant Muslim populations.

Taking up the vision of the Hindu Mahasabha, the Rashtriya Swayamsevak Sangh (RSS), was birthed in 1925, which propagated further the idea of Hindu nationalism and the vision of a Hindu nation. As history reveals, the RSS (more recently referred to as *Sangh Parivar*, or *Sangh*, reflecting the addition of affiliate/associated organizations) eventually distanced itself from the all-inclusive political vision of the Indian National Congress—which subsequently was led by Mohandas Karamchand Gandhi—as well as from ongoing freedom struggles against the British Raj (British colonial rule). While concerted efforts were being made to oust the British Raj, the RSS did not participate, arguing that the law—even colonial law—must be respected.[6]

The RSS was banned for a brief period from 1948 to 1949 after Gandhi was assassinated by a close associate of both the RSS and

---

and clashes between different religious communities in various regions. See, "Communalism—Meaning and Issues," http://www.insightsonindia.com/2014/11/07/communalism-meaning-and-issues/, accessed on August 23, 2015. It can also be defined as artificially induced feelings of "separateness" based on religion in order to gain political capital.

6 Shamsul Islam, *Know the RSS: Based on Rashtriya Swayamsevak Sangh Documents* (New Delhi: Pharos Media & Publishing Pvt. Ltd., 2014), 30. See also Vinay Lal, *Veer Savarkar: Ideologue of Hindutva*, https://www.sscnet.ucla.edu/southasia/History/Hindu_Rashtra/veer.html, accessed March 2, 2016.

the Hindu Mahasabha.⁷ After the lifting of the ban, and as the RSS became active again, several Hindu-Muslim riots broke out between 1969 and 1993.⁸ Central to these riots was the effort by the RSS to create a "Hindutva," or Hindu homeland, a commitment that began before Independence and has grown stronger every decade since.

During this period, however, Christians and other minorities such as Sikhs remained largely unaffected by the violence, as the RSS focused its energies on Muslims, whom its leaders regarded as a greater threat. According to the United Christian Forum for Human Rights, there were only thirty-two registered cases of communal violence against Christians between 1964 and 1996.⁹ Regarding this, Chad Bauman rightly states that until the end of the 1990s, Indian Christians were largely unaffected, despite being accused, in some circles, of being a "foreign" element and suspected of divided loyalties.[10]

---

7   In a letter written to the head of the RSS, Golwalkar, dated September 11, 1948, Sardar Patel, as the first Union Home Minister of Independent India, stated: "It was not necessary to spread poison in order to enthuse the Hindus and organize for their protection. As a final result of the poison, the country had to suffer the sacrifice of the invaluable life of Gandhiji." Opposition turned more severe when the RSS men expressed joy and distributed sweets after Gandhi's death. This letter is quoted in full in Desraj Goel, *Rahstriya Swayamsevak Sangh*, http://www.kractivist.org/letter-sardar-vallabhai-patel-to-rss-chief-guru-golwalkar-1948-godse-mustread/, accessed March 2, 2016.

8   Sarbeswar Sahoo, "Religious Violence and the Developmental State in Rajasthan," in *Perspectives on Violence and Othering in India*, ed. R. C. Tripathi and Purnima Sing (New Delhi: Springer, 2016), 176. Sahoo notes that five judicial commissions have exposed the role of the RSS in various communal riots in the past: Ahmadabad (1969), Bhivandi (1970), Tellicheri (1971), Jamshedpur (1979), Kanyakumari (1982), Mumbai (1992-93), and others.

9   S. M. Michael, "Culture and Religious Identity of India from Dalit and Minorities Perspectives," in *Mobilization of Backward Communities in India*, ed. B. V. Bhosale (New Delhi: Deep and Deep Publications Pvt. Ltd., 2004), 3.

10   Chad M. Bauman, "Hindu-Christian Conflict in India: Globalization, Conversion, and the Coterminal Castes and Tribes," *Journal of Asian Studies* 72,

However, the trend began to change when the Bharatiya Janata Party (BJP), the political wing of the RSS, came into political power. In 1996, a Catholic Health Center near Latur (Maharashtra) was attacked. Bibles were burned, and Christians were physically assaulted.[11] Gradually, the violence against Christians grew, with fifteen recorded incidents of anti-Christian violence in 1997 and the number reaching ninety in 1998.[12] Between 1998 and 2016, the number of attacks on Christians continued to increase, with the number reaching close to two hundred incidents annually according to the annual report on persecution published by the Evangelical Fellowship of India.[13] However, these figures are not the exact representation of the state of persecution in India, as there are many anti-Christian activities that do not get reported or come to the notice of the larger Christian community.

The most severe form of anti-Christian violence, which has been classified as a "genocide" by the Human Rights Law Network, and as a pogrom by the Organization for Minorities of India, broke out in December 2007, after an altercation between Christians in the Kandhamal region of Odhisha state and Swami Lakshmanananda Saraswati, a local leader of the Vanavasi Kalyan Ashram (VKA), an RSS affiliate organization. According to the Human Rights Law Network, the VKA aims to "Hinduise the adivasis (tribals) through conversion and reconversion activities."[14] These riots, which lasted for a few days,

---

no. 3 (August 2013): 633; http://digitalcommons.butler.edu/cgi/viewcontent.cgi?article=1271&context=facsch_papers, accessed April 23, 2015.

11 Ram Puniyani, ed., *Ghar Wapsi: Conversions and Freedom of Religion* (Delhi: Media House, 2015), 27.

12 Sushil Aaron, *Christianity and Political Conflict in India: The Case of Gujarat* (Colombo: Regional Centre for Strategic Studies 23, 2002), 47.

13 Evangelical Fellowship of India, "Hate and Targeted Violence against Christians in India," *Report 2015,* March 2, 2016, http://files.ctctcdn.com/523942c3501/271ca9a9-f085-4006-a08b-051ed9cd51c8.pdf.

14 "Genocide in Kandhamal," *Human Rights Law Network,* http://idsn.org/uploads/media/Orissa_report_-_Human_Rights_Law_Network.pdf, accessed May 26, 2015; John Dayal, "August 2008 Anti-Christian Pogrom

subsided but then broke out again in much greater magnitude in August 2008, resulting in between 75 and 123 deaths, according to the Multiple Action Research Group (though the government has confirmed only 54 deaths), as well as dozens of cases of sexual assault and rape, destruction of more than 5,000 homes and 264 churches, and displacement (temporary or permanent) of more than 25,000 Christians.[15]

Rajini Majhi, who was burned at the orphanage at Bargarh, Odisha State.
Source: "Photos of Orissa Violence," *Christian Persecution India* (blog), September 10, 2008, http://christianpersecutionindia.blogspot.in/2008/09/photos-of-orissa-violence.html.

Widow and orphan of a dismembered victim.
Source: "Indian Christians—Photos of Persecution and Death in Orissa," *Christian View* (blog), September 27, 2008, http://christianlook.blogspot.in/2008/09/indian-christians-photos-of-persecution.html.

---

in India Saw 'Rivers of Blood on the Road,'" *Organization for Minorities of India*, http://www.minoritiesofindia.org/august-2008-anti-christian-pogrom-in-india-saw-rivers-of-blood-on-the-road, accessed June 7, 2016; Vrinda Grover, ed., *Kandhamal: The Law Must Change Its Course* (New Delhi: Multiple Action Research Group, 2010), 32.

15 Grover, *Kandhamal*, 17.

It is of course impossible to identify each of the perpetrators of these acts, given that they are carried out as mob actions. Nevertheless, according to Bauman, who has extensively researched anti-Christian violence in India, more often than not, these acts of violence are devised and executed by the "Family of the Sangh," that is, the RSS.[16] As is evident, these attacks on the Kandhamal Christians during 2007-8 were not just isolated incidents but part of a sequence of well-planned and concerted efforts of the *Sangh Parivar*, through which a systematic suppression and marginalization of religious minorities as the Other is being carried out. Because of these events, communal violence against minorities—especially Christians—has now become a regular occurrence in India. This is particularly true in pockets of North and Central India, where Christians make up a tiny minority. As per another recent report, numbers of "reported" incidents of violence against Christians in 2015 rose to more than 350.[17]

In most cases, these victims of violence are not given due justice in the courts of law. For instance, Anto Akkara has documented that, in the seven years since the Kandhamal violence, there has been little justice for the victims and not much has changed for them. Many victims continue to live in refugee camps, being displaced from their native villages. The government has done little to bring justice to the victims or to prosecute the perpetrators.[18]

---

16 Chad M. Bauman, *Pentecostals, Proselytization, and Anti-Christian Violence in Contemporary India* (New Delhi: Oxford University Press, 2015), 3.

17 Open Doors, a Christian nonprofit relief agency based in the United States, stated that, in 2015, "more than 350 Christians were physically attacked, at least nine Christians were killed for their faith and at least three women were raped." See Mark Woods, "India: 8,000 Christians Targeted by Violence and Persecution in 2015," *World*, http://www.christiantoday.com/article/india.8000.christians.targeted.by.violence.and.persecution.in.2015.report.says/77222.htm, accessed on February 20, 2015.

18 In a written memorandum submitted to the president of India, Dr. Pranab Mukherjee, Kandhamal Christians have highlighted the gross injustice being done to them in the courts of law. Elaborating on the injustice, the memorandum pointed out that of the approximately 3,300 complaints

The history of Christianity in North India is recent compared to that of South India. While, according to tradition, Christianity reached South India as early as 52 CE with the arrival of the biblical apostle Thomas, it largely remained concentrated in the two southern states of Kerala and Tamil Nadu. The northeastern states were not introduced to Christianity until 1626, with the arrival of Jesuit missionaries.[19] The northern and central parts of India were not exposed to Christianity until much later, in the early nineteenth century.[20] This explains the smaller, and more vulnerable, populations of Christians in North and Central India in comparison to southern India.

A major reason why Christians in India, particularly in North and Central India, have remained marginalized and vulnerable to violence is because a large proportion of them come from Dalit and Tribal backgrounds, groups who had been subject to social and economic deprivation—due to caste-based discrimination in the case of Dalits, and due to lack of education and other opportunities in the case of Tribals.[21]

Christian victims made to the police, only 820 cases were registered. The police investigated only 518 cases while the remaining complaints were dismissed as "false reports." Seven years later, only 247 of the 518 registered cases have been disposed of, while the rest remain pending before Indian courts. In 30 murder cases that have been handled by the courts, there have been only 2 convictions "due to shoddy investigation by the police and intimidation of the witnesses in the court premises," according to the memorandum of complaint. See Anto Akkara, "Amid Mounting Injustice, Church in Odisha Promotes Kandhamal Martyrs' Day," *National Catholic Register*, September 17, 2015, http://www.ncregister.com/daily-news/amid-mounting-injustice-church-in-odisha-promotes-kandhamal-martyrs-day/#ixzz42CVHpMQ0.

19   Pathika Dhara Sharma, "Christianity in the Northeast," *The Telegraph*, [Calcutta Edition], September 9, 2011, http://www.telegraphindia.com/1110909/jsp/northeast/story_14484991.jsp, accessed March 3, 2016.

20   Raj Bahadur Sharma, *History of Christian Missions: North India Perspective* (New Delhi: Mittal Publications, 1998), vi.

21   Goldie Osuri, *Religious Freedom in India: Sovereignty and (anti) Conversion* (London: Routledge, 2013), 137.

Christians from Dalit backgrounds have become doubly marginalized and disenfranchised as well. In addition to marginalization because of their status as Dalits, they also are marginalized as Christians, for instance, through laws that effectively prevent them from benefiting from affirmative action through the various "Freedom of Religion" laws (also known as anti-conversion laws), coincidently enacted by various BJP-led states. These laws are often misused to target and falsely accuse Christians of converting people by deception and of rendering them vulnerable to being penalized for violating the law.[22] Likewise, such laws are being used to restrict the religious freedom of those who seek to embrace the Christian faith. Regarding this John Dayal states, "Anti conversion laws in six Indian states, which require one must 'inform the local government that you want to change your faith,' encourage violence against new or potential converts."[23]

While trying to discern the causes behind the persecution of Christians, one of the most commonly stated is the charge that Christians have been converting people by allurements or by force. If allurements or force had been employed, one would expect a rise in that number. That is not the case, however. Despite problems with under-reporting, the 2011 Census data on religion show that the percentage of Christians in India has remained steady at about 2.3 percent.[24]

---

22 Thus, for instance the "Freedom of Religion Bill," which is basically meant to protect the freedom of individuals to practice and embrace the religion of their choice, is now being used to file police cases against Christians on the pretext that Christians are involved in converting people through allurement and fraudulent measure. In many cases, a local person is bribed to bear false witness against the Christian being charged.

23 John Dayal, "August 2008 Anti-Christian Pogrom in India Saw 'Rivers of Blood on the Road,'" *Organization for Minorities of India*, http://www.minoritiesofindia.org/august-2008-anti-christian-pogrom-in-india-saw-rivers-of-blood-on-the-road/, accessed June 7, 2016.

24 Census 2011—Official Site, http://www.census2011.co.in/religion.php, accessed March 4, 2016.

The problem of anti-Christian violence becomes even more serious when, at times, the political parties and national leaders turn a blind eye to it or appear complicit. For instance, in April 2014, before the nation's elections for the central government, the current prime minister denied that he was aware of any attacks on members of the Christian community and their places of worship in India, a claim vigorously condemned by Christian leaders.[25] Similarly, since the BJP has come into power in the central government, Prime Minister Modi's administration failed to acknowledge a series of attacks on churches in Delhi, a silence so striking that even international newspapers such as the *New York Times* have commented on it.[26]

Considering these attacks on Christians and the government's subsequent silence and/or complicity, many Christians have expressed that their sense of security has been compromised and that they have become much more keenly aware of their minority status and their vulnerability in parts of the country.[27]

As a response to these events, we interviewed four church leaders in India to determine what theological responses were emerging because of these experiences of violence, silencing, trauma, and marginalization. Each of these four leaders in our case studies is part of the movement of independent churches in India, whose adherents

---

25 Greg [No Last Name Given], "Christian Leaders Condemn Modi's Ignorance on Anti-Christian Attacks: *SILENT VOICE* Exposes His Lies," *Silent Voice* (blog), April 17, 2014, https://silentmaj.wordpress.com/2014/04/17/christian-leaders-condemn-modis-ignorance-on-anti-christian-attacks-silent-voice-exposes-his-lies/, accessed March 2, 2016.

26 The Editorial Board, "Modi's Dangerous Silence," the *New York Times*, February 6, 2015, http://www.nytimes.com/2015/02/07/opinion/modis-dangerous-silence.html?_r=0, accessed March 4, 2016. See also Anto Akkara, "India under Modi Sees Increase in Attacks on Christians, Critics Charge: Growing Number of Atrocities Worries Religious Minorities," http://aleteia.org/2014/10/01/india-under-modi-sees-increase-in-attacks-on-christians-critics-charge/#sthash.jzrIZppE.dpuf, accessed March 4, 2016.

27 Rowena Robinson, *Boundaries of Religion: Essays on Christianity, Ethnic Conflict and Violence* (New Delhi: Oxford University Press, 2013), 165.

have been particularly hard-hit by the violence.[28] We interviewed them to discover their stories and how they have responded to persecution and have made sense of their Christian faith in the midst of it.

Case Studies

We were sitting in our home after the worship service got over; it was Sunday afternoon. Two unidentified men who were opponents of Christ entered our house. They said that they were interested to know about Jesus. Later on, behind them, fourteen more men entered. They had their faces covered by handkerchiefs. They started beating me with wooden and iron rods and with chairs. I was badly injured. When I fell on the floor, I cried out loudly to the Lord in prayer and asked him to help me face this test of faith.

Veer

It was stories like this that prompted us to explore the unique ways that Christians in India have responded to persecution. Through a grant from the Nagel Institute at Calvin College, Grand Rapids, Michigan, we conducted extensive interviews with four case studies, all of whom personally witnessed or experienced, or whose close family suffered trauma in one of the violent outbreaks or pogroms against Christians from the period of 1986 to the present, but especially from 2007 to 2015.[29]

Participants

For this study, we were seeking specifically theological responses to the catastrophes that our interviewees had suffered. As such, our case studies are all clergymen from independent churches. Three

---

28 The movement of independent churches refers to self-governing, indigenous churches composed of predominantly first-generation Christians, who are actively involved in evangelism and, in many cases, also in social work activities among the poor.

29 All of our research has been submitted to an Institutional Review Council made up of faculty from Georgetown University in Washington, DC, and Calvin College in Grand Rapids, Michigan. The names of the participants as well as other identifying markers are pseudonymous in order to protect their identities.

out of the four participants are clerics serving in various Pentecostal denominations within India; the fourth is an evangelical cleric. We selected these Christian leaders based on the purposive sampling technique, in which we chose for our interviews those who could offer insights into certain events or experiences. For each of our interviewees, either they or one of their close family members has directly experienced persecution. They come from four different parts of India: Dehradun (North), Jaipur (West), Kandhamal (East), and Bangalore (South). All four participants are male. We were unable to identify female ministers who would have added different theological perspectives to the study. In most parts of India, the number of female Pentecostal, evangelical, or independent house church ministers remains small. We chose independent church ministers because their churches have been unique targets for violence. They are not as well-funded or as prominent as Catholic or Thomas churches or those from more traditional, mainline Protestant denominations. Because of this, they are more likely to come under attack.[30] Below, we first introduce each participant and his story of persecution. Once they all have been introduced, we follow with a discussion of their theological responses to those events.

Case Study #1: Shaurya

Shaurya comes from a family whose members are part of the Tribal, or Adivasi, class within India—indigenous people groups that tend to populate rural regions and that often occupy the lower rungs of

---

30 In addition to being more vulnerable financially and structurally, the independent churches are also vulnerable because (1) for the most part they are run by Indians and not foriegners; (2) they are based in urban, poor, or tribal areas; (3) they have large healing ministries that draw the poor to attend and thus raise suspicions. That said, some of the worst attacks on churches and on clergy have been directed at Catholic churches. Dilshad Gardens Church (Delhi) is one of many examples of Catholic churches that have been attacked in part because they are so prominent and because the clergy—both priests and nuns—are more visible because they are most likely to be in clerical outfits or habits.

the social hierarchy. His parents, who suffered heavy losses in the Kandhamal pogrom of 2008, live in Odisha Province in East India, in a Tribal village amid dense forests. Roads are poor, and access is difficult. Shaurya's family attended an indigenous Baptist church after his father converted from Hinduism. Nevertheless, even after his conversion to Christianity, relations with their Hindu neighbors were good.

This is not to say that there were no tensions. In 1986, Swami Laskhmananda and his followers burned Shaurya's parents' church to the ground and continued to harass them thereafter.[31] Despite this, Shaurya claims, relations with most of their Hindu neighbors continued to be tolerant. This tolerance was strained even further, however, when, on August 28, 2008, a mob arose, instigated and led by the members of Bajrang Dal, the VHP, and similar member organizations of the RSS, also known as *Sangh parivar*.[32] They attacked Shaurya's parents' rural village, seeking to harm Christians of any age and gender. They burned houses, destroyed livestock, and killed hundreds, according to Shaurya.[33] One of his family members was killed and his body dismembered, but most of his family members survived by fleeing into the dense forest. Once the attack subsided, the refugees feared returning, huddling in the forest for three days without food or water. Eventually, the authorities found them and relocated them to a refugee camp run by the Odisha provincial government. The conditions there, he reported, were filthy, and many fell desperately ill.

---

31 Swami Laskhmananda was subsequently killed by unknown assailants in August 2008. His death became the pretext of the Kandhamal pogrom that claimed the lives of more than one hundred people and displaced more than 50,000 Christians from their native locations.

32 According to The National People's Tribunal on Kandhamal, *Final Report* (New Delhi, August 22-24, 2010), 33, http://www.sabrang.com/cc/archive/2012/jan2012/citizens%20tribunal%20Kandhamal%20Report%20Full.pdf, accessed February 28, 2017, "almost all victim-survivors who gave their testimonies to the Tribunal referred to members of the RSS, BJP, Bajrang Dal and VHP as being part of the violent mobs that attacked them and their villages." This was reinforced by local police.

33 See note 13 above for more official estimates of injuries and death.

Finally, after five months some of the refugees were given permission to return. Still others, as of early 2016, had not been able to return home. Those who returned found their homes destroyed and now live in perpetual fear. Relations with their former Hindu neighbors are strained. "Socially, Christians have lost their previous confidence in their neighbors of other faiths," Shaurya explains. He notes that "even though many Hindu neighbors confessed their guilt and want to join hands as before," the returnees "are suspicious and fearful of them." Shaurya reports constraints on religious freedom as well. For instance, he reports increased restrictions on public religious activity, including open air evangelizing, which now, he claims, is almost impossible.

For these reasons, Shaurya operates with fear and mistrust of authorities and alienation from social-cultural others. He is careful to avoid members of radical Hindutva organizations, whom he can identify by their distinctive clothing. Moreover, he has no contact with Muslims or Sikhs, other groups also undergoing persecution. He lives inside a Bible College compound "with almost no interaction with people of other faiths."

Shaurya also, however, receives strength and encouragement from other Christians. The persecutions, he states, "have been a blessing in disguise." Other Christian groups have raised money for his family to help them recover. One group organized special prayer meetings for the Christians in Kandhamal. After an initial period of depression and hopelessness, Shaurya began to research and found Christian books and resources that were new to him but that introduced him to a theology of suffering, books that comforted him through times of extreme pain. Finally, he is witnessing a new unity of purpose among Christians of varying denominations, who are standing together in the face of this adversity.

Case Study #2: Pranav

Pranav lives with his wife and two sons in an urban area of the state of Karnataka, in the south-central region of India. As a child, his family was Hindu, but when a Christian sexton prayed for his ailing sister, who was subsequently healed, the mother, along with the entire family, became Christians. Soon after his sister's healing, Pranav joined a Pentecostal church.[34] Like Shaurya's father, Pranav continued to have excellent relations with his Hindu neighbors and co-workers. He describes a story about his Hindu employer's reverence for both Hindu practices and the Christian Bible: "My boss was a devout Hindu, but every day before beginning our duties, we would gather together, and he had a New Testament respectfully placed on one of the shelves. Every morning, he would do his 'puja' and then take out the New Testament, kiss it, and place it back in its place." Because of experiences like this, Pranav did not perceive Hindus and Christians to be hostile to one another.

In 1982, Pranav started a small Bible study in his living room, which, thirty-five years later, has grown to be a large church of more than four hundred people. Pranav oversees this church, out of which several branch churches have opened as well. Once, while traveling to a rural village where a few dozen people had converted to Christianity, Pranav and his companions suddenly found themselves surrounded by 150 to 200 Hindu villagers, who began to beat them. While he was trying to reason with the village elder, a fight suddenly broke out among the village instigators. They began to fight each other, and thus Pranav and his companions were spared any further beatings. Despite this, Pranav was able to avoid arrest only after reasoning with the police officers.

This event was followed by many years marked by attacks of vandalism but no physical injuries. Then, on Christmas Day 2012, in one of their branch churches located in a coastal town in Karnataka, as he tells it, some *gundas* ("rowdies") broke into the church at 8:30 in the morning, during the Sunday School hour, and began beating the teachers and the children, leaving many of the children injured

---

34 Pentecostal churches are not identical with independent churches. But, in most cases in North India, the independent churches also happen to be Pentecostal in their practices.

and bleeding. This violence was followed in 2014 by a public strike by the RSS against a branch church, occasioned by the false testimony of an embittered husband of a recent convert. Later, other branch churches were attacked, threatened, and, in one case, burned to the ground. Church members throughout the region report that in the local villages, hostilities are high, with many pastors having been physically attacked with no provocation. Many of the Christians in the villages have fled to the cities or have stopped attending church out of fear.

While emboldened and organized, Pranav and his co-religionists recognize that the threat of violence is growing. Just recently, his church received a written death threat from a radical Hindu group that read: "Now no more Bible, only Gita; no more Christians, only Hindus. We are ready to die for Hinduism." Because of these ongoing threats, Pranav is prepared for the possibility that he might die for his faith.

Case Study #3: Veer

Veer is a fifty-year-old male, married, with one daughter. He grew up in the state of Punjab in North India, in a rural village whose populace was half Christian and half Sikh. After attending a Methodist missionary school, Veer committed his life fully to Christ at a revival meeting at age sixteen, when he received a powerful experience of "anointing" for a vocation in ministry. Thereafter, he attended a Bible College, and received both a BA and a BTh. He now pastors an independent church in a large city in the state of Rajasthan in the northwest part of India.

Veer speaks positively about Hindus in general. He states that he has received encouragement and sympathy from his Hindu friends over the years. Nevertheless, he, too, has experienced persecution from radical Hindu groups. On Sunday, April 29, 2007, he was at his home, which adjoined his church building. Several hostile men, with faces covered in handkerchiefs, broke in and began beating him with iron and wooden rods and with chairs, destroying musical instruments and other valuables within the home as well. While they were beating him, he began to recite to himself scripture verses, many of which Veer had long interpreted as personal promises and which now fortified him during the attack. This only enraged his attackers further. He relates that while beating him, "they abused me verbally and said that today we will see how your Jesus will come and protect you." These statements would prove to be ironic, as just as they were speaking, some reporters in a news media van happened to drive by. They saw the commotion, stopped, entered the home, and began video recording the beating, which caused the attackers to flee.

Bloodied and severely injured after the attack, Veer stumbled outdoors and found the strength to make a speech to the bystanders who had assembled in response to the commotion. His speech was reminiscent of Peter's speech in Acts 3:11-26, where he relayed similar themes of innocence, faith in the name of Jesus, and forgiveness. After his speech, Veer returned to his house and collapsed, having sustained injuries that required a week of hospitalization.

Ultimately, Veer's attackers were arrested; however, the investigation has dragged on in court for ten years, with the verdict still pending. Like the other attackers, they claimed that he was converting people by offering financial allurements, which he has vigorously denied.[35] Nonetheless, like the others, he continues to make a clear distinction between the radical attackers and average Hindus: "We love our country and we thank God for our country," he explains. "The persecutors are very few, and, when we were attacked, many Hindu friends came and said that what happened with us was wrong."

Case Study #4: Vihaan

Our final participant, Vihaan, is thirty-seven years old, and married with three children. Vihaan's extended family members are all Hindu except for him and one elder brother. Vihaan converted to Christianity in 1996. In 2003, after attending one year of Bible College, he left to plant a Pentecostal, independent church in a large city in the state of Uttarakhand, in the far north of India.

---

35 In fact, most of the clergy of the independent churches are in dire financial straits themselves. They are neither salaried nor supported by foreign missions organizations. Their churches are not affluent and do not have the resources to make such allurements.

Vihaan has always had good relations with his Hindu neighbors. He sees them as generally "peace loving" and adapting well to the multicultural environment that is India. He speaks of sharing meals with Hindu friends and being invited into their homes. For him, average Hindus are often powerless just as are Christians—being exploited, he claims, by ideologues and politicians and thus sharing a similar experience of marginalization.

One fall evening, on October 11, 2011, Vihaan and his church members were praying in the church. They are a fervent congregation, and they had been fasting and praying for two full days. Vihaan recounts the events that followed: "Suddenly men belonging to RSS, Bajrang Dal, and Veer Savarkar Sangathan forcefully entered the worship hall in which the fasting prayers were going on. They started destroying the furniture, sound system, and musical instruments." He adds that they ransacked the building and threatened to burn the small children with fire, all the while accusing the Christians of coercion and of encouraging prostitution. Events soon escalated. "At that time my youngest daughter . . . was very young, and they took hold of her and tried to hit her, but God saved her from their hands. Then they attacked a sister from our church and ripped her stomach open . . . and she had to be immediately rushed to the hospital." In the aftermath of this violence, Vihaan expresses both bitterness toward some churches, which have withheld aid, and gratefulness for those who have helped because of these traumatic events.

Trauma and Memory in Response to Catastrophe

In recent years, considering acts of genocide, mass killings, and terror, a new theory—trauma theory—has emerged as a field of study that evaluates the effects that trauma and catastrophe have on survivors' cognitive processes. These studies show that the effects of trauma are significant and long lasting. Because of these experiences, identity markers shift. Individual and communal identity becomes shaped by that trauma, influencing the community's social, symbolic, and metaphysical structures of meaning.[36] Trauma theorists analyze these cognitive shifts at both the individual and the communal levels.

Theological Responses to Trauma

By examining these sociolinguistic and cognitive shifts, we can thus identify how our participants responded to the trauma. Many of these responses result in trauma sufferers finding ways to cope that are positive and life affirming and that result in theological innovations--centering new facets of their religious life and decentering others.

Drawing from coping strategies identified in post-holocaust studies, trauma studies, and memory studies, we found that our participants employed several of those selfsame strategies to make sense of their trauma. Several scholars of trauma theory have suggested that most coping strategies fall under three categories: those of resistance, remembrance, and/or realization (i.e., the effort to "realize" a better future). In the following sections, we discuss specifically how each of these strategies has been employed among our participants.

Resistance

> *When [one church attack] happened, the police came and put me in custody. Then the Senior Superintendent of Police (a Hindu) came to meet me. He called me close to him and said that when he was a child, he used to participate in Sunday School. He said that he knew that false allegations are made because of the anti-Christian propaganda of the radical and extremist groups. Then, he offered me a cup of tea.*
>
> *Vihaan*

When first faced with the type of traumatic injustice that Vihaan experienced, a common strategy is to resist by seeking redress from the authorities—to hope and expect that the authorities will somehow change or influence the perpetrators to change. Vihaan, in his appeal

---

36 See David G. Garber Jr., "Trauma Theory and Biblical Studies," *Currents in Biblical Research* 14, no. 1 (2015): 26; Gil Zukerman and Liat Korn, "Post-Traumatic Stress and World Assumptions: The Effects of Religious Coping," *Journal of Religion and Health* 53 (2014): 1676.

to authority, perceived God's sovereignty in the acts of the police official, concluding, "The Lord gave us favor in the eyes of the state machinery and in times of great sorrow, we received help from them." It was this experience of divine justice that served as a positive coping response to the violence and catastrophe.

Pranav relates how an extensive police inquest into the charges against his church resulted in a finding of innocence and an end to the persecutions. Nevertheless, Pranav is not naive. Unlike Vihaan, Pranav contends that pastors who lodge complaints with the police often receive no justice. "The police," he argues, "tend to take sides with the persecutors, and many innocent pastors have been put in prison based on false charges." Therefore, while still being willing to appeal to police, Pranav and others are also skeptical that they will help. Shaurya and Veer share his skepticism. They still cling to hope for some legal redress, but they place their hope in God rather than in the local judicial authorities.

While resistance also can take the form of militant or active protest, it just as often shows up as resistance to the psychic pressures brought about by the trauma of the events. If a dominant social group has the power to produce its version of the narrative as the legitimate history, hence silencing—and also delegitimizing—other versions, then the peripheral group often resists these national myths and histories that silence their own. They can do so by sharing their own narratives and by moderating their language.

This second form of resistance, then, can involve self-conscious changes in language. Our participants noted how their language and discourse had changed as a way of mollifying or alleviating tensions with their persecutors. Shaurya counsels people to abandon a pejorative phrase, *anya-jati* (literally, "Other Backward Caste"), used by a minority of Christians to refer to Hindus or people of other faith. Pranav has changed his language and his approach to Hindus in response to the trauma. Gone is the brash, binary language of the missionaries. "We are not called to say that Christian faith is right and other faiths are wrong," he asserts, a decided departure from previous missionary efforts based on colonial models.

Both Shaurya and Pranav have abandoned the binary, confrontational approaches of the colonial missions' model as a response to the trauma. While at first glance, their efforts to humanize may not seem to fit the category of resistance, we can see that we are dealing here with a form of resistance that challenges the discursive models that, at the very least, contributed to the persecution in the first place.

Once activities have escalated to the point of violence, types of resistance such as appeals to the authorities or efforts to change language often fail to produce the desired effect. When political efforts break down, many survivors resort to physical, militant, or defensive resistance. But resistance takes other forms as well. Another form that it can take is that of intensified piety, which results in even deeper religious behavior. This type of resistance, in turn, works to strengthen and shape social identity, making resistance both political and personal.

Shaurya, for instance, despite a short period of disorientation and despair after the events, nevertheless, quickly regained his composure and found new meaning in suffering. Now, he claims, he finds suffering to be "an intrinsic part of Christian life." He reports finding hope in the smallest victories in the aftermath of the pogroms: "While some of our dear ones lost their lives, it is purely God's miracle that others could run away to the forest and manage to survive. Even in the forest, God provided them food and water to survive. Though they didn't get normal food daily, God provided them with wild food and water to drink from the streams. Like the Israelites, God took care of Kandhamal people in the forest." Shaurya has thus formed a "counter identity" as a strategy of resistance, for which suffering is a necessary component.

Veer, Vihaan, and Pranav all express gratitude for the persecutions they have experienced. It has heightened their sense of commitment and love for and by Jesus. It has shaped their Christian identity and has increased their faith. Pranav acknowledges, however, that such a perspective is difficult to sustain. He recounts the feeling of fear that occurs in the face of persecution: "So, I believe that all of us have to go through that complex of fear; mouth becoming dry and you are facing death; but after praying and committing our lives to God, fear was gone . . . we have nothing to fear." Creating new identities that embrace suffering as meaningful and ultimate was one of the most striking and consistently positive responses among our participants.

Another form that resistance takes is that of guarding one's own dignity in the face of the dominant group's message to subaltern, peripheral groups that they are deviant, dangerous, and threatening. In this case, resistance means maintaining honor and religious integrity when society heaps upon a group only dishonor.

As Pranav's words demonstrate, once one's social identity is politicized and marked, it takes enormous psychic power to maintain this discursive resistance in the face of relentless humiliation, degradation, physical threat, and social ostracism.[37] Pranav admits that it is difficult to find "leaders with integrity," that is, leaders who are willing to persist in the face of this marginal social identity.

Because of these crushing social pressures that discursive resistance must face, those who resist are deeply in need of reassurance from outside. All our participants mentioned being reassured by outsiders. Shaurya was encouraged by a visit from a Christian team from the European Union. Pranav describes the powerful consolation he experienced when pastors from all around the region quit their services en masse upon hearing of the attack on his church and gathered together 1,500 congregants for a mass demonstration and protest on the National Highway. Veer reports that Christians from many parts of India paid for all his extensive medical care in the aftermath of the beating. In these ways, our participants report that consolation gives them a strong sense of stabilization and affirmation of their status and their dignity as persecuted Christians and as human beings.

---

37 See Marion A. Kaplan, *Between Dignity and Despair: Jewish Life in Nazi Germany* (New York: Oxford University Press, 1998), 231.

By the same token, when consolation does not come from those who are expected to give it, the sufferers often feel betrayal, anger, or sadness. Vihaan expresses that sadness when he notes that, in India, the independent churches, which experience the bulk of the persecution, "are almost, like, separated or considered second class by the Christians from mainline and big established churches."[38] He claims that representatives of some of these "mainline churches" in India blamed him and his church members for somehow bringing the attacks on themselves, a charge he vehemently rejects. Perhaps because of this sense of abandonment, Vihaan expresses a renewed sense of solidarity with others who are undergoing persecution.

These various forms of consolation, which survivors seek both from God and from their fellow religionists and which they offer to others, serve as powerful forms of resistance by building up dignity and affirming one's spiritual commitments. Alternately, however, when consolation does not come, it makes resistance more difficult for those who are experiencing trauma.

Resistance, then, takes many forms. It can be political, militant, or discursive. It can take the form of physical resistance against evil or of creative reimagining of history, identity, and one's own humanity in the face of extreme trauma. It can take the form of changes in language and of consolation toward other sufferers. In all these forms, resistance is a common and necessary form of positive adaptation to social trauma.

Remembrance

> *While I was being carried in the police van to the police station, I was reminded of the words of Jesus, when he said, "Do not worry about what you will say, when they will take you before the officers and magistrates; because God himself will give you strength and wisdom to speak all that you ought to speak" [Matt 10:19-20]. Then I was also reminded of the Bible verse, "Do not fear; I am with you" [Acts 18:10].*
>
> *Vihaan*

---

38 Representatives of the independent churches in India have at times charged that the mainline churches sometimes fail to give them credence or respect.

Collective remembering, or social memory, is probably the most central coping strategy for trauma. Collective memory has a deep connection to social identity in that it highlights certain narratives that exemplify or typify trauma.[39] Remembering includes repetition of the events and creating ritual typologies and archetypes that allow social groups either to endure ongoing suffering or to create meaning out of the suffering.

Among Jews or Christians, an important way in which collective remembering takes form is in the survivors discovering their own experiences in the archetypes of the Bible. These typologies or archetypes often get resignified in the life of the community through new rituals. Survivors enact a strategy called "transtemporal" identification, in which they enact biblical archetypes in their own bodies despite being separated from the biblical characters in both geographic location and in time. What results from these transtemporal enactments is that suffering, and catastrophe actually enhance the import of biblical archetypes—survivors are living those archetypal experiences in the here and now.[40]

When Shaurya reads the narratives about Paul's persecutions in the New Testament, he indeed sees himself and his church members "trans temporally," as re-enacting those ancient archetypes. Because Shaurya experiences his own identity in this way, he pities those in the Christian West who do not have the opportunity to find this kind of transtemporal meaning in scripture. He claims that because of this, Christian faith is "more real" in India than in the West.

---

39 Chris Weedon and Glenn Jordan, "Collective Memory: Theory and Politics," *Social Semiotics* 22, no. 2 (April 2012): 143.

40 David G. Roskies, *The Literature of Destruction: Jewish Responses to Catastrophe* (Philadelphia: Jewish Publication Society, 1988), 107.

Pranav relates how his church members also embraced biblical archetypes to find meaning in suffering by seeing themselves as re-enacting—or trans temporally experiencing—the persecutions in the New Testament book of Acts. He tells how his associate pastors ask him why they are being attacked, beaten up, and threatened with physical violence. "I say to them," he reports, "'you are making a difference in people's lives through your preaching.' I remind them of the book of Acts and how the Church was persecuted because they preached the gospel."

Veer also shares this practice of re-enacting scripture trans temporally. When he staggered out to the crowd that had assembled outside to witness his beating, still dripping with blood, he proclaimed a speech to them in which he trans temporally re-enacted the speeches of Peter and Paul in Acts. In the interview, Veer repeatedly quoted Psalm 91:14-15. He knows it by heart, and he claims that he recites it every day. Veer has internalized that statement as a personal promise across time and space. In these ways, Veer is an example of how those experiencing trauma resignify the Bible and understand its meaning to be about their time and their circumstances specifically.

That said, however, even these timeless archetypes often break down. For many who suffer, the archetypes lose their power in the face of true horror and terror.[41] Pranav relates how some churches, in the aftermath of the pogroms, shrunk from fifty to fifteen members because of fear of further persecutions. Vihaan expressed great personal discouragement as well. He even considered abandoning his ministerial vocation altogether, admitting that he had struggled with theodicy in the aftermath of the suffering. How can God be just, he asks, toward those who never hear the gospel? Why are good, law-abiding people persecuted? Why are those in the cities protected while those in the villages have no protection against persecution? Despite these questions, for Vihaan the breakdown of archetypes was only

---

41 Ibid., 568.

temporary. Ultimately, in his time of prayer, he found comfort in those same biblical archetypes.

Shaurya, after his experiences, admitted that he had considered quitting his theological studies out of despair. For him, too, however, the archetypes reasserted themselves, and Shaurya ultimately found great comfort in seeing himself in Pauline archetypes of suffering. Even Veer, who expresses great boldness in the face of the physical violence he endured, admits that he feels discouraged at times.

The significant role of suffering in the Christian scriptures, and the archetypes, idioms, and linguistic signs associated with it, serve to anchor the experiences of survivors in a realm that stands above and outside history, and in this way, they offer hope. This form of collective memory has given our participants a powerful transtemporal experience of participating in the world of scripture in their very bodies.

Another element of memory that is crucial in transforming the collective memory of survivors of trauma is ritualization. David Roskies has argued that new rituals are one of the hallmarks of experiences of trauma. Whether through grief or celebration, ritual acts anchor collective memory. In this way, ritual, as a form of remembrance, serves to ground people who have been traumatized and to allow them to find meaning and hope, ultimately shaping their social identity in the process.

> *When our church in Udupi was under opposition, I invited pastors [from] all the other churches and said, "Today, it is our church being attacked, and tomorrow it will be yours; day after tomorrow it will be yours. So, we need to come together and stand together and raise our voice together." There was a very positive response from all the pastors, and as a result we started having once a month fasting prayers. Then we also started having all-night prayers from district to district and Taluk to Taluk. So, we began to gather together. There was a spirit of encouragement and unity among the Christians.*
>
> *Pranav*

Among our participants, these rituals included fasting. Here, too, biblical archetypes provide the models for these new rituals. Veer describes fasting and praying with his church every Saturday, following the models of Acts 13:2 and 14:23. Pranav relates how pastors from all over the surrounding regions gather regularly to fast. Veer also has added regular fasting to his devotional practices.

Often, in the wake of trauma, Roskies adds, survivors employ traditional rituals that they now understand in new ways, hence eliciting new ways of remembering. What changes, he argues, is not necessarily the basic practice of the ritual but the fervency and passion with which it is enacted.[42] Pranav relates how, before the persecution, his focus was on evangelism and an internal change through Christ. In the aftermath of persecution, his piety was no longer individualistic. Because of this, he recounts developing new modes of prayer in which he views prayer as actively engendering social, as well as individual, change:

> After persecution, prayer took a much more important place in my life. I have been touched by passages such as in Acts 1:14 ("They all came together and prayed"); Acts 2:1 ("They all gathered at the day of Pentecost and prayed"); Acts 3:1-2 ("On the hour of prayers, they went and prayed in the Temple" and God raised a lame man); Acts 4:30 ("The place, where they prayed, it shook"). So, I began to focus on passages like these, and I realized the great need for prayers in a Christian's life.

Not only has his piety become more communal and less individual, it also has extended beyond his own church community—"from district to district and Taluk to Taluk." Veer and Vihaan also claim that prayer, fasting, and scripture reading have become new and more urgent mandates precisely because of the experience of persecution. These are clear examples of the ways that transformed rituals and liturgies have provided positive strategies for coping with extreme trauma in the experiences of our participants.

Whether it is through re-enactment of biblical archetypes or through ritualization of ancient liturgies and practices of piety that are re-envisioned considering catastrophe, remembrance in all these cases serves to construct social identity and to provoke action and vision

---

42 Ibid., 73.

for change. When employed in these ways, remembrance becomes a positive strategy for psychic coping.

Realization

> We thank Lord Jesus for the nation of India. The truth is that Jesus loved and came for everyone in this world. He loves every one of us equally. Jesus came to give eternal life to all people. In our nation, people go here and there (to holy cities) to find peace and eternal life. But, Jesus came so that we may have hope of eternal life.
>
> Veer

A final important strategy for coping with trauma is to imagine that the traumatic events a group experiences lead to a new and positive future. Roskies has observed that realization can include re-envisioning in the way of intensifying modes of remembrance, reshaping meaning, imagining and inspiring a new future, and transforming social identity.[43] These forms of realization of a different future spark hope in a community and empower it through a stronger, more enduring social identity.

Some of our participants expressed this hope for a new future by showing great hope in their Hindu neighbors. Vihaan trusts his Hindu neighbors and sees them as victims of exploitation just as the Christians are. "Actually," he adds, "the Hindu community is not harmful and generally they are peace loving; and as it is clear, we belong to a multi-cultural and multi-religious country." In the aftermath of their own experiences of exploitation, Vihaan explains, "People feel happy if someone comes and offers to pray for them. They may not necessarily accept Jesus, but they will never oppose Christians or the message of Christ." Because of this, he reports hopefully, "those who know us will never attack us." Because of this, he has great hope for a

---

43   Ibid., 5, 107. See also Elizabeth O'Donnell Gandolfo, "Remembering the Massacre at El Mozote: A Case for the Dangerous Memory of Suffering as Christian Formation in Hope," *International Journal of Practical Theology* 17, no. 1 (2013): 74, 77; Weedon and Jordan, "Collective Memory," 144.

better future that will allow him to work closely with Hindus, as well as other peripheral social groups.

Veer is confident in a spiritually rich and fulfilling future, precisely because of the persecution he endured. "Yes," he rejoices, "my faith in the Lord Jesus Christ has increased much more after persecution. The Lord used this event to bless me and to bless my ministry. *Agey kadam barha chukey, pichey kabhi na dekhengey*! I have taken steps forward (toward Jesus) now I will never turn back!"

Veer recognizes that suffering is not easy, but he also is strengthened by knowing that Christ shares his suffering:

> *Even Jesus while he was in the garden of Gethsemane, he knew that the pain he would endure would be overwhelming. He knew how painful it would be on the cross. Jesus knew the nails that would pierce his body. But, thanks to the Lord! He also said, "Not my will but thine be done." Then the angels came and comforted him.*

All our participants express hope, boldness, confidence, and transformation through the experience of suffering. They hold no animosity toward Hindus and love their country and its traditions. They imagine a future in which they can preach with boldness and in which lives will be transformed.

Conclusion

> *I think that for Indian Christians, who go through persecution or who live in a context of opposition, persecution has become part of our identity as Christians.*
>
> Pranav

Throughout history, survivors of trauma have had to find ways to make sense of the violence. Patterns emerge among those who cope in ways that are positive for psychic and spiritual thriving and wellness as well as in ways that are destructive for such thriving. Our participants who have suffered violence in the recent Hindutva pogroms have discovered ways to cope that have resulted in spiritual thriving amid violence. Chief among them has been through resisting that violence—either actively or through discursive resistance—through remembering, by constructing new rituals and patterns and by re-enacting biblical archetypes, and through realizing a new future by creating vehicles for hope during suffering. Our participants demonstrate that these resources are effective and instrumental in a variety of social, historical, and cultural contexts.

Veer's final words call out to Christians worldwide to partner with them in this transformation:

> *First, we need prayers from the body of Christ. We have received this ministry by the grace of the Lord Jesus. We cannot serve the Lord by our own strength. We need God's wisdom and support from his body so that we may be able to together progress in his plans. We thank God that the ministry is growing and many believers from other faiths are getting added to the Church. I request everyone to pray for us. God bless you!*

Chapter 10

Religious Freedom among the Marginalized in Bangalore, India

Rebecca Samuel Shah
and
Timothy Samuel Shah

On September 6, 2017, the *Indian Express* reported that the governor of the Indian state of Jharkhand had given her approval to the "Freedom of Religion Bill, 2017," a bill that had passed through the BJP-held Jharkhand Assembly the previous month.[1] Controversial in its nature and cryptic in its name, this bill has ignited a firestorm of controversy. Among its provisions is a requirement that "whoever converts any person from one religion/religious faith to another . . . shall take prior permission for such proposed conversion from the District Magistrate concerned by applying in such form as may be prescribed by rules."

---

1 Prashant Pandey, "Jharkhand Guv Approves Freedom of Religion Bill, Land Act; BJP Welcomes Move," *Indian Express,* September 6, 2017, http://indianexpress.com/article/india/jharkhand-guv-approves-freedom-of-religion-bill-land-act-bjp-welcomes-move/.

Violation of this provision is subject to punishment of a year in prison and a fine of up to 5,000 rupees.[2]

Even more significant, the bill outright prohibits any "attempt to convert, either directly or otherwise, any person from one religion/religious faith to another by the use of force or by allurement or by any fraudulent means, nor shall any person abet any such conversion."[3] While the bill attempts to define "force" and "fraud," it does so in extremely vague generalities and entirely omits any effort to define the term "allurement."[4] Violation of this provision can be punished by imprisonment of up to three years and a fine of up to 50,000 rupees.

Finally, the bill specifically singles out minors, women, and members of the Scheduled Castes and Scheduled Tribes (i.e., those Indian citizens commonly referred to as outcastes or untouchables) as groups particularly vulnerable to the threat of forced conversion. Any attempt to convert a member of one of these groups—if the attempt entails "force," "fraud," or "allurement"—automatically increases the maximum punishment from three to four years of imprisonment and from fifty thousand to 100,000 rupees.[5]

This bill, despite posturing as a "Religious Freedom Bill," constitutes the imposition of enormous restrictions on the freedom of people of all faiths to communicate their beliefs to others. Its passage has

---

2 "[Jharkhand Freedom of Religion] Bill, 2017," text available at http://files.constantcontact.com/523942c3501/9c2fd470-ffb4-4c21-a485-9138a10a2896.pdf.

3 Ibid.

4 "'Force' shall include a show of force or threat of injury of any kind including threat of divine displeasure or social ex-communication . . . 'Fraud' shall include misrepresentation or any other fraudulent contrivance." Ibid. Under the text of the law, then, to suggest that one ought to convert to a new religion for the sake of avoiding divine displeasure is tantamount to "forced" conversion—and such force can be entirely affected merely by the verbal communication of one's beliefs about the nature of divinity and of what the divine might consider to be displeasing.

5 Ibid.

been opposed by many, most notably the Catholic Church and other Christian communities present in Jharkhand. Nonetheless, it is not without its defenders. Responding to the governor's approval of the bill, Pratul Shahdev, a spokesperson for the Hindu nationalist Bharatiya Janata Party (BJP), stated, "The anti-national forces involved in religious conversion in Jharkhand will now have to face a jail term."[6] Another member of the BJP, chief whip Radha Krishna Kishore, justified the necessity of the bill by pointing to the growth of the Christian population in Jharkhand between 2001 and 2011. Referencing this demographic change, Kishore asked, "And who are the people being converted? The poor, the Dalit,[7] and the tribal population living in interior areas."[8] Even those who oppose the bill have frequently based their objections not on the impropriety of its restrictions on religious freedom, but rather on the fact that the Jharkhand penal code already outlaws and punishes conversions that are the result of coercion or allurement, though these pre-existing codes were neither as punitive nor as vague as the new bill.[9]

The passage of this bill, even with its stringent restrictions on religious expression, is not necessarily surprising. Anti-conversion laws of a similar nature have previously been passed in the Indian states of Odisha (formerly Orissa, 1967), Madhya Pradesh (1968), Gujarat (2003), and Chhattisgarh (2006), and there have been many other attempts in other states to pass similar legislation throughout India's history.[10] Nor

---

6   Pandey, "Jhakhand Guv."

7   Dalit, which means "broken," refers to untouchables or members of the outcastes in India.

8   Prashant Pandey, "Jhakhand Passes Anti-Conversion Bill, Govt Rejects Demand for More Scrutiny," *India Express,* August 13, 2017, http://indianexpress.com/article/india/jharkhand-passes-anti-conversion-bill-govt-rejects-demand-for-more-scrutiny-4794360/.

9   Ibid.

10   Harsh Mander, "Why Jharkhand's Anti-Conversion Bill Is against Constitution and Not Necessary," *Hindustan Times,* September 12, 2017, http://www.hindustantimes.com/columns/why-jharkhand-

is it particularly surprising to see such initiatives in a world where 74 percent of the global population lives in countries with high or very high restrictions on the exercise of religious freedom.[11]

What is surprising, however, is the increasing amount of sympathy for such initiatives among prominent thinkers in Western liberal democracies. Today, there is widespread criticism of what were once widely thought of as universal principles of religious freedom. A growing number of scholars attack these principles as neo-colonial impositions of parochial, Western concepts. These scholars, who include Elizabeth Shakman Hurd, Winnifred Fallers Sullivan, Saba Mahmood, Peter Danchin, and others, are part of an emerging school of what might be termed "religious freedom skeptics." One can detect the skepticism even in the titles of their recent books—titles like *The Impossibility of Religious Freedom* or *Beyond Religious Freedom* or *Politics of Religious Freedom*.[12]

---

s-anti-conversion-bill-is-against-constitution-and-not-necessary/story-FIhGsnxuqIItvniVAoiLQO.html.

11 Pew Research Center, "Trends in Global Restrictions on Religion," June 23, 2016, http://www.pewforum.org/2016/06/23/trends-in-global-restrictions-on-religion/, accessed February 13, 2018.

12 Winnifred Fallers Sullivan, *The Impossibility of Religious Freedom* (Princeton: Princeton University Press, 2005); Elizabeth Shakman Hurd, *Beyond Religious Freedom: The New Global Politics of Religion* (Princeton: Princeton University Press, 2015); Winnifred Fallers Sullivan et al., *Politics of Religious Freedom* (Chicago: University of Chicago Press, 2015). The emerging school of religious freedom skepticism is not limited to a few books, but in fact includes a substantial and rapidly growing number of books, edited volumes, journal articles, and op-ed pieces. A few additional examples include Brent Nongbri, *Before Religion: A History of a Modern Concept* (New Haven: Yale University Press, 2012); Talal Asad, "Thinking about Religious Beliefs and Politics," in *The Cambridge Companion to Religious Studies*, ed. Robert Orsi (Cambridge: Cambridge University Press, 2012); Elizabeth Shakman Hurd and Winnifred Fallers Sullivan, eds., "Symposium: Rethinking Religious Freedom," *Journal of Law and Religion* 29, no. 3 (2014); Saba Mahmood and Peter Danchin, eds., "Contested Genealogies of Religious Freedom," special

But such religious freedom skepticism does not confine itself to ivory towers. These fashionable Western academic criticisms are increasingly aligned with—and joined by—criticisms coming from within non-Western countries that perceive religious freedom as an attempt by the West, particularly the United States, to impose Western/American culture, values, and political arrangements of secularism, religion-state separation, liberalism, and individualism on non-Western cultures—cultures in which such values and arrangements are alien, unwelcome, and unworkable.

Instead of importing allegedly universal but Western values, it is argued that cultures should develop their own local practices and arrangements for addressing religious differences and promoting religious accommodation and toleration. The aim should not be to maximize adherence to an abstract and supposedly universal principle. Rather, the aim should be to develop "local practices" and arrangements that respect the "lived" religious forms of ordinary people as well as the embeddedness of religious commitments in the numerous other identities and commitments—cultural, ethnic, political—that define them. This ethic of localism, opposed to an ethic of universalism, foreswears the neo-colonial agenda of imposing Western-inspired religious forms and norms on the world's irreducible religious diversity. Instead, it encourages people to get along and live in peace on their own terms, rather than the terms defined by NGOs and human rights experts in Washington or Geneva. In other words, the aim should not be a universal liberal utopia grounded in the Universal Declaration of Human Rights, but rather a makeshift modus vivendi that is "beyond religious freedom" insofar as it reflects local lived religion and its forms and practices.

In this chapter, we critique this whole line of reasoning by focusing on the case of India. We argue, largely based on our field work in India, that the weakest and most vulnerable members of Indian

---

issue, *South Atlantic Quarterly* 113, no. 1 (2014); and the online blog "The Politics of Religious Freedom," *The Immanent Frame,* https://tif.ssrc.org/category/exchanges/religion-world-affairs/the-politics-of-religious-freedom/.

society—especially women who are also Dalits (untouchables) and are therefore doubly marginalized—have been ill-served by the very kinds of local practices and arrangements much valorized by fashionable Western scholars today. These arrangements essentially treat religious identity in India in non-individualist terms, as a static communal reality into which one is born, and in which one must irrevocably remain. Our field work demonstrates that, on the contrary, India's doubly marginalized benefit in demonstrable ways to the extent that they can break free and break out of the cultural and religious and legal straitjackets imposed by these local, indigenous practices. Indeed, they benefit politically, economically, psychologically, and socially to the extent that they are able to exercise—despite severe and growing challenges and opposition—what we believe is the universal human right to religious freedom, as articulated, for example, in Article 18 of the Universal Declaration of Human Rights: "Everyone has the freedom of thought, conscience and religion; this right includes freedom to change his religion or belief, and freedom, either alone or in community with others and in public or private, to manifest his religion or belief in teaching, practice, worship and observance."[13] We argue, furthermore, that the doubly marginalized Dalit women with whom we have talked would benefit even more if this right were afforded much greater legal and social respect and protection than is the case in India today.

To understand the relationship between anti-conversion laws and caste in post-Independence India, such as the "Religious Freedom Bill" recently passed in Jharkhand, it is necessary to provide a brief description of India's longstanding "local" legal arrangements governing caste identity and religious identity. In the past twenty years, more and more states in India have enacted anti-conversion laws. Called "Freedom of Religion" laws, they use the same language as the recent Jharkhand bill, seeking to restrict conversions that take place because of "force," "allurement," or "threat." However, laws limiting conversion

---

13 Universal Declaration of Human Rights, http://www.un.org/en/universal-declaration-human-rights/, accessed February 13, 2018.

in India extend back to the colonial era. More than a dozen princely states enacted "anti-conversion," "apostasy," and "public safety" acts. By the time India gained independence from the British in 1947, nearly seventeen states had enacted legislation to limit and/or restrict conversion.

Among these prominent laws were the Rajgargh State Conversion Act of 1936, the Patna Freedom Act of 1942, the Sarguja State Apostasy Act of 1945, and the Udaipur State Anti-Conversion Act of 1946. The Sarguja State Apostasy Act of 1945 in today's Chhattisgarh requires that any person attempting to convert from one religion or religious tradition to another first notify the government three months in advance, with the additional provision that no conversion can take place without express approval from the authorities. The act is abundantly clear that it deals with conversions from "the Hindu religion" to "an alien religion."[14] The Rajgarh Act of 1936 and the Udaipur Anti-Conversion Act of 1946 included open threats from government officials to Christian missionaries who were converting Tribals (Adivasis) and untouchables. The local Rajput king of Rajgarh went so far as to ban the preaching of Christianity and prohibit the entry of Christian missionaries into the Kingdom of Rajgarh.[15]

Donald Eugene Smith in his classic book *India as a Secular State* describes the situation of British agent Lieutenant Colonel A. S. Meek, who in 1936 was responsible for governing the Indian city of Udaipur, one of the largest cities in the Indian state of Rajasthan, until its raja came of age. The British agent, aware that the young raja's father had strenuously sought to limit the number of conversions to Christianity, and seemingly motivated to preserve the status quo, stated that "the Udaipur State should remain in so far as customs of its population as it was on the death of its late ruler . . . all teaching designed to secure

---

14 Donald Eugene Smith, *India as a Secular State* (Princeton: Princeton University Press, 1963), 178-79.

15 Ibid., 177-78.

any change in the mode of religion being prohibited."[16] Nonetheless, the Catholic bishop of Ranchi, upset by the policy pursued by the British agent, argued that any action taken to prevent the population of Udaipur from following the religion of their choice was morally impermissible. Smith has tracked the extensive correspondence between Meek and two secretaries in the Foreign and Political Department in New Delhi, F. V. Wylie and B. J. Glancy, which emerged as a response to the Bishop's challenge.

Wylie, learning of the challenge to the British agent's policy, suggested that Udaipur enact a law like the one in Rajgarh, which severely restricted any form of conversion and banned any preaching of Christianity. Glancy nonetheless resisted this suggestion, arguing that "the kernel of this legislation is that a change of religion, in the absence of official sanction, constitutes a penal offense. We should, I think, in some quarters expose ourselves to severe criticism if we proceed along these lines." The proposal to enact official legislation along the lines of the laws in Rajgarh was dropped, but the existing restrictions on conversions were not loosened. Throughout the remainder of his tenure as agent, Meek would pass regulations banning the entry of lay preachers into the state of Udaipur and prohibiting ordained clergymen from remaining within the state any more than eight hours per quarter (or ninety-six hours with special permission). All these regulations, in turn, were superseded by the Udaipur State Anti-Conversion Act of 1946, which more closely resembled the anti-conversion law in Rajgarh and was passed about a year and a half after the young raja assumed office.

Fast forward about sixty years. In 2008, the state legislature in Rajasthan passed the "Freedom of Religion" or Rajasthan Dharma Swatantrya Bill. Jogeshwar Garg, the leader of the BJP in Rajasthan, said, "This bill was the need of the hour. Problems of fanaticism,

---

16 This quote and all information in the following paragraph regarding Meeks's correspondence come from ibid., 179-80.

terrorism, and secessionism have always arisen in areas where Hindus were reduced to a minority by large scale conversions."[17]

It is notable that the most prominent early laws restricting conversion, which were passed in Rajgarh in modern Madhya Pradesh, Patna in modern Bihar, Sarguja in modern Chhattisgarh, and Udaipur in modern Rajasthan, were enacted by Hindu rulers in princely states, which were areas not controlled by the British Empire. During British rule Hindus were ruled by ancient Hindu laws called the *Dharmasastras*. Hindus were not directly ruled by the ancient texts as such, but as interpreted by local scholars, priests, and Brahmin pundits who interpreted the rules and advised the lawyers on their application. Gradually the common law judges did away with the pundits in deciding what rules were applicable, applying them to various cases and modifying them to the prevailing customs of the locality, family, or even the caste group. Apart from variations in the application of laws introduced by caste customs, the Hindu law had to be applied differently to different members of different castes. In most cases there was one rule for the twice-born upper varnas, and another set of rules for the Sudras.[18]

Hindu Personal Law thus gave the castes significant autonomy and juridical power to sue and be sued, acquire, hold, and manage property. According to legal scholar Marc Galanter, prior to the formulation of the Indian Constitution, the courts regarded castes as "corporate units" that were not only "wholly religious" but also "autonomous and self-sufficient entities whose order proceeds from

---

17 "Religious Freedom Bill Passed in Rajasthan," *The Hindu*, March 21, 2008, http://www.thehindu.com/todays-paper/tp-national/Religious-Freedom-Bill-passed-in-Rajasthan/article15188629.ece.

18 The three upper varnas include the Brahmins, the Kshatriyas, and the Vaishyas. The Sudras include all residual people who are not members of an upper varna, the untouchables as well as converts to Hinduism.

internal organs."[19] Furthermore, court rulings as early as 1895 indicate widespread recognition of a form of caste autonomy existing among communities of non-Hindus, including Christians, Sikhs, Jains, and Muslims.[20]

In 1909, in *Mudaliar v. Masilamani*, the Madras High Court ruled in favor of a woman who was being denied her property by her brother-in-law following the death of her husband. The brother-in-law called into question the validity of the woman's marriage and therefore her claim to the deceased's inheritance claiming at the time of her marriage, she was a Christian while he was a Hindu. The defendant claimed that immediately upon her marriage, she "abandoned her cross in place of the sacred ashes" and lived alongside her husband as a dutiful Hindu wife. Justice Nair reversed the degree of the lower court and restored the property to the defendant, stating that it was not the place of the court to judge whether a marriage was valid. In support of the caste autonomy, the justice maintained that if the caste treated the defendant and her deceased husband as members of the caste, "it appears to me, an unjustifiable interference for the Courts to declare those marriages null and void."[21]

While the British government did not actively support either the privileges or the disabilities of caste groups, its policy of non-

---

19 Marc Galanter, "The Religious Aspects of Caste: A Legal View," in *South Asian Politics and Religion*, ed. Donald E. Smith and the Council on Religion and International Affairs (Princeton: Princeton University Press, 1966), 288.

20 "It has been held by this Court in *Abdul Kadir vs Dharma* I.L.R. (1895) 20 Bom. 190 that there may be a community among Mahomedans, having its own usages and forming a caste within the meaning of Bombay Reg. II of 1827. That is a distinct recognition by this Court of the existence and legal validity of the institution of caste, in some form or other, among Mahomedans." *Bai Jina v. Jina Kalia Kharwa*, decided on March 14, 1907, https://www.legalcrystal.com/case/331775/bai-jina-vs-kalia-kharwa.

21 *Muthusami Mudaliar And Anr. v. Masilamani And Ors.*, decided on December 1, 1909, https//indiakannon.org/doc/71373.

interference in social and religious matters saw it exert little effort to intervene in many cases where upper-caste Brahmins excluded outcastes on the basis that it was a "local custom" or "right." For the most part, recognized authorities within the caste could not be overruled by the civil courts. The courts would entertain neither suits in cases involving dignity or acceptance of a member or members, nor disputes within a caste, even if the dispute involved the expulsion of one person or a group. The courts tried to restrict their involvement to claims involving civil and property cases and avoided cases involving social standing or caste-related deference. Under limited circumstances, courts would be willing to punish offenses against religions or religious states, but only when these offenses were not the result of intra-caste disputes.

In one case the courts were unwilling to intervene to protect the claims of a Sudra who had taken to wearing a Brahmin's sacred thread. After a Brahmin tore the thread from the Sudra's neck, the Sudra went to court claiming that he had suffered an injury to his religious susceptibilities. The court, however, did not regard the action of one Hindu tearing a sacred thread from another Hindu as an expression of a religiously motivated offense. Since he was an outcaste, the Sudra's original decision to wear the thread was "not part of his religion vis-à-vis other Hindus," but rather as an attempt to claim a higher rank.[22] Therefore, the court refused to intervene because it decided that the injury was not to his religious state, which would have been an offense, but only to his dignity.

Scholars such as Marc Galanter and Chandra Mallampalli provide many examples of local authorities who acquiesced to demands from higher castes that the disabilities and disadvantages faced by outcastes be maintained.[23] Generally, this support was provided because these

---

22 Galanter, "The Religious Aspects of Caste," 282.

23 Ibid. See also Marc Galanter, *Law and Society in Modern India* (Delhi: Oxford University Press, 1989); Chandra Mallampalli, *Christians and Public Life in Colonial South India* (London: RoutledgeCurzon, 2004); and Chandra Mallampalli, *Race, Religion, and Law in Colonial India* (Cambridge: Cambridge University Press, 2011).

authorities recognized each caste's autonomy and authority to apply internal sanctions against those who defied their rules. People could thus be legally and legitimately "outcasted" or punished if they defied the rules designed and applied by caste authorities.

Following Indian independence, Article 341 of the Indian Constitution of 1950 envisaged a new order for the place of caste in Indian life. Article 341 gave the president the important task of identifying the "castes, races or tribes or parts of or groups within castes, races or tribes which shall for the purposes of the Constitution be deemed to be Scheduled Castes." It authorized the government to provide benefits and preferences to members of the Scheduled Castes and Scheduled Tribes—also known as outcastes or untouchables—including reserved seats in legislatures and local bodies, reserved places in government educational intuitions, and other welfare measures.[24]

Article 341 was a deliberate attempt to recognize the integrity and autonomy of all groups within Indian society. It was also a clear message to higher castes and groups that the government would no longer favor or recognize rank ordering among groups in the country. However, despite the Constitution's emphatic commitment to providing new aid for minority groups—apparent in the preamble, which seeks "to secure to all its citizens . . . equality of status and opportunity"—only Hindus were listed under the Scheduled Castes category. Non-Hindus were excluded as recipients of preferences based on purely religious classification in spite of the presence of evidence of social and economic backwardness and in spite of evidence that others regarded them as outcastes.[25]

---

24 Constitution of India, https://www.india.gov.in/my-government/constitution-india/constitution-india-full-text, accessed February 12, 2018.

25 Satish Deshpande and Geetika Bapna, "Dalits in the Muslim and Christian Communities: A Status Report on Current Social Scientific Knowledge," prepared for the National Commission for Minorities of the Government of India, 2008, http://ncm.nic.in/pdf/report%20dalit%20%20reservation.pdf.

In August 1950, a Presidential Order defining Scheduled Castes was issued, which was exceptional because it authorized the government to use communal criteria to provide compensatory discrimination to previously disadvantaged peoples. Although the Constitution sought to redress many of the wrongs that outcastes experienced because of religious discrimination, post-Independence policies such as the Presidential Order have actively affirmed the religious dimension of caste in India. As Galanter points out, religion was used not to include marginalized groups for access to better treatment but as a means of "disqualification of individuals and groups who otherwise meet the criteria, thereby inevitably discouraging conversion."[26] By including only Hindu, Jain, Sikh, and Buddhist Scheduled Castes as potential recipients of aid, the Presidential Order automatically restricts freedom of religion by placing a heavy price on conversion out of these religions to Christianity and Islam.[27] Furthermore, the order violates the constitutional command to render equal treatment for all citizens.

Even as the Presidential Order under the Indian Constitution was closing the door for Christians and Muslims to access government benefits, the Congress was instituting an inquiry into the "abuses" of religious freedom by missionaries in India. Led by Dr. M. B. Niyogi, the committee conducted interviews across North India and prepared a report entitled *Report of the Christian Missionary Activities Enquiry Committee*[28] to shed light on additional concerns about conversion, which included public order, social cohesion, and national security in the new nation. This report's scathing criticisms of missionary activities included recommendations to restrict conversions; in fact, the committee recommended prohibiting "any attempt or effort (whether successful

---

26 Marc Galanter, *Competing Equalities: Law and the Backward Classes in India* (Berkeley: University of California Press, 1984), 144.

27 In 1956, an amendment to the Presidential Order was passed to include Sikhs, and in 1990, a similar amendment was passed to include Buddhists.

28 *Report of the Christian Missionary Activities Enquiry Committee, Madhya Pradesh*, 2 vols. (Nagpur: Madhya Pradesh, 1956).

or not), directly or indirectly to penetrate into the religious conscience of persons (whether of age or underage) of another faith."[29]

Suspicions about the motivations of converts and assumptions about the gullibility of poor converts expressed by Niyogi and his fellow committee in 1956 paved the way for a slew of harsh anti-conversion legislations. In 1967-68, the states of Orissa (now Odisha) and Madhya Pradesh enacted local laws called, respectively, the Orissa Freedom of Religion Act (enacted in 1967) and the Madhya Pradesh Dharma Swatantrya Adhiniyam (enacted in 1968). In 1977, in a prominent case challenging the validity of the Orissa and Madhya Pradesh Acts, *Rev. Stainislaus v. State of Madhya Pradesh and Orissa*, the Indian Supreme Court upheld legal restrictions on conversion in Madhya Pradesh and Orissa. The discussion in the case focused on Article 25 of the Indian Constitution, which states: "Subject to public order, morality and health and to the other provisions of this Part, all persons are equally entitled to freedom of conscience and the right freely to profess, practice and propagate religion."[30]

The meaning of the term "propagate" was at the center of the Court's decision. The Court distinguished between the right to "transmit" one's religion, which it allowed, and the right to "convert" a person to a different religion, which it did not recognize.

The Court upheld the restrictions on efforts to convert as set out by the Madhya Pradesh and Orissa High Courts as constitutional because in its view, the efforts to convert themselves impinge on "freedom of conscience" and "public order." The Court reasoned that "if a person purposely undertakes the conversion of another person to his religion, as distinguished from his effort to transmit or

---

29 Smith, *India as Secular State*, 211.

30 Article 25(1) of the Constitution of India, accessible at https://indiankanoon.org/doc/86224/.

spread the tenets of his religion, that would impinge on the 'freedom of conscience' guaranteed to all the citizens of the country alike."[31]

In 2002, the state of Tamil Nadu in the south passed the Tamil Nadu Prohibition of Forcible Conversion of Religion Ordinance. (Both Madhya Pradesh and Orissa are northern states.) The law was later repealed on May 18, 2004. However, at the time it was passed it included a penalty, which was not included in the Madhya Pradesh or Orissa statutes, for those forcibly converting minors, women, or members of Scheduled Castes and Tribes. Those who sought to convert members of these groups could be subject to four years of imprisonment and a fine of 1,000 rupees, whereas conversions aimed at other groups could only be punished with three years of imprisonment or a fine of 500 rupees.[32] To track conversions, the Tamil Nadu Ordinance required members of the public to inform the district magistrate about any conversions in the district. A failure to do so would result in a year's imprisonment and/or a fine of 1,000 rupees. The ordinance included such vague terms as "allurement," "convert," "force," and "fraudulent means." The district magistrate in Tamil Nadu was empowered to launch criminal proceedings against a person or persons who "facilitated" conversions through threat, force, or fraudulent means.

In April and May 2014, India's national parliamentary elections saw landslide victories that gave the BJP an outright majority in India's lower house of Parliament, the Lok Sabha. Since that time, there have been renewed calls for a national anti-conversion bill. In March 2017, Home Minister Rajnath Singh called for a debate on an anti-conversion law, calling opponents of the law anti-democratic and anti-secular.

---

31 *Rev. Stanislaus v. State of Madhya Pradesh and Orissa*, decided January 17, 1977, https://indiankanoon.org/doc/1308071/.

32 "Tamil Nadu Prohibition of Forcible Conversion of Religion Act, 2002," text available at http://www.lawsofindia.org/pdf/tamil_nadu/2002/2002TN56.pdf.

Interestingly, the BJP's push for a national anti-conversion law came a few days after the Indian Supreme Court ruled that anyone who reconverted to Hinduism whose parents, grandparents, or great-grandparents had converted to Christianity could return to the "fold of the community and regain his membership (and therefore benefits) that were available to members of Scheduled Castes."[33] These benefits include grants for housing, education, or vehicles, as well as reserved seats in government colleges and legislative bodies. This ruling came as the result of a petition from a Mr. Manu, whose great grandfather had converted to Christianity but who at the age of twenty-three had abandoned his Christian faith and adopted Hinduism. Claiming a Hindu faith, Manu applied and received an official outcaste certificate, which gave him eligibility to fill affirmative action style quotas for Scheduled Castes for government jobs. His employer, on discovering his Christian heritage, nonetheless dismissed him. Manu brought his case to court.

To support their opinion, the judges during the case quoted from the 1975 case *G. M. Arumugam v. S. Rajagopal*: "In our opinion, when a person is converted to Christianity or some other religion the original caste remains under eclipse and as soon as during his/her lifetime the person is reconverted to the original religion the eclipse disappears and the caste automatically revives."[34] The Court went on to state, "Unless the practice of the caste makes it necessary, no expiatory rites need be performed [for his reconversion] and, ordinarily, he regains his caste unless the community does not accept him. In fact, it may not be accurate to say that he regains his caste; it may be more accurate to say that he never lost his caste in the first instance when he embraced another religion."[35]

It is no exaggeration to say that such arrangements—however reflective they are of indigenous values, cultural autonomy, and the

---

33   *K. P. Manu, Malabar Cements Ltd v. Chairman, Scrutiny Committee*, decided February 26, 2015, https://indiankanoon.org/doc/98912765/.

34   See *K. P. Manu v. Chairman*, quoting *G. M. Arumugam v. S. Rajgopal & Others*, decided December 19, 1975.

35   *K. P. Manu v. Chairman*.

integrity of "local" arrangements and practices—are on their face in flagrant conflict with the principle essential to the rule of law in a constitutional republic, namely, that the law be isonomic. In any constitutional republic, the law must render to all citizens equal treatment and equal rights, regardless of their religious identity, their social status, or their caste status. The only justification for departures from the isonomic principle, according to both international standards and India's own Constitution, would be an unavoidable necessity to protect "public order" or the rights and liberties that animate and undergird the constitutional order itself.

If the local arrangements governing conversion in India banned all conversion outright on the belief that all forms of religious switching, in any direction, were inherently destabilizing and threatening to public order, it might be at least plausible (if not in the end justifiable) to think that genuine public order considerations were in play.

But these arrangements, both in their conceptualization and in their application, do not discourage conversions across the board but only discourage conversion in one direction: from Hinduism to either Christianity or Islam. This is the case even though it could plausibly be argued that conversions from, say, Islam to Hinduism in Muslim-majority areas of India (Kashmir or West Bengal) threaten social stability and public order in those areas, areas already characterized by social and political volatility. But no such contextual changes in practice are in place in India, where conversion away from Hinduism is always disparaged, regardless of circumstance. It is manifestly true that no impartial, reasonable, or plausible public order consideration could justify the differences that are, as it were, "baked into" India's local arrangements regarding caste and religion.

If these arrangements cannot be justified on the grounds of public order considerations, the only remaining justification must be rooted in virtue of some constitutional principle. And indeed, arguments justifying differences in treatment on constitutional principles are in fact very old and have been made in many ways by influential figures in India, including Mohandas Gandhi himself.

The argument that attempts to justify restricting the conversion of lower castes based on constitutionally protected rights and liberties has two basic parts. One part is that the Dalits (or the Sudra, Outcastes, Harijans, or Tribals) do not have the mental capacity, educational attainment, and in short, the basic capability and agency to make an informed and responsible choice in religious matters in the first place. Any "choice" made by a member of one of these groups to convert would not and could not, ipso facto, be a genuine choice. Precisely to shield them from making a false choice, a paternalistic state must in effect treat them as wards of the state and set up a system of laws, incentives, and even penalties to maintain the status quo with respect to their religious identity and religious community. Precisely to protect the "freedom" that is the hallmark of a constitutional republic, one must make religious conversion difficult if not effectively impossible. According to this argument, Dalits and Tribal do not have the minimum requisite agency to exercise religious freedom and the freedom to change one's religion.

The other part of the argument is that Dalit and Tribal conversion, where it does occur, robs Dalits and Tribal of whatever little agency they might have had prior to their conversion. Since, it is supposed, they do not have the capacity to convert from genuine choice, any conversion that does occur must happen through forms of manipulation, fraud, coercion, and inducement that make those who convert subject to some group or individual that is exercising agency on their behalf. In other words, as the argument goes, any conversion that occurs among Dalits or Tribal is not an individual act on the part of the one who converts but a transitive process in which some other agent acts upon someone else to induce them to convert. In this transitive process, the one who converts becomes a pawn—an object—of a conversionary group, whatever its agenda might be.

The main burden of the remainder of this chapter is to demonstrate that these two arguments are badly flawed. We see two main problems with them.

First, the overwhelming finding from our research, from hundreds of in-depth interviews of Dalit women, is that these human beings—doubly marginalized as they are—undoubtedly have all the requisite capacities to be informed and effective agents in religious matters.

Over the past eight years, we have interviewed hundreds of Dalit[36] women who were micro-credit clients. With generous support from the Religion and Innovation in Human Affairs Program at Boston University and the John Templeton Foundation, we were privileged to interview more than three hundred Dalit women entrepreneurs over three years in one of Bangalore's most notorious slums. In total we conducted more than one thousand in-person surveys with women from Hindu, Muslim, mainline Protestant, and Catholic backgrounds. During the first of three waves of interviews we unexpectedly discovered that 23 percent of our sample had identified themselves as "converts." These women were all converts from Hinduism and belonged to independent, Pentecostal churches. This fortuitous result provided the opportunity to examine the role of conversion to this vibrant and encompassing form of Christianity.[37]

---

36 I use the term "Dalit," which means "broken," to refer to outcastes or untouchables.

37 To examine the results of this research in more detail, see Rebecca Samuel Shah, "Religion and Economic Empowerment among the Enterprising Poor," *The Review of Faith and International Affairs* 11, no. 4 (2013): 41-45; Rebecca Samuel Shah and Timothy Samuel Shah, "Pentecost amid Pujas: Charismatic Christianity and Dalit Women in Twenty-First-Century India," in *Global Pentecostalism in the 21st Century*, ed. Peter L. Berger and Robert W. Hefner (Bloomington: Indiana University Press, 2013), 194-219; Rebecca Samuel Shah and Timothy Samuel Shah, "How Evangelicalism—Including Pentecostalism—Helps the Poor: The Role of Spiritual Capital," in *The Hidden Form of Capital: Spiritual Influences in Societal Progress*, ed. Peter L. Berger and Gordon Redding (London: Anthem, 2011), 61-90; Rebecca Samuel Shah, "Religious Innovation and Economic Empowerment in India: An Empirical Exploration," in *Religion and Innovation: Antagonists or Partners?* ed. Donald A. Yerxa (London: Bloomsbury Academic, 2016), 176-93; and Rebecca Samuel Shah, "Christianity among the Marginalized: Empowering Poor Women in India." in *Christianity and Freedom*, vol. 2, *Contemporary Perspectives*, ed. Allen

Baglur slum is situated beneath a busy elevated expressway that whisks passengers from the city's new international airport to the designer-decorated offices of Infosys or Microsoft. Baglur bears no resemblance to the high-end apartment complexes that surround the slum on all four sides. It is a maze of litter-strewn lanes, open sewers, and numerous cramped huts. After dusk, few auto-rickshaws or taxi drivers are willing to drive beyond the railway lines that divide respectable neighborhoods from Baglur and its surrounding smaller slums. At first glance, Baglur looks like your typical slum. It is crowded and filthy; it is located near a busy highway; the neighborhood is dangerous and most of the "respectable" buildings like schools and offices are situated on the other side of the railway tracks.

But Baglur is a bit different. Dotted all over the slum are numerous prayer rooms and small independent churches. These independent churches—reminiscent of "storefront" churches in urban America—are self-supporting micro-communities, separate from all mainstream denominations. They unabashedly proclaim the full use and manifestation of the Pentecostal gifts of the Spirit. They are situated right in the middle of slum areas that are home largely to Dalits and poor members of the lower castes. Most of the congregants are Dalit converts and the Pentecostal pastors are also Dalits. It is not unusual for members to be sole supporters of the work of the independent church. Most of the independent "storefront" churches in Baglur are supported by the members' tithes and donations. Many the churches meet in rented storefronts in the slum and on the main road, while others have raised enough capital from their members and from other local middle-class churches to build their own structures. The converts in our study were all members of these "storefront" churches. Many of them were co-equal leaders in the church and organized weekly Bible Study and fasting and prayer meetings in their homes.

D. Hertzke and Timothy Samuel Shah (New York: Cambridge University Press, 2016), 107-32. The data cited in this chapter are also found in more detail in an unpublished 2013 report, "Tithing and Thrift Among the Enterprising Poor in India," in the author's possession.

We have spent hundreds of hours talking with Dalit women from different faiths. Most of them are the sole breadwinners for their families. Most often women apply for and get a business loan to provide income for their families. In some cases, the women take loans for their husbands' taxi service or small business and work as domestic servants to pay back the loan on their husband's behalf. According to the National Commission for Minorities Report of 2008, Dalit Muslims are unquestionably the worst off in terms of all the key social and economic indicators compared to Dalits in Hindu, Sikh, and Christian communities. In 2008, 47 percent of Dalit Muslims were below the poverty line in urban areas.[38]

One of the women interviewed is Shanu Munisa. Shanu and her husband Imtiaz are Muslim Dalits (outcastes) who live in Razak Palaya, a predominantly Muslim village and one of the poorest communities in north Bangalore. After talking about her work and business interests, sitting in their half-finished hut, Shanu was asked, "Where do you think God is?" Looking up from the floor, Shanu replied, "He is here," placing her hand on her chest. How did she know that God was with her? Shanu pointed outside, beyond the debris and toward a small shrine, or a *darga* as it is called, which was situated about one hundred feet away from the village gate. "When I am sad, or when I worry about food, my home, or my children, I go to the *darga* to talk to God and I bring home a *gulab* [rose]. I know God is with me because just as the fragrance of the rose fills my hut, I can feel God's presence with me."[39]

Shanu, like many other Dalit Muslim women in Razakpalaya, is a successful small business owner. She applied for and qualified for a

---

38 Satish Deshpande, *Dalits in the Muslim and Christian Communities: A Status Report on Current Social Scientific Knowledge*, prepared for the National Commission for Minorities, Government of India, 2008, http://ncm.nic.in/pdf/report%20dalit%20%20reservation.pdf, accessed February 8, 2018.

39 An in-person interview conducted by Rebecca Samuel Shah in a predominantly Dalit Muslim village called Razakpalaya in Karnataka, India. Field notes were recorded in English in a journal (August 12, 2014).

small business loan. Along with Imtiaz and her younger brother Aslam, they run a small but successful silkworm business. They raise the cocoons and then collect the silk threads, which are sold to the weavers in India temple towns such as Kanchivaram to weave Indian silk. It is clear to me that women like Shanu are fully capable of exercising agency. They are fully capable of making choices and taking decisions about their faith, their economic wellbeing, and the wellbeing of their family. They make such all-important decisions—often life-or-death decisions—almost every day of their lives. So much for the argument against conversion because of Dalits' and Adivasis' lack of agency.

The other overwhelming finding from this study is that the Dalit women who were interviewed who convert have not become objects or pawns of someone else—that is, they are not deprived of agency. On the contrary, their agency, dignity, and all-around empowerment are demonstrably enhanced in ways that are radically and completely inconsistent with the allegation that converts become dupes or pawns of some conversionary group or agenda external to themselves.

In their paper *The Economic Lives of the Poor* (2006), MIT economists Abhijit V. Banerjee and Esther Duflo conducted a study of the consumption and income generation patterns of the poor—those living on less than $1 a day—in thirteen countries. The researchers discovered that the poor in various countries did not utilize all their available resources to improve their caloric intake or their health. For the average poor household, spending on food accounted for between 56 and 74 percent of their total income in urban households and between 56 and 78 percent in rural households. In India, for example, an average 5 percent of the poor person's income went toward the purchase of non-food items or "temptation goods," including alcohol and tobacco, and 10 percent of the median family income went toward spending on festivals and family events.[40]

---

40 Abhijit V. Banerjee and Esther Duflo, "The Economic Lives of the Poor," *SSRN Electronic Journal*, 2006, https://economics.mit.edu/files/530, accessed February 13, 2018.

For many of the poor clients in our sample in Bangalore, spending 20 to 30 percent of their monthly income on "temptation goods" can significantly reduce their ability to save and invest in durable goods and assets and that yield long-term benefits such as a house, a refrigerator, or a good-quality English-medium education for their children in a private school. Among women who identify themselves as recent converts to Christianity, we see the lowest levels of spending on temptation goods. As we see in table 10.1, 30 percent of converts spent more than 500 rupees a month on temptation goods compared to 60 percent of Hindu women, 70 percent of Muslim women, and more than 50 percent of Roman Catholic women. It is worth noting that there is little variation in the level of income of women from various religious traditions. The average income for women in 2013 ranged between 7,500 and 10,000 rupees a month. Data from the three tables for monthly spending on temptation goods for the three years that we interviewed women reveal that converts maintained a uniquely restrained pattern of spending on temptation and non-essential items over three years.

Table 10.1. Percentage of women and their monthly spending in rupees on temptation goods in rupees *(paan,* betel leaves, lottery tickets, chips, biscuits, chocolates, tea/coffee, intoxicants, cigarettes)

2013

	Less than 100	100-199	200-299	300-399	400-499	500 and above
Hindu	2	8	11	16	2	61
Muslim	0	3	12	14	0	71
Catholic	0	6	18	16	2	58
Mainline Protestant	0	8	17	0	0	75
Convert	0	27	17	26	0	30

Source: Unpublished India data collected for the John Templeton Foundation-funded Tithing and Thrift Among the Enterprising Poor Project, 2011, 2012, 2013.

A household that wishes to purchase a television, washing machine, refrigerator, or any other durable asset often must purchase the goods in installments or borrow money to purchase them outright (table 10.2). Since 2000, the Indian market has been flooded with consumer durables that are designed for low-income families. Godrej, an Indian manufacturer, designed a refrigerator for 12,000 rupees ($200) to target aspiring consumers with lower incomes.

Table 10.2. Percentage of women who owned a television, washing machine, or refrigerator in 2013

	Television with Cable Connection	Washing Machine	Refrigerator
Hindus	90	56	50
Muslims	83	41	40
Catholics	92	51	45
Protestants	91	50	33
Convert	**89**	**64**	**61**

Source: Unpublished India data.

A refrigerator and a washing machine can be regarded as more beneficial investments for a family than a television. Watching television is a good leisure activity but being able to provide a family with fresh food and clean clothes is significantly better for the health and welfare of the family. A television, washing machine, and refrigerator all cost around 12,000 to 15,000 rupees. While television ownership is prevalent among women in all religious traditions, we see converts to Christianity more likely to invest in washing machines (64 percent) and refrigerators (61 percent).

The demand for and the cost of labor are both rising in Bangalore as they are all over urban India. Many of the women we interviewed worked two or three jobs as maids in the luxury apartments that surround the slum. A maid can earn anywhere between 1,000 to 3,000 rupees a month for doing four hours of work for one family. We found that nearly 60 percent of converts discussed their salary with their employers (table 10.3). While such discussions and negotiations did not always yield the desired results, which were additional hours or better wages, the converts were sufficiently self-confident and empowered to make the attempt in the first place, despite their gender, income level, and low-caste status.

Table 10.3. Percentage of women who discussed their salary with their employer

	Hindus	Muslims	Catholics	Mainline Protestants	Converts
Percentage of women who discussed salary with employer	33	22	33	9	59

Source: Unpublished India data.

Poverty can be a closed system, yet access to religious networks and communities may open a door out of the closed world of domestic violence. The Indian National Family Health Survey (NFHS), one of the largest surveys of women and children in the country, reported that only one out of four women surveyed who had been a victim of domestic violence told someone and sought outside help. The largest background differentials of those seeking are by religion. In India overall, 32 percent of Christian women are likely to seek outside help, compared to 24 percent of Hindu women and 22 percent of

Muslim women.[41] Table 10.4 provides the results of our survey on this pivotal dimension.

Table 10.4. Percentage of women who ever experienced domestic violence who sought help

	Hindus	Muslims	Catholics	Mainline Protestants	Pentecostal Convert
Told No One	90	100	73	75	**43**
Told Family Member (s)	7	0	8	0	**0**
Told Pastor/ Pastoral Team	3	0	0	25	**57**
Told Priest/ Parish Priest (Roman Catholic)	0	0	19	0	**0**
Told Priest at Temple (Hindu)	0	0	0	0	**0**
Told Imam	0	0	0	0	**0**

Source: Shah, "Christianity Among the Marginalized," 125.

The notable finding here is the dramatic difference in agency of the Pentecostal converts, who were much more likely to act (telling a pastor) when faced with domestic abuse. Of the converts to Pentecostal Christianity in the study who ever experienced domestic violence, 57 percent reported their abuse to a pastor or a member of a pastoral team. None of the Muslim women in the sample who experienced

---

41 For more information, see table 16.17 in *The National Family Health Survey* (NFHS-4), 2015-16, International Institute for Population Sciences Deonar, Mumbai 400 088, http://rchiips.org/nfhs/, accessed February 13, 2018.

domestic violence ever talked to anyone, even a family member, about their abuse.

Strikingly, converts were more likely to tell their pastor about instances of domestic violence than members of their own family. The impact of religious leaders (who are men) may have an empowering impact on women who experience domestic violence because the men who victimize them are more likely to listen to other men than to women counselors or social workers. In the sample area, male pastors from the local Pentecostal churches regularly visited the homes of converts to offer prayer and counseling, and these regular visits may "shame" some abusive husbands into curbing their violent behavior.

Religious communities and networks could assist women in dealing with violent and dangerous husbands. The benefits of being involved in religious networks and communities go beyond the opportunity to form meaningful social relationships with others—as significant and important as these relationships may be. Being involved in religious networks and communities gives people a sense of belonging to a wider religious group in which they are embedded. Women who face violence and domestic abuse may be more likely to share their problems with a community of people they trust and with whom they feel connected on a deep level. These communities may include male leaders or members who could assist the abused women by counseling the abusive husband.

The upshot of all of this is that the Dalit women we have studied are, first, fully capable of understanding and exercising religious freedom—a right whose character and value they are fully capable of appreciating and putting into practice in their own lives. Despite the ongoing and now growing challenges to that right, Dalit women who become Pentecostals experience dramatic gains in dignity, agency, and sense of equality when they exercise a core part of religious freedom and choose to convert from one faith to another. These gains are so significant and so multidimensional that they radically call into question the objections to the right to religious conversion currently being propagated by both Western scholars and the purveyors of Hindutva ideology in India.

"The value of a man was reduced to his immediate identity and nearest possibility. To a vote. To a number. To a thing. Never was a man treated as a mind."

These words were found in a suicide note on January 17, 2017, when Rohith Vemula, a 26-year-old Dalit PhD student of Sociology at Hyderabad Central University, took his life. In August 2016, Rohith, along with five other Dalit graduate students, were suspended from the university for allegedly attacking a university official during a protest. Rohith's words illustrate the ways in which Indian society and law continue to perpetuate a profoundly imprisoning and oppressive discourse about Dalits. Anti-conversion legislation reduces converts to victims and to objects—it treats them as hapless things rather than minds. It perpetuates a long-standing inclination of those in authority—whether they be the rulers of princely states like Udaipur or Indian Supreme Court justices—to view converts, particularly those from the so-called weaker sections of Indian society, as passive dupes who need to be saved from those who would mislead and take advantage of them. Most of the recent anti-conversion legislation singles out Scheduled Castes and Tribes and women for extra protection from people who may convert them.

But as the stories of Dalit women Christian converts make clear, the right to religious freedom is not a Western, neo-colonial plot. Its nature and its value lie precisely in the demonstrable ways in which it safeguards and enhances the agency and dignity of vulnerable human beings, such as poor Dalit women, who would otherwise be at the mercy of highly oppressive local practices, cultures, laws, and political systems. These human beings do indeed possess authentic agency and authentic dignity. They are not just things. They are minds, and they have a right to make their own religious commitments.

Chapter 11

The Burned Church
Christians and Pluralism in India
Paul S. Rowe

June 2015: As I walked through the charred remains of Saint Sebastian's Church in the Dilshad Garden neighborhood of Delhi, India, I could not help but think of the charred remains of churches attacked in other parts of the world in anonymous incidents of sectarian violence. Just less than two years previously, in August 2013, Christian churches had become collateral damage in a conflict between the Egyptian government and the Islamist Muslim Brotherhood in a spasm of violence.[1] Islamists have long misidentified Christians as a sort of fifth column of Western interests in Arab society. Christian institutions make soft targets that reveal the impotence of the Egyptian regime. By attacking a church, radical religious nationalists targeted the liberal tolerance of the regime and challenged its ability to protect religious minorities. They were also attempting to force state authorities to

---

1 Martin Chulov, "Egypt's Coptic Christians Report Fresh Attacks on Churches," *The Guardian* August 15, 2013, https://www.theguardian.com/world/2013/aug/15/egypt-coptic-christians-attacks-churches, accessed February 17, 2017.

choose between a single religious vision for the country and a form of secularism that allows many religions to partner with the state. Churches in other faith settings are therefore important bellwethers of the overall freedom for religious belief and practice under the state.

But this was India: an established democratic state with constitutionally enshrined religious freedom and a tradition of secularism. Nevertheless, Indian authorities had apparently attempted to limit the importance of this burned-out church. Its adherents were told that an electrical short circuit had sparked and led to a conflagration. No crowd had attacked the church. Its basic structure remained, though the inside had been destroyed. A neighboring Orthodox church and Hindu temple had not been affected by the fire. As our group departed the burned-out church, I noticed that the police had set up a checkpoint on the other side of the road. I turned to a colleague and remarked that the police must be there to prevent future short circuits.

Does a burned church stand as an indicator of the future of religious freedom in India? Today, India, like many other countries around the world, is facing a crisis in defining the essential characteristics of religion's role in politics. Will India continue to embrace its constitutionally enshrined secularism, or will it provide some sort of special place to religion in Indian public life? The way that Indians answer this question will set the stage on which interreligious relations play out. For Indian Christians, a small minority population in a country of hundreds of millions of Hindus and Muslims (not to mention other minority groups), this stage will be extremely important to their participation in Indian public life. Indian secularism, or public religion, will either embrace a multitude of religious perspectives in a system of pluralism, or it will seek to enshrine a religious viewpoint as the dominant one and force all others to adapt. Tragically, limitations on the free practice of religion also limit the ability of people of faith to commit to the common good through civil activism. In other words, a pluralist form of civil society provides opportunities for all religious groups, both those of the majority and the minorities, to contribute via socially concerned agencies.

In 2014, Indians elected the Hindu nationalist Bharatiya Janata Party (BJP) to its first majority government. Rooted in the ideology of Hindutva, the BJP presents itself as a modern party that seeks to preserve India's Hindu identity. Its defense of the Hindu identity threatens to redraw Indian secularism in a way that limits the participation of other religious groups. What is more, the BJP's constituency engages in flagrant vigilantism and intimidation of religious minorities to discipline them as one would an unruly child. What is the future of religious freedom and activism in India under such a government?

In this chapter, I seek to present a defense of Christian participation in governance through the lens of social movement theory. I am interested in the way in which pluralist forms of interest representation strengthen religious civil society in democratic and liberal environments. Pluralist interest representation should not be confused with a postmodern, pluralist form of secularism; rather, it refers to the participation of various groups and their competition for influence on an equal footing under a neutral administration. Pluralism is challenged by regimes that seek to monopolize interests under government control in a form known as corporatism. When the government seeks to embrace a religious group or form, it restricts pluralism and instead embarks upon a form of corporatist interest representation that defines the nation as a singular religious community. Under a religious nationalist movement, pluralism may therefore be threatened. This is the contemporary crisis that Indian Christians face today.

Indian Secularism under Threat

The series of fires and attacks on church buildings in the city of Delhi that took place in early 2015 raised increasing concerns among Indian Christians and others about the status of the Christian minority in India. On January 3, vandals broke into the Church of the Resurrection in Rohini and burned the Christmas crèche. On January 14, three vandals broke the glass of a church in Vikaspuri. On February 2, unidentified thieves broke into St. Alphonsa's Church in Vasant Kunj and stole the communion chalice.² Falling on the heels of the victory of the Hindu nationalist Bharatiya Janata Party in federal and state elections in 2014, the attacks sent a chill throughout the Christian minority of India. Was this a sign that religious tolerance was under threat? During his visit in late January, US President Barack Obama delivered a speech on Indian Independence Day that drew attention to the need to preserve tolerance of multiple religious traditions in the world's largest democracy. He stated, "India will succeed so long as it is not splintered along the lines of religious faith—so long as it's not splintered along any lines—and is unified as one nation."³

Unity in diversity is a slogan of US politics, but any attempt to unify a nation under one vision must deal with reality: nations are diverse environments in which people embrace many ideas, faiths, and ways of life. On the surface, India is a country with a clearly defined Hindu majority: the official Census of India reported in 2011 that just under 80 percent of the population self-identified as Hindus, whereas Muslims accounted for 14.2 percent, Christians for 2.3 percent, and Sikhs for 1.7 percent.⁴

Hindu nationalists have traditionally seen the relative homogeneity of the Indian population as its most significant identifying feature. Hindutva (meaning "Hindu-ness") was originally articulated by V. D. Savarkar in his 1928 book of the same name. Savarkar's nationalism sought to unify South Asians through an argument about indigeneity. Hindutva was premised on the assertion that Hindu culture was an essential characteristic of the Indian nation. It demanded the defense

---

2 Kunal Anand, "Yet Another Church Attack Adds to the List of Increasing Violence Against Christianity" *India Times*, March 23, 2015, http://www.indiatimes.com/news/india/delhi-saw-5-attacks-on-christian-institutions-in-the-last-3-months-230230.html, accessed February 17, 2017.

3 Barack Obama, "Remarks by President Obama in Address to the People of India," January 27, 2015, https://www.whitehouse.gov/the-press-office/2015/01/27/remarks-president-obama-address-people-india.

4 Census 2011, http://www.censusindia.gov.in/2011census/Religion_PCA.html, accessed February 17, 2017.

of Indian national pride and held that Indian institutions, including its Constitution, should preserve Hindu national traditions. Savarkar argued that India should be a Hindu state—a Hindu *rashtra*.

Savarkar's ideology was taken up by the Rashtriya Swayamsevak Sangh (RSS), established by K. P. Hedgewar in 1925 and led by M. S. Golwalkar from 1940 to 1973. The RSS was a patriotic youth organization that promoted martial virtues, Hindu devotion, and community service to the Hindu homeland. The RSS became the leading force of a wide variety of Hindu nationalist movements known as the *Sangh Parivar* (family of organizations). For a time, the RSS was officially banned when one of its cadres was held responsible for the assassination of Mahatma Gandhi. But the Hindutva movement remained an important force in the Indian democratic opposition throughout the 1950s to the 1970s. By the 1980s, Hindutva rose to challenge the dominant liberal form of nationalism championed by the Indian National Congress. By the 1980s, the breakdown of the liberal national consensus benefited subnational movements among the Sikhs, Tamils, and others. It also led to the rise of the BJP as the political party of the Hindutva movement. In 1998, the BJP was appointed to lead its first coalition government, which was returned to power in 1999. After losing the 2004 elections, the BJP formed the opposition until its dramatic majority government win in 2014.

While the *Sangh Parivar* tended to be both nationalist and protectionist in its ideological outlook, the BJP has embraced neo-liberal reforms while emphasizing a more militaristic foreign policy and criticizing accommodations made to India's minority religious groups, Muslims and Christians. Hindutva under the BJP has sought to promote a "unity through uniformity" that would strengthen the national identity and thereby the military and economic prowess of the Indian (Hindu) nation.[5] The party gained popularity in the 1980s amid

---

5 Achin Vanaik, "Making India Strong: The BJP-Led Government's Foreign Policy Perspectives," in *Hindu Nationalism and Governance*, ed. John McGuire and Ian Copland (New Delhi: Oxford University Press, 2007), 380.

several controversies. Even prior to the rise of the BJP, the Hindutva movement had actively supported state legislation to control conversion in the form of "religious freedom" laws that required converts to go through onerous official proofs that changes of religion did not come as the result of coercion. In the 1980s, the celebrated Shah Bano case, in which the Indian courts upheld a separate personal status law that was viewed to unfairly punish Muslim women, provided an opportunity for the BJP to take up the cause of a Uniform Civil Code, promised but never delivered under the Indian Constitution. In the early 1990s, the BJP targeted a mosque that dated back to the Mughal period (the Babri Masjid) in the city of Ayodhya allegedly constructed over a Hindu shrine that marked the birthplace of the Hindu god Ram. While BJP party leaders railed against the perceived insult the mosque presented to Hindu heritage, elements within the *Sangh Parivar* staged an attack on the mosque that led to its destruction on December 6, 1992. Elements within the movement have also engaged in direct attacks against minority populations, most notably during the Gujarat riots of February and March 2002. These two months of violence followed an incident in which a train filled with Hindu pilgrims caught fire near the Godhra station, killing fifty-nine people. Many Hindutva activists blamed the fire on the local Muslim community. Attacks on Muslims cultivated defensive retaliation, leading to more than one thousand deaths, most of the victims from a Muslim background.

Despite the *Sangh Parivar*'s institutional diversity, it does not shy away from defining the Indian nation in a monistic way. Celebration of the Hindu way of life is coupled with explicitly anti-Muslim, anti-Christian, and anti-Western rhetoric. Martha Nussbaum writes that

> the ideas that India was always a Hindu nation, that this Hindu identity encompassed all India's diverse elements with considerable coherence from an early date, and that this identity is linked with glorious achievements, power, and insight—these ideas are of profound importance to the politics of Hindutva today. Equally important is the idea that Muslims have been the primary sources of disruption

and trouble in India from at least the eleventh century CE, bringing violence and separatism where before there were unity and peace.[6]

The putative unity of Indian Hindutva denies the legitimacy of liberal pluralism on multiple levels. It demands a uniformity of Indian cultural and religious traditions to enshrine the dominance of a Hinduism defined by the movement. This Hinduism tends to be a northern-Indian Vaishnavite form that venerates the god Ram and celebrates his martial qualities—that ideally embody the Indian state.[7] It questions the desirability of Indian legal pluralism as represented by personal status law. It seeks to impose limits on the free choice of Indians in matters of religion through anti-conversion legislation. Through vigilantism and attacks on sacred sites, it seeks to intimidate minority religious groups and perspectives and to deny the legitimacy of other narratives of Indian heritage.

The long-term impact of religious nationalism on India's conception of secularism remains to be seen. India's Constitution has committed the state to secularism under the forty-second amendment. Nevertheless, constitutional secularism has never been attached to a full separation of church and state as much as position of state neutrality on issues of religion. It is also paradoxically combined with a constitutional commitment to interfere in religious issues such as caste (both banned and subject to government reservations) and personal status law. Ran Hirschl points out that secularism is thus combined with a selective accommodation of religion in the Indian case.[8] Ashis Nandy argues that the content of Indian secularism, championed by even the Hindu nationalists, "comes as a part of a larger package consisting of a set of

---

6 Martha Nussbaum, *The Clash Within: Democracy, Religious Violence, and India's Future* (Cambridge, MA: Belknap Press of Harvard University Press, 2007), 213.

7 Thomas Blom Hansen, *The Saffron Wave: Democracy and Hindu Nationalism in Modern India* (Princeton: Princeton University Press, 1999), 175-77.

8 Ran Hirschl, *Constitutional Theocracy* (Cambridge, MA: Harvard University Press, 2010), 30.

standardized ideological products and social processes—development, mega science, and national security being some of the most prominent among them."⁹

Hindutva simultaneously criticizes Western rationality all the while embracing the developmental alternatives presented by Western modernization, to justify intimidation and even violence, paradoxically in the name of both Hindu *dharma* and secularism. Though religion in the form of Hindu culture is central to the definition of India, the political theology of Hindutva insists on Hinduism as an organizing principle rather than a devotional faith. In Nandy's words, "Urban, Westernized, middle-class, Brahmanic, Hindu nationalists and Hindu modernists often flaunt Gandhi's tolerance as an indicator of Hindu catholicity but contemptuously reject that part of his ideology which insisted that religious tolerance, to be tolerance, must impute to other faiths the same spirit of tolerance."¹⁰ Stanley Tambiah points out that in spite of the Western rationalist form of Hindutva, "RSS literature berates sections of the 'de-Hinduized intelligentsia' who are influenced by Western education and culture."¹¹ In India, Western education of this sort would commonly be provided by Christian institutions, and fairly or unfairly, Christian groups would be associated with Western culture. Such a form of secularism provides the bedrock upon which bids to enshrine a dominant religious perspective may grow, and bids to maintain the autonomy of other religious traditions may easily come under strain.

Diversity and Pluralism

The unity through uniformity championed by the Hindutva movement does not recognize the dramatic diversity of Indian society. Below

---

9 Ashis Nandy, "The Politics of Secularism and the Recovery of Religious Tolerance," in *Secularism and Its Critics*, ed. Rajeev Bhargava (Delhi: Oxford University Press, 1998), 333.

10 Ibid., 344.

11 Stanley J. Tambiah, "The Crisis of Secularism in India," in *Secularism and Its Critics*, ed. Rajeev Bhargava (Delhi: Oxford University Press, 1998), 435.

the surface lies an extreme diversity of beliefs, social movements, organizations, and practices, even within the Hindu mainstream. Indian faiths include ascetics and Epicureans, pacifists and martial arts enthusiasts, meat eaters and vegetarians. Hundreds of distinctive ethnic, cultural, and caste groups subsist within the majority and minority religious groups. Small local organizations and national movements represent some of this diversity by providing social outlets, educational opportunities, and services of all kinds to citizens. They may also contribute more directly to the politics of the nation by representing the key interests of society. Ironically, it is this very diversity of forms and interests that contributes to the unity of the Indian state. While various groups may have profound disagreements about core values, or seek very different ends, they have a shared interest in maintaining the freedom that contributes to their success. According to Amartya Sen, it is in fact these very disagreements that have enriched Indian society since its earliest history, for "the form as well as the interpretation and understanding of secularism in India can be linked to the history of the acceptance of heterodoxy."[12] Pluralist democrats in secular India survive by supporting the very society that provides them with the freedom to live and breathe. Any attempt to limit those freedoms, even in the effort of achieving a greater unity of purpose, will only serve to undermine the very system that grants success to religious civil movements.

How do minority religious groups succeed and even thrive in a society in which they are otherwise marginalized? Among others, Christian social movements in Indian civil society have managed to survive as relevant and often influential organizations. Despite their marginal numbers, Christians have had a significant impact on Indian politics, economics, and society, as will become plain in the remainder of this chapter. Indian pluralism has allowed Christians to enjoy wider freedoms to organize and live out their faith as a means of sharing it with fellow Indians and in identifying with fellow

---

12 Amartya Sen, *The Argumentative Indian* (New York: Picador, 2005), 21.

Christians throughout the world. It has also benefited other religious and nonreligious movements, many of which have grown to become important factors in Indian society and politics. Efforts to constrain the religious freedoms of Christians, or followers of any other religion, will only serve to limit the more fundamental freedoms that contribute to the success of religion in that country. Pluralism is the life force of Indian democracy and the glue of Indian unity. For this reason, Indian unity is best preserved through a system that maximizes the freedoms of religious minorities to practice their faith with a view to ministering to the whole of society. Democratic and pluralist societies thrive when religious groups are afforded a high level of independence from state authority. But profound religious differences can often seem threatening—to religious minorities, to religious traditionalists seeking to maintain the status quo, and to the nonreligious. Still, religious faith has proven to be a resilient factor in human relations in the twenty-first century. Conflicts and controversies between people of different religious faiths and between the religious and nonreligious remain central questions in the world of politics. How do we learn to live together despite profound differences in the way that we see the world?

One of the greatest challenges of politics in the contemporary age is the need to protect religious pluralism in a way that defends the widest latitude for freedom for all. As religion has taken center stage in the conduct of global politics, the threat of religious intolerance and antireligious tyranny has risen in tandem. In their groundbreaking work on religious resurgence in global politics, Monica Duffy Toft, Daniel Philpott, and Timothy Samuel Shah argue that religious pluralism is the most effective means by which competition among religious organizations may be managed. Pluralism provides an opportunity for religious organizations to thrive and contribute back to society and expands the exercise of freedom in democratic settings. They note that "when religious actors are given substantial independence from the state, they are given the capacity to perform a range of positive functions in society."[13] Efforts to curtail the influence of religion are self-defeating because "sustained and systematic efforts to repress religious actors not only tend to fail to secure their objective of weakening religion but also open up a Pandora's box of social and political evils."[14] The state enforcement of antireligious dogma (either targeted at a specific religion or at religion as a phenomenon) is associated with broader limitations on free speech and association, in addition to constraining societal innovation and open trade in ideas. It tends to lead religious actors toward more radical forms of action, including antisocial behavior and violence, as they feel excluded from their own social environments. Like it or not, the world is a place of plural religions. Healthy societies must work toward preserving a place for religious diversity no matter how divisive these differences may seem.

Modern democracies have developed multiple ways to allow religion and religious actors to participate in politics. More important in many ways than even the right to vote is the ability to organize in groups and to present one's views openly without fear of reprisal. Citizens may practice their religious beliefs individually, but almost all religions are practiced in communities of faith, meaning that religion is lived out in groups of like-minded individuals. These groups, particularly in the case of religious actors, have a life outside the confines of the state. They pre-exist the modern state and operate autonomously from it, based in social structures that unite people of faith. Stephen Monsma argues that such "social structures found in every society receive their right to exist and their powers not from the state nor from autonomous individuals freely entering into contractual arrangements, but from God—or, for the more secularly minded, from the necessary, inherent nature of human society."[15] Religious freedom therefore undergirds

---

13 Monica Duffy Toft, Daniel Philpott, and Timothy Samuel Shah, *God's Century: Resurgent Religion and Global Politics* (New York: W. W. Norton, 2011), 217.

14 Ibid., 220.

15 Stephen Monsma, *Pluralism and Freedom* (Lanham, MD: Rowman & Littlefield, 2012), 126.

the pluralist state in the modern age. Without religious freedom, there is no strong basis for political pluralism.

In domestic politics, religion has a role at multiple levels. Government leaders and elite call upon religion to summon support from the nation. The religious ideas of a particularly influential leader or leaders may have a role in decision-making. Religious leaders may command power or authority by their influence over the faithful. Religious organizations have an influence on politics through activism, through lobbying, or even directly by creating political parties that run for office. It is less common to see the activities of religious organizations in serving the faithful or fellow citizens as a means of communicating religious interests. But if the belief commitments of the religious movement stress the need to engage in service to the poor or downtrodden of a society, these activities are also means by which the interests of the religious movement are pursued.

Faith and Pluralism

Recent research into the role of religion in pluralist political environments has shone a light on the way that religion mobilizes groups and helps to constitute communities of purpose. Toft, Philpott, and Shah argue that the role of religious organizations in the politics of nations must be understood as a product of the religious beliefs of the group that form the core of an organization. These beliefs include what is called political theology, defined as "the set of ideas that a religious actor holds about what is legitimate in political authority."[16] These beliefs motivate the faithful to engage in efforts to promote the social wellbeing of fellow human beings, to spread their beliefs to those who have not heard them, to engage in reforming negative social behaviors, or to protect the faithful from threats to their religious freedom. As a result, religious organizations become political actors, extending their efforts to promote change or to represent the interests of their community. The way in which they behave is the product of their peculiar political theology and the environment of which they are

---

16 Toft, Philpott, and Shah, *God's Century*, 27.

a part. Some political environments are conducive to the free exercise of religion. Others are restrictive.

In other faith majority societies Christians inevitably operate as sub-state groups (civil society). Dominant groups will likely represent some constellation of the more numerous religious perspectives, except in those societies where no one religious tradition represents the majority. Majority Muslim societies such as Egypt, Jordan, Indonesia, and Malaysia, majority Buddhist societies such as Sri Lanka and Nepal, or the majority Hindu society of India present many similar challenges for their native Christian populations, even though there are many important differences among these countries when it comes to governance, the economy, and political freedoms. Mehran Tamadonfar and Ted G. Jelen point out that "locally dominant religious traditions are likely to seek to impose some version of the sacred canopy" (a unifying set of religious ideas about how the society should be governed) "while the opponents (religious or secular) of such traditions will seek alternatives."[17] As a result, Christian communities in societies dominated by other religious traditions often take up subaltern and alternative discourses that will challenge the dominant powers in those states. When the political theology of the group in question strengthens their identification with marginalized people, the calling of Christian organizations to serve the poor and downtrodden is a means of demonstrating both political efficacy and the pursuit of their own interests as a representative institution of the faith adherents.

The idea that service to the community could be a form of interest representation is perhaps not immediately apparent. Civil society activism at its heart is about representing the desires, values, and needs of the group. Representation may take the form of providing an outlet for someone to simply get involved or to make a difference. It may also take the form of declaring an interest, a policy preference, or a call to vote in a particular way. Civil organizations, including religious

---

17 Mehran Tamadonfar and Ted G. Jelen, "Conclusion," in *Religion and Regimes*, ed. Mehran Tamadonfar and Ted G. Jelen (Lanham, MD: Lexington Books, 2014), 246.

ones, are therefore said to represent the interests of a group. They are a representative form of interest aggregation.

Interest aggregation may take multiple forms. One form is competitive nationalism. Sometimes the group unites around a shared notion of identity. Their purpose, rooted in a belief in shared group identity, is to protect the interests of the group itself. Their beliefs are nationalistic in nature, and the group—its survival, the promotion of its shared culture, or the expansion of its numbers—is the central focal point of what is important to the group. In extreme cases, such as a fascist state, nationalism may take the form of a religion, enshrining the nation as the most important social good and subordinating all other interests to that of the state.

A second form of interest aggregation is the corporatist form. In this case, identity remains the important focal point of the group, but identity forms the basis for group recognition by governing authorities. Corporatism may take a relatively limited form: some European states channel funds to established churches or create representative organizations of minority groups such as Muslims who represent the interests of those constituencies. In other cases, corporatism takes a more ideological or programmatic form, where a leading religious group uses its influence in the government to require special privileges or protections for that religious organization.

A final form of interest aggregation is the pluralist form, in which the free choice of members constitutes the organization. Identity is not the focus; rather, shared ideas and interests are the pillars of pluralist forms of social organization. Pluralist religious organizations are formed out of the shared interests and desires of members. They provide opportunities for participation rather than categorization. These organizations may work in partnership with governing authorities, but they are not created or recognized by such authorities. Such organizations have wide latitude to articulate their interests in partnership with state authorities or in opposition. Their funding, legitimacy, or survival does not depend on the state; indeed, they may thrive by presenting an alternative (or "prophetic") perspective to the dominant forces in society.

Christianity and Pluralism in India

Interest aggregation among Indian Christians is well positioned to take advantage of pluralist social concern. Competitive nationalism is unlikely to benefit a diffuse and tiny minority such as Christians, nor does it fit well with a political theology of free choice in matters of religion, often the hallmark of evangelical efforts throughout the country. Though corporatism links the protection of the minority group to the state, it has limited benefits. The minority is likely to remain a minority community, and its relative success or failure to impact society and government is rooted not in the vibrancy of the community but in the strength of its link to the governing apparatus. In authoritarian societies, corporatism is a common model for the survival of minority communities, but in democratic states, there are far greater opportunities in taking up the social concerns of interested members of the religious community and channeling their enthusiasm to achieve goals for the good of both the group and society at large.

India's democratic model therefore provides an excellent backdrop to the successful organization of the Christian community. While concentrated in northeast and southern India, Christian churches and organizations dot the landscape throughout the country. Over the course of four extended visits to India since 2009, I have personally encountered the panoply of Indian Christian activities throughout its many states. These include children's homes and after-school programs run by churches and parachurch organizations in Himachal Pradesh, West Bengal, Assam, Meghalaya, Tamil Nadu, Karnataka, and Kerala. Small rehabilitation centers and occupational training centers are commonly run by Christian organizations. In Delhi, Varanasi, and West Bengal, I have toured Christian ministry centers that seek to provide gainful employment to former sex workers and lower-caste groups. One of the most noteworthy of these is Freeset, an organization that works to provide alternatives to the sex trade in the Sonagachi red light district of Kolkata, purportedly one of the largest such districts in the world. World Vision, the world's largest Christian aid agency, is actively involved throughout low-Human Development Index states (with only small and fragmented Christian populations) in community development. Extending the reach of the Indian church, the World Vision approach deliberately includes all religions, partnering with other faiths and Christian community leaders on the ground.

During our June 2015 study tour of Bangalore, our group of scholars were introduced to several innovative and leading forms of social service organizations initiated by Christian churches and parachurch organizations. The Divya Shanti Christian Association (DSCA) operates as "one of the largest and most well-established community development organizations working in the three slums of northern Bangalore."[18] Located very close to these slum areas, the Christian organization has followed through on its proximity to minister to Muslim, lower-caste, and migrant communities in the area. Our group saw the impact of DSCA on these slums, specifically its ability to promote educational opportunities and entrepreneurialism among women in the area. Though DSCA prioritizes social activism within the slum, it was also interesting to note the number of small churches that dotted the community.

In Vellore, Tamil Nadu, our group visited the Christian Medical College and Community Health and Development Organization, originally founded in 1918 and now one of the leading health and training organizations in India. We met with medical professionals who attested to the national impact of the training center, including those who left with medical training to work in underserviced areas of Odisha state and other parts of India. Just outside Chennai, we visited an occupational training center run by Christians where young men are provided with employable trades.

---

18 Rebecca Samuel Shah and Timothy Samuel Shah, "Pentecost amid Pujas: Charismatic Christianity and Dalit Women in Twenty-First Century India," in *Pentecostalism in the 21st Century*, ed. Robert W. Hefner (Bloomington: Indiana University Press, 2013), 202.

These organizations complement the social work of government in addition to representing the political-theological call of Christians to serve the "least of these." Where government resources are inadequate to the task, Christian pluralist social concern provides a substitute that accomplishes two tasks: it provides an outlet for the free practice of religious devotion while also benefiting the larger community. Pluralist social forms therefore allow maximal expansion of the full pursuit of religious freedom rooted directly in the community without some of the divisive effects of identity politics (as represented in competitive nationalistic systems) or the authoritarian impact of government regulation (as demonstrated in corporatist systems).

At the same time, internal competition within the Christian community contributes to the health of pluralist institutions. The internal diversity of the Christian community also contributes to the vibrancy of Christian civil society. Indian Christians follow diverse paths and respond to many different demands for religiosity and tradition. The syncretic approach to religion embraced by Hinduism has had a strong effect on Christian religious practice. Selva Raj and Corinne Dempsey observe that "popular Christianity in India is neither homogenous nor uniform but essentially plural and diverse, formed by era, region, caste identity, and local earthly and spiritual need. In significant ways this plurality reflects the pluriform cultural, ethnic, linguistic, and religious landscape of India."[19] They go on to identify numerous ways in which the lines between Christian and non-Christian religious practices are blurred in India. Christian practices are thereby made accessible to other faith groups and open the church to the participation of those outside. This commitment to identification with Indian society is revealed by Christian commitments to celebrate major

---

19 Selva J. Raj and Corinne G. Dempsey, "Introduction," in *Popular Christianity in India: Riting between the Lines*, ed. Selva J. Raj and Corinne G. Dempsey (Albany: State University of New York Press, 2002), 5.

holidays and feasts with their Hindu neighbors, a practice observed by Carman and Rao in the state of Telangana.[20]

At first it might seem paradoxical that a small, marginal community of Christians in India is divided into a vast plurality of independent churches, from Catholics to Anglicans to Baptists to Pentecostals, and many more. In his study of charismatic movements in Tamil Nadu, P. N. Thomas counts at least 1,864 churches in the city of Chennai alone, including both massive megachurches and small fellowships.[21] The greatest number of these are independent Pentecostal and other charismatic congregations. However internal competition among the Indian churches to attract parishioners and supporters has also contributed to their innovation, organization, and activism. Though historically it was Protestant groups in Europe and the New World that were known for such sectarian tendencies, modern scholarship demonstrates how mainline churches, including Catholics and Orthodox, have also adapted their organizational forms to cater to a diverse array of interests among the faithful. Robert Calderisi notes that India's Catholics have proven just as prolific as their Protestant and Orthodox compatriots in institution-building. He notes how the archbishop of Kerala alone managed to establish ten different training institutions and a hospital, all of which have been funded locally among the faithful. "Our role is certainly out of all proportion to our numbers," the archbishop notes.[22] Indeed, this is demonstrated by the dramatic role that Christian organizations play in the Indian context. According to Lancy Lobo,

> The church in India . . . covers 25 percent of the entire voluntary sector operations in India though Christians are a mere 2.3 percent of the total population. The church is the single most important

---

20 John Carman and Chilkuri Vasantha Rao, *Christians in South Indian Villages, 1959-2009* (Grand Rapids, MI: Eerdmans, 2014), 190.

21 P. N. Thomas, *Strong Religion, Zealous Media: Christian Fundamentalism and Communication in India* (Thousand Oaks: Sage, 2008), 57.

22 Robert Calderisi, *Earthly Mission: The Catholic Church and World Development* (New Haven: Yale University Press, 2013), 131-32.

NGO in India that has activities in education and health, rural and urban development, caring for widows and orphans, aged and handicapped, leprosy patients, and doing relief, reconstruction and development work in times of floods, famines, droughts, cyclones and hurricanes.[23]

The ability of Christian organizations to punch above their weight demonstrates some of the social significance of Christian civil organizational life to the wider politics of India, even in those sectors that do not appear directly tied to religious freedom or the defense of religious heritage.

The vibrancy of Indian Christianity must be understood in the context of globalized religion and the long-term development of religion as what Peter Beyer calls a "functional system" of globalization. Christian religious activity is not territorial or culturally rooted in the way that Hinduism is. It relates to a worldwide tradition of beliefs that have transnational implication—beliefs that may spread through evangelization and mesh with individual local cultures to produce authentic Christianities in those environments. The spread of global Christianity has been closely tied therefore to the development of modern globalization. The development of Christian traditions in places like India came because of mission activity, beginning in the early decades after the death and resurrection of Jesus Christ. As a result, many of the existing Christian communities and organizations have their roots in mission activity. The long history of Christian mission activity helps to explain the large number of Protestant and Pentecostal churches that have grown in number and vibrancy, particularly over the course of the last half-century. It also contributes to the widespread feeling among Hindutva activists that much of Indian Christianity, and especially the evangelical impulse, has its roots in Western colonialism. Even today, much of Christian activity in India, as throughout the global South, comes because of Western Christian interest in funding and extending the faith throughout the world.

---

23 Lancy Lobo, *Globalization, Hindu Nationalism, and Christians in India* (Jaipur: Rawat Publications, 2002), 150.

However, the most notable accomplishments of Indian Christianity have come as a result of its identification with the oppressed and subaltern groups within Indian society. The most recognizable face of Christianity in India, Mother Teresa, is at once a product of both globalization and Christian pluralist social concern. Though originating outside India, Christianity has taken on a distinctively Indian interest in the improvement of a highly segregated, caste-based society. Christianity's traditional field of growth in India resided in the northeast and southwest, among lower-caste Hindus and the southeast Asian tribes of India's mountainous eastern interior. Tribal Nagas, Mizos, and Khasis from the northeast of India embraced Christianity in large numbers during the late 1800s and 1900s, and have built many churches, Christian educational institutions, and parachurch agencies in the states of Nagaland, Mizoram, and Meghalaya.

While traditional churches, even those that in the past grew because of evangelization among lower-caste groups, are increasingly unable to draw supporters among the poor, the most expansionary Christian movements in India speak to the plight of the poor and the oppressed. P. N. Thomas credits the success of charismatic groups in India to their contribution to the "creation of networks and solidarities that have been critical to the survival of people dispossessed by globalisation."[24] At the same time, globalization has provided new opportunities for such churches to share their message back to the world, complete with a theology of worldly success that seeks to harness the expansion of worldwide capitalism for personal success. During the June 2015 visit to Bangalore, several scholars on my team visited the Garden City Assembly of God International Worship Centre, where a senior pastor Ernest V. George delivered an impassioned sermon inspiring the faithful to overcome through the power of Christ—a sermon that was broadcast over the Internet to a global faithful.

---

24 Thomas, *Strong Religion*, 63.

A Waning Commitment to Pluralism?

Pluralism has also contributed to the increasing power and influence of the Hindutva movement. Its ability to harness public support through mass mobilization at *yatra* processions and demonstrations speaks to the power of the local *shakhas* and *pracharaks* who have led it since the foundation of the RSS. However, the conflation of Hindutva and secularism indicated by actions such as the provisions of anti-conversion laws and state acquiescence with actions such as the destruction of the Babri Masjid in Ayodhya or the 2002 riots in Gujarat demonstrate the anti-pluralist approach taken by many supporters of the BJP and the *Sangh Parivar*.

Returned to power, the BJP has made symbolic moves to try to enshrine the public practice of putatively religious forms that are championed by the Hindutva movement. Though largely symbolic, the idea of yoga as a mandatory subject of instruction has been embraced in Prime Minister Modi's home state of Gujarat and much discussed throughout the nation as many schools begin to contemplate similar moves. In late December, even the leftist government of Tripura made the surprising decision to accept the idea of implementing mandatory yoga instruction, a move that indicated its desire to pre-empt the rise of BJP support in the state.[25]

Of far greater concern is the interplay of forces within the Hindutva movement that convey the BJP government's inability or unwillingness to rein in the more radical elements. The Vishva Hindu Parishad (World Hindu Organization) and its youth wing, the Bajrang Dal, a prominent set of organizations in the *Sangh Parivar*, have undertaken an ongoing campaign to intimidate Christians suspected of challenging anti-conversion laws in several states of North India. Perhaps this is most dramatically demonstrated in the least developed states of eastern

---

25 "Left-Ruled Tripura Makes Yoga Must for Students," *Times of India*, December 31, 2015, http://timesofindia.indiatimes.com/city/agartala/Left-ruled-Tripura-makes-yoga-must-for-students/articleshow/50388276.cms, accessed January 7, 2016.

India, namely, Bihar, Odisha, and Jharkhand, states where RSS *shakhas*, the VHP, and other elements of the *Sangh Parivar* have been active. The dramatic expansion of Christian endeavors in these states over the past several years has drawn Christian organizations into conflict with the purveyors of Hindutva. Perceiving Christian evangelical efforts as a threat to the Hindu identity of the majority population of the state, Hindutva activists have engaged in several campaigns of violence. The most dramatic of these violent acts included the murder of Australian Christian missionary Graham Staines and two of his children in the Keonjhar district of Odisha in January 1999 and the massive outbreak of violence against Christian communities in Odisha after the assassination of Swami Lakshmananda in August 2008. However, even everyday intimidation of churches held to be engaging in evangelical activities in defiance of anti-conversion laws is the stock in trade of such organizations.[26] Mob vigilantism is rarely confronted by local police and often suborned by governing BJP authorities or their allies such as the Biju Janata Dal or the Shiv Sena.

In essence, the rise of Hindutva presents a specific challenge to Christianity's enjoyment of pluralist freedoms of organization and spread in the years to come. Hindutva's advocacy of a Hindu *rashtra*, in which the state takes on a project that enshrines a specific notion of Hindu heritage in Indian society, suggests the increasing embrace of a statist, competitive nationalist vision of Indian religion based on identity rather than free choice or belief. State corporatism that privileges one form of religious *dharma* over others may continue to provide deep cover for substate groups that are granted free license to define the law and may constrain the law in ways that demand Christians increasingly to register and limit their efforts to the Christian community. They may also reinforce a statist mentality that seeks to limit the global relationships of the Indian Christian community with

---

26 See, e.g., "Bajrang Dal Activists Vandalize Christian Building in Bihar," *The Hindu*, January 12, 2015, http://www.thehindu.com/news/national/other-states/bajrang-dal-activists-vandalise-christian-building-in-bihar/article6780498.ece, accessed January 7, 2016.

co-religionists elsewhere under the rubric of protecting Indian heritage. Still, the challenge of Hindu nationalism and state corporatism has provided a new opportunity for India's Christians to take up a new cause in favor of the nation's newly disenfranchised. As Christians organize to confront the challenges of vigilante movements and take their concerns to the courts and to the Indian public, they demonstrate the social power of pluralist social concern in action.

Conclusion

A burned church represents the folly of a society that would lay aside the benefits of pluralism for the dubious pursuit of unity in uniformity. In his recent journalistic account of changes in the social and political life of modern India, Simon Denyer responds to the many significant political challenges that have led Indians to be pessimistic about the country's progress. In the past years, several high-profile cases of rape and injustice have drawn justified criticisms that India is a deeply flawed society. Church burnings and attacks on the religious freedom of Christians among others could be added to the list of grievances that Indian patriots have against their own country. Nevertheless, Denyer concludes on an optimistic note that while injustices and corruption remain endemic in India, the passion of ordinary Indians to address those problems is rooted in its democratic impulse and in the diversity and liberalism common in Indian society. In his words, "Democracy has not only held India together against all the odds; it has also given voice to the voiceless and allowed the underprivileged to begin raising their bowed heads and asking questions of the supposed superiors."[27] One might add that India's embrace of pluralist forms of interest representation, even in the field of something as divisive and controversial as religion, has managed to give voice to the voiceless. Christian organizations have had a central role in accomplishing this end.

Indian Christianity is part of a larger pluralist society that has demonstrated strong democratic credentials throughout the decades

---

27 Simon Denyer, *Rogue Elephant: Harnessing the Power of India's Unruly Democracy* (New York: Bloomsbury, 2015), 405.

following independence in 1947. Pluralist representation of religion matches well the traditional Indian embrace of secularism as neutrality among religions, all the while providing religion an important role in the promotion of India's economic and political development. Indian Christians have thrived within this pluralist environment and have engaged in a remarkable number of social projects and services to the wider community that are essential to the health of Indian society. Among these one might include some of the best elementary, secondary, and higher educational institutions in the country, the Christian Medical College at Vellore and its various community programs throughout the country, numerous children's homes, rehabilitation centers, relief and development projects, and churches that provide spiritual and social homes for hundreds of thousands of Indian citizens.

Pluralism of this sort is best preserved in a society that seeks to promote the success of free choice in the matter of religion. Deepening efforts to define Indian citizenship through appeal to the Hindu heritage, demonstrated by the Hindutva movement and the *Sangh Parivar*, are therefore counterproductive. The very pluralism that has allowed the Hindutva movement to gain such an influential place in Indian politics is supported by the perpetuation of competitive and diverse voices in the realm of civil society. The best means to enhance both Indian celebration of its distinctive Hindu traditions and the freedom of religion and belief is through a deepened commitment to the pluralist notion that free choice that leads to a harmonious civil society.

It would be a mistake for Hindu nationalists to presume that soft authoritarian corporatism will help them to "discipline" religious minorities. The soft authoritarian impulse may appear to regulate the cultural impact of such groups, but the experience of most states eager to regulate religion suggests that unregulated religious activity will grow despite efforts by government or vigilante groups to control their expansion. On the other hand, while Christians will survive in a non-pluralist society, the sustainability of their civil activities, and those of other social movements, is only threatened by the move to more identity-focused forms of interest representation and majoritarian forms of democracy. This means that religious activity will not be curtailed, but the social capital encouraged by religious civil society will have a limited impact. The desire to restrict religious dissent will not succeed, and the positive benefits that accrue to people of all faiths will be restrained. Christian civil society has been particularly significant in its impact on social indicators of health, prosperity, education, and positive civil relations. A limited Christian civil society will be restricted in its ability to provide these services and all Indian society will be worse off as a result. The flames that gut the church will inevitably spread.

Bibliography

Aaron, Sushil. *Christianity and Political Conflict in India: The Case of Gujarat.* Colombo: Regional Centre for Strategic Studies 23, 2002.

Akkara, Anto. "Amid Mounting Injustice, Church in Odisha Promotes Kandhamal Martyrs' Day." *National Catholic Register*, September 17, 2015. http://www.ncregister.com/daily-news/amid-mounting-injustice-church-in-odisha-promotes-kandhamal-martyrs-day/#ixzz42CVHpMQ0. Accessed March 2, 2016.

------. "India under Modi Sees Increase in Attacks on Christians: Critics Charge Growing Number of Atrocities Worries Religious Minorities. " http://aleteia.org/2014/10/01/india-under-modi-sees-increase-in-attacks-on-christians-critics-charge/#sthash.jzrIZppE.dpuf. Accessed March 4, 2016.

Allen, John L., Jr. "'Kandhamal' Tells the Whole Story of Anti-Christian Persecution." *Crux*, July 28, 2015, https://cruxnow.com/faith/2015/07/28/kandhamal-tells-the-whole-story-of-anti-christian-persecution/. Accessed February 12, 2018.

Anagol, Padma. "Feminist Inheritances and Foremothers: The Beginnings of Feminism in Modern India." *Women's History Review* 19, no. 4 (2010): 523-42.

Anand, Kunal. "Yet Another Church Attack Adds to the List of Increasing Violence Against Christianity." *India Times*, March 23, 2015. http://www.indiatimes.com/news/india/delhi-saw-5-attacks-on-christian-institutions-in-the-last-3-months-230230.html. Accessed February 17, 2017.

Andrews, C. F. "A Pilgrim's Progress." In *Religion in Transition*. London: George Allen & Unwin, 1937.

------. *What I Owe to Christ.* New York: Abingdon Press, 1932.

Apte, Mahadev. "Home as the Extension of Self in Marathi Autobiographies." In *House and Home in Maharashtra,* edited by Irina Glushkova and Anne Feldhaus. Delhi: Oxford University Press, 1998.

Asad, Talal. "Thinking about Religious Beliefs and Practices." In *The Cambridge Companion to Religious Studies,* edited by Robert Orsi. Cambridge: Cambridge University Press, 2012.

Bacote, Vincent. "A Perennial Moment of Opportunity." *Comment,* August 7, 2012. https://www.cardus.ca/comment/article/3395/a-perennial-moment-of-opportunity/2012.

"Bajrang Dal Activists Vandalize Christian Building in Bihar." *The Hindu,* January 12, 2015. http://www.thehindu.com/news/national/other-states/bajrang-dal-activists-vandalise-christian-building-in-bihar/article6780498.ece. Accessed January 7, 2016.

Bakker, Janel K. *Sister Churches: American Congregations and Their Partners Abroad.* New York: Oxford University Press, 2013.

Banerjee, Abhijit V., and Esther Duflo. "The Economic Lives of the Poor." *SSRN Electronic Journal,* 2006. https://economics.mit.edu/files/530. Accessed February 13, 2018.

Basu, Sanjukta. "Karwan e Mohabbat: Uncovering How Violence Against Minorities Has Been Normalised." *First Post,* December 21, 2017. http://www.firstpost.com/india/karwan-e-mohabbat-uncovering-how-violence-against-minorities-has-been-normalised-4098127.html. Accessed February 12, 2018.

Bauman, Chad M. "Conversion, and the Coterminal Castes and Tribes." *Journal of Asian Studies* 72, no. 3 (2013): 633-53. http://digitalcommons.butler.edu/cgi/viewcontent.cgi?article=1271&context=facsch_papers. Accessed April 23, 2015.

------. "Hindu-Christian Conflict in India: Globalization, Conversion and the Coterminal Castes and Tribes." *Journal of Asian Studies* 72, no. 3 (August 2013): 633-53.

------. *Pentecostals, Proselytization, and Anti-Christian Violence in Contemporary India.* New Delhi: Oxford University Press, 2015.

Bayly, Christopher A. *Indian Society and the Making of the British Empire.* Cambridge: Cambridge University Press, 1987.

Befus, David. "Discovering a Role in God's Provision." In *The Local Church in a Global Era: Reflections for a New Century,* edited by Max Stackhouse, Tim Dearborn, and Scott Paeth. Grand Rapids, MI: Eerdmans, 2000.

Bhakiaraj, Paul J. "Identity and Community." In *South Asia Bible Commentary*, edited by Brian Wintle. Grand Rapids, MI: Zondervan, 2015.

Blocker, Jack S. *American Temperance Movement: Cycles of Reform*. Boston: Twayne Publishers, 1989.

Borthwick, Paul. *Western Christians in Global Mission: What's the Role of the North American Church?* Downers Grove, IL: Intervarsity Press, 2012.

Bosch, David J. *Transforming Mission: Paradigm Shifts in Theology of Mission*. Maryknoll, NY: Orbis, 1991.

Boucher, Megan C. "Ten Talents: The Role of Church-Based Progress in the Microfinance Industry." *Missiology* 40, no. 2 (2012).

Bradley, Tamsin. "A Call for Clarification and Critical Analysis of the Work of Faith-Based Development Organizations (FBDO)." *Progress in Development Studies* 9, no. 2 (2009).

Branson, Mark Lau, and Juan F. Martinez. *Churches, Cultures, and Leadership: A Practical Theology of Congregations and Ethnicities*. Downers Grove, IL: Intervarsity Academic, 2011.

Brautigam, Michael. "A Queen with a Throne? Harnack, Schlatter, and Kuyper on Theology in the University." In *The Kuyper Center Review*, vol. 5, *Church and Academy*, edited by Gordon Graham. Grand Rapids, MI: Eerdmans, 2015.

Brosius, Christiane. "The Scattered Homelands of the Migrant: Bollyworld through the Diasporic Lens." In *Bollyworld: Popular Cinema Through Transnational Lens*, edited by Raminder Kaur and Ajay J. Sinha. New Delhi: Sage Publications, 2005.

Brown, M. Judith. "Who Is an Indian?" In *Missions, Nationalism, and the End of Empire*, edited by Brian Stanley and Alaine M. Lo. Grand Rapids, MI: Eerdmans, 2003.

Bussau, David, and Russell Mask. *Christian Microenterprise Development: An Introduction*. Costa Mesa, CA: Regnum Books, 2003.

Butler, Judith. *Giving an Account of Oneself*. New York: Fordham University Press, 2005.

Calderisi, Robert. *Earthly Mission: The Catholic Church and World Development*. New Haven: Yale University Press, 2013.

Carman, John, and Chilkuri Vasantha Rao. *Christians in South Indian Villages, 1959-2009*. Grand Rapids, MI: Eerdmans, 2014.

"Census 2011." http://www.census2011.co.in/religion.php. Accessed March 4, 2016; February 17, 2017.

Chandorkar, Leena. *Eye Me Myself: A Study of Six Women's Autobiographies*. Delhi: New Century Publications, 2002.

Chaturvedi, Benarsidas, and Marjorie Sykes. *Charles Freer Andrews: A Narrative.* London: George Allen & Unwin, 1949.

Chitnis, Suma. "Exploring Tradition and Change among Women in Marathi Culture." In *Faces of the Feminine in Ancient, Medieval, and Modern India,* edited by Mandakranta Bose. New York: Oxford University Press, 2000.

"Christian Leaders Condemn Modi's Ignorance on Anti-Christian Attacks: SILENT VOICE Exposes His Lies." *Silent Voice,* April 17, 2014. https://silentmaj.wordpress.com/2014/04/17/christian-leaders-condemn-modis-ignorance-on-anti-christian-attacks-silent-voice-exposes-his-lies/. Accessed March 2, 2016.

Chulov, Martin. "Egypt's Coptic Christians Report Fresh Attacks on Churches." *The Guardian,* August 15, 2013. https://www.theguardian.com/world/2013/aug/15/egypt-coptic-christians-attacks-churches. Accessed February 17, 2017.

Clarke, Gerar. "Faith Matters: Faith-Based Organisations, Civil Society and International Development." *Journal of International Development* 18 (2006).

Clarke, Sathianathan. "Dalit Theology: An Introductory and Interpretive Theological Exposition." In *Dalit Theology in the Twenty-First Century: Discordant Voices, Discerning Pathways,* edited by Sathianathan Clarke, Deenabandhu Manchala, and Philip Peacock. New Delhi: Oxford University Press, 2010.

Clendinnen, Inga. *True Stories.* Sydney: ABC Books, 1999.

"Communalism—Meaning and Issues." *Insights,* November 7, 2014. http://www.insightsonindia.com/2014/11/07/communalism-meaning-and-issues/. Accessed August 23, 2015.

Corbett, Steve, and Brian Fikkert. *When Helping Hurts.* Chicago: Moody, 2009.

Cornwell, Grant H., and Eve W. Stoddard. *Globalizing Knowledge: Connecting International and Intercultural Studies.* Washington, DC: Association of American Universities and Colleges, 1999.

Cottle, Michelle. "Rick Warren's Resurrection." *Newsweek,* December 2012, 30.

Coward, Harold. "Gandhi, Ambedkar, and Untouchability." In *Indian Critiques of Gandhi,* edited by Harold Coward. Albany: State University of New York Press, 2003.

Das, Bhagwan. *Thus Spoke Ambedkar.* Vol. 4. Bangalore: Ambedkar Sahitya Prakshan, 1980.

Daughrity, Dyron, and Jesudas Athyal. *Understanding World Christianity: India.* Minneapolis: Fortress Press, 2016.

Dayal, John. "August 2008 Anti-Christian Pogrom in India Saw 'Rivers of Blood on the Road.'" *Organization for Minorities of India*. http://www.minoritiesofindia.org/august-2008-anti-christian-pogrom-in-india-saw-rivers-of-blood-on-the-road/. Accessed June 7, 2016.

de Brijne, Ad. "Not without the Church as Institute." In *The Kuyper Center Review*, vol. 5, *Church and Academy*, edited by Gordon Graham. Grand Rapids, MI: Eerdmans, 2015.

Denyer, Simon. *Rogue Elephant: Harnessing the Power of India's Unruly Democracy*. New York: Bloomsbury, 2015.

Deshpande, Satish and Geetika Bapna. *Dalits in the Muslim and Christian Communities: A Status Report on Current Social Scientific Knowledge*. Paper prepared for the National Commission for Minorities, Government of India, 2008. http://ncm.nic.in/pdf/report%20dalit%20%20reservation.pdf. Accessed February 8, 2018.

Deshpande, Sudhanva. "The Consumable Hero of Globalised India." In *Bollyworld: Popular Cinema Through Transnational Lens*, edited by Raminder Kaur and Ajay J. Sinha, 186-206. New Delhi: Sage Publications, 2005.

Duraisingh, Christopher. "Gospel and Identity in Community." *International Review of Missions* 85, no. 336 (1996).

Dwyer, Rachel. *Filming the Gods: Religion and Indian Cinema*. New York: Routledge, 2006.

Eaton, Richard. "Temple Destruction in Pre-Modern India." In *Demolishing Myths or Mosques and Temples: Readings in History and Temple Desecration in Medieval India*, edited by Sunil Kumar, 93-139. Gurgaon: Three Essay's Collective, 2008.

Ebrahim, Antoor. "NGO Behaviour and Development Discourse: Cases from Western India." *Voluntas: International Journal of Voluntary and Nonprofit Organizations* 12, no. 2 (2001).

Editorial Board. "Modi's Dangerous Silence." *New York Times*, February 6, 2015. http://www.nytimes.com/2015/02/07/opinion/modis-dangerous-silence.html?_r=0. Accessed March 4, 2016.

Embree, Ainslee T. *Utopias in Conflict: Religion and Nationalism in Modern India*. Delhi: Oxford University Press, 1992.

Evangelical Fellowship of India. "Hate and Targeted Violence against Christians in India." *Report 2015*. March 2, 2016. http://files.ctctcdn.com/523942c3501/271ca9a9-f085-4006-a08b-051ed9cd51c8.pdf.

Eveleigh, Alexandra M. M. "Pembroke College (Cambridge) Mission, 1885-1995: An Administrative History." Unpublished MA thesis, University College London, 1997.

Fikkert, Brian, and Russell Mask. *From Dependence to Dignity: How to Alleviate Poverty through Christ-Centered Microfinance*. Grand Rapids, MI: Zondervan, 2015.

Flegg, C. G. *'Gathered under Apostles': A Study of the Catholic Apostolic Church*. Oxford: Clarendon Press, 1992.

Flett, John C. *The Witness of God: The Trinity, Missio Dei, Karl Barth, and the Nature of Christian Community*. Grand Rapids, MI: Eerdmans, 2010.

Frykenberg, Robert E. *Christianity in India: From Beginnings to the Present*. Oxford: Oxford University Press, 2008.

------. *Constructions of Hinduism: At the Nexus of History and Religion*. New Delhi: Critical Quest, 2009.

------. "Constructions of Hinduism at the Nexus of History and Religion." *Journal of Interdisciplinary History* 23, no. 3 (1993).

Galanter, Marc. *Competing Equalities: Law and Backward Classes in India*. Berkeley: University of California Press, 1984.

------. *Law and Society in Modern India*. Delhi: Oxford University Press, 1989.

------. "The Religious Aspects of Caste: A Legal View." In *South Asian Politics and Religion*, edited by Donald E. Smith and the Council on Religion and International Affairs. Princeton: Princeton University Press, 1966.

Gandhi, Leela. *Affective Communities: Anticolonial Thought, Fin-de-Siècle Radicalism, and the Politics of Friendship*. Durham: Duke University Press, 2006.

Gandhi, Mohandas K. *An Autobiography or The Story of My Experiments with the Truth*. Translated by Mahadev Desia. Ahmadabad: Navjeevan Publishing House, 1991.

------. *Collected Works of Mahatma Gandhi*. 98 vols. New Delhi: Publication Division, 1976.

Gandolfo, Elizabeth O'Donnell. "Remembering the Massacre at El Mozote: A Case for the Dangerous Memory of Suffering as Christian Formation in Hope." *International Journal of Practical Theology* 17, no. 1 (2013).

Garber, David G., Jr. "Trauma Theory and Biblical Studies." *Currents in Biblical Research* 14, no. 1 (2015).

"Genocide in Kandhamal." *Human Rights Law Network*. http://idsn.org/uploads/media/Orissa_report_-_Human_Rights_Law_Network.pdf. Accessed May 26, 2015.

Gilespie, Mary. *Television, Ethnicity and Cultural Change*. London: Routledge, 1995.

Gnanavaram, M. "'Dalit Theology' and the Parable of the Good Samaritan." *Journal for the Study of the New Testament* 15, no. 50 (1993): 59-83.

Goel, Desraj. *Rahstriya Swayamsevak Sangh.* http://www.kractivist.org/letter-sardar-vallabhai-patel-to-rss-chief-guru-golwalkar-1948-godse-mustread/. Accessed March 2, 2016.

Golwalkar, Madhavarao S. *Bunch of Thoughts.* 3rd ed. Bangalore: Bikrama Prakashan, 1966.

------. *We or Our Nationhood Defined.* Nagpur: Bharat Prakshan, 1939.

Grover, Vrinda, ed. *Kandhamal: The Law Must Change Its Course.* New Delhi: Multiple Action Research Group, 2010.

Hansen, Thomas Blom. "In Search of the Diasporic Self: Bollywood in South Africa." In *Bollyworld: Popular Cinema Through Transnational Lens,* edited by Raminder Kaur and Ajay J. Sinha. New Delhi: Sage Publications, 2005.

------. *The Saffron Wave: Democracy and Hindu Nationalism in Modern India.* Princeton: Princeton University Press, 1999.

Harish, Ranjana. "Pen and Needle: The Changing Metaphors of Self in Autobiographies by Women in Post-Independence India." *Indian Literature* 46, no. 4 (2002).

Harper, Susan Billington. *In the Shadow of the Mahatma: Bishop V. S. Azariah and the Travails of Christianity in British India.* Grand Rapids, MI: Eerdmans, 2000.

Hauerwas, Stanley, and William H. Willimon. *Resident Aliens: Life in the Christian Colony.* Nashville, TN: Abingdon, 1989.

Hedlund, Roger. *Indian Christianity: An Alternative Reading.* New Delhi: Christian World Imprint, 2016.

Heifetz, Ronald A. *Leadership Without Easy Answers.* Boston: Harvard University Press, 1994.

Heifetz, Ronald A., and Marty Linsky. *Leadership on the Line: Staying Alive Through the Dangers of Leading.* Boston: Harvard Business Review Press, 2001.

Heirich, Max. "Change of Heart: A Test of Some Widely Held Theories about Religious Conversion." *American Journal of Sociology* 83, no. 3 (1977): 653-80.

Hirschl, Ran. *Constitutional Theocracy.* Cambridge, MA: Harvard University Press, 2010.

Hoedemaker, L. A. "The People of God and the Ends of the Earth." In *Missiology: An Ecumenical Introduction,* edited by A. Camps, L. A. Hoedemaker, and M. R. Spindler. Grand Rapids, MI: Eerdmans, 1995.

Howell, Brian M., *Short-Term Mission: An Ethnography of Christian Travel Narrative and Experience.* Downers Grove, IL: Intervarsity Press Academic, 2012.

Hunter, James D. *To Change the World: The Irony, Tragedy, and Possibility of Christianity in the Late Modern World.* New York: Oxford University Press, 2010.

Hurd, Elizabeth Shakman. *Beyond Religious Freedom: The New Global Politics of Religion.* Princeton: Princeton University Press, 2015.

Hurd, Elizabeth Shakman, and Winnifred Fallers Sullivan, eds. "Symposium: Rethinking Religious Freedom." *Journal of Law and Religion* 29, no. 3 (2014).

"Indian Christians—Photos of Persecution and Death in Orissa." *Christian View*, September 27, 2008. http://christianlook.blogspot.in/2008/09/indian-christians-photos-of-persecution.html.

Islam, Shamsul. *Know the RSS: Based on Rashtriya Swayamsevak Sangh Documents.* New Delhi: Pharos Media & Publishing Pvt. Ltd., 2014.

Iyadurai, Joshua. "Multiple Identities of Converts in India: An Interdisciplinary Perspective." *Dharma Deepika* 16 (January-June 2012): 27-41.

------. "Religious Experiences of College Students: The Christian Students of Chennai (Madras) City." Unpublished study conducted at the University of Madras, Chennai, 2003.

------. *Transformative Religious Experience: A Phenomenological Understanding of Religious Conversion.* Eugene, OR: Pickwick Publications, 2015.

Iyer, Mani. "Mani Iyer," *Conversions in India—Testimonies*, January 31, 2009. https://conversionsinindia.wordpress.com/2009/01/31/mani-iyer/. Accessed November 29, 2017.

James, William. *The Varieties of Religious Experience.* New York: Barnes and Noble Classics, 2004 [1902].

Jenkins, Philip. *The Next Christendom: The Coming of Global Christianity.* 3rd ed. New York: Oxford University Press, 2011.

Kakar, Sudhir. "Indian-ness: So What Really Makes Us Indians?" *Little India*, http://www.w3c.org/TR/1999/REC-html401-19991224/loose.dtd.

Kamat, Sangeeta. "The NGO Phenomenon and Political Culture in the Third World." *Society for International Development* 46, no. 1 (2003).

Kaplan, Marion A. *Between Dignity and Despair: Jewish Life in Nazi Germany.* New York: Oxford University Press, 1998.

Kapoor, Jayasudha. "Chit Chat with Jayasudha." *Idlebrain.com*, March 1, 2006. http://www.idlebrain.com/news/2000march20/chitchat-jayasudha.html. Accessed November 29, 2017.

------. "I Hated Every Minute of It." *Rediff.com*, May 13, 2000. https://www.rediff.com/movies/2000/may/13jaya.htm. Accessed November 29, 2017.

Kapur, Anju. "Theorizing Women Writing in India." *South Asia Bulletin* 14, no. 1 (1994): 114-21.

Kapur, Jyotsna. "Putting Herself into the Picture: Women's Accounts of the Social Reform Campaign in Maharashtra." *Manushi: A Journal about Women and Society* 56 (1990): 28-37.

Keller, Timothy. *Generous Justice: How God's Grace Makes Us Just*. New York: Riverhead Books, 2010.

Keum, Jooseop, ed. *Together towards Life: Mission and Evangelism in Changing Landscapes*. Geneva: WCC Publications, 2013.

Kim, Yosep. *The Identity and the Life of the Church: John Calvin's Ecclesiology in the Perspective of Anthropology*. Eugene, OR: Pickwick Publications, 2014.

King, Richard. "Orientalism and the Modern Myth of Hinduism." *Numen* 46, no. 2 (1999): 146-85.

Korten, David C. "Community Organization and Rural Development: A Learning Process Approach." *Public Administration Review* 40, no. 5 (1980).

Korten, David C., and Rudi Klauss, eds. *People-Centered Development: Contributions Toward Theory and Planning Frameworks*. West Hartford, CT: Kumarian Press, 1984.

Kosambi, Meera. *Crossing Thresholds: Feminist Essays in Social History*. Ranikhet: Permanent Black, 2007.

Kudva, Neema. "Uneasy Partnerships? Government-NGO Relations in India." Berkeley: University of California, Institute of Urban and Regional Development, 1996.

Laing, Mark. "Missio Dei: Some Implications for the Church." *Missiology* 37, no. 1 (2009).

Lal, Vinay. *Veer Savarkar: Ideologue of Hindutva*. https://www.sscnet.ucla.edu/southasia/History/Hindu_Rashtra/veer.html. Accessed March 2, 2016.

------, ed. *Political Hinduism: The Religious Imagination in Public Spheres*. New York: Oxford University Press, 2009.

Lederle, Matthew. *Philosophical Trends in Modern Maharashtra*. Bombay: Popular Prakashan, 1976.

"Left-Ruled Tripura Makes Yoga Must for Students." *Times of India*, December 31, 2015. http://timesofindia.indiatimes.com/city/agartala/Left-ruled-Tripura-makes-yoga-must-for-students/articleshow/50388276.cms. Accessed January 7, 2016.

Lobo, Lancy. *Globalization, Hindu Nationalism, and Christians in India*. Jaipur: Rawat Publications, 2002.

Lofland, John, and Rodney Stark. "Becoming a World-Saver: A Theory of Conversion to a Deviant Perspective." *American Sociological Review* 30, no. 6 (1965): 862-75.

Luhrmann, T. M. *When God Talks Back: Understanding the American Evangelical Relationship with God*. New York: Alfred A. Knopf, 2012.

Mahadevan, Anand. "I the Convert." *Out Look* 27 (October 2008). https://www.outlookindia.com/magazine/story/i-the-convert/238770. Accessed November 27, 2017.

Mahava Prasad, M. *Ideology of Hindi Film*. New Delhi: Oxford University Press, 2000.

Mahmood, Saba, and Peter Danchin, eds. "Contested Genealogies of Religious Freedom." Special issue, *South Atlantic Quarterly* 113, no. 1 (2014).

Mallampalli, Chandra. *Christians and Public Life in Colonial South India*. London: RoutledgeCurzon, 2004.

——. *Race, Religion, and Law in Colonial India*. Cambridge: Cambridge University Press, 2011.

Mander, Harsh. "Why Jharkhand's Anti-Conversion Bill Is against Constitution and Not Necessary." *Hindustan Times*, September 12, 2017. http://www.hindustantimes.com/columns/why-jharkhand-s-anti-conversion-bill-is-against-constitution-and-not-necessary/story-FIhGsnxuqIItvniVAoiLQO.html.

Mani, Braj Ranjan. *Debrahmanizing History: Dominance and Resistance in Indian Society*. New Delhi: Manohar, 2005.

Mann, James. "Why Narendara Modi Was Banned from the US." *The Wall Street Journal*, May 2, 2014.

Manu, K. P. *Malabar Cements Ltd vs Chairman, Scrutiny Committee for Verification of Community Certificate*, February 26, 2015. Bench: Dipak Misra, V. Gopala Gowda. https://indiankanoon.org/doc/98912765/. Accessed February 9, 2018.

Marsden, George M. *Fundamentalism and American Culture: The Shaping of Twentieth-Century Evangelicalism, 1870-1925*. New York: Oxford University Press, 1980.

McGavran, Donald A. *The Bridges of God: A Study in the Strategy of Missions*. New York: Friendship Press, 1955.

McPhee, G. Arthur. *The Road to Delhi: Bishop Pickett Remembered, 1890-1981*. Bangalore: SIACS Press, 2005.

Melanchthon, M. J. "Theological Education for Transformation: India." *Colloquium* 47, no. 2 (2015): 237-56.

Menon, Dilip. *The Blindness of Insight: Essays on Caste in Modern India.* Delhi: Navayan, 2006.

Michael, S. M. "Culture and Religious Identity of India from Dalit and Minorities Perspectives." In *Mobilization of Backward Communities in India*, edited by B. V. Bhosale. New Delhi: Deep and Deep Publications Pvt. Ltd., 2004.

Ministry of Tribal Affairs. *Report of the High Level Committee on Socioeconomic, Health and Educational Status of Tribal Communities of India.* Delhi: Government of India, 2014, 31. http://www.kractivist.org/wp-content/uploads/2014/12/Tribal-Committee-Report-May-June-2014.pdf. Accessed February 12, 2018.

Mishra, Vijay. *Bollywood Cinema: Temples of Desire.* London: Routledge, 2002.

Moltmann, Jürgen. *Ethics of Hope.* Translated by Margaret Kohl. Minneapolis, MN: Fortress Press, 2012.

Monsma, Stephen. *Pluralism and Freedom.* Lanham, MD: Rowman & Littlefield, 2012.

Morgan, Timothy C. "Purpose Driven in Rwanda: Rick Warren's Sweeping Plan to Defeat Poverty." *Christianity Today* 49, no. 10 (2005): 32-36, 90-91.

Mosse, David. "Process-Oriented Approaches to Development Practice and Social Research." In *Development as Process: Concepts and Methods for Working with Complexity*, edited by David Mosse et al. New Delhi: India Research Press, 2001.

Myers, Bryant. *Walking with the Poor: Principles and Practices of Transformational Development.* Maryknoll, NY: Orbis, 2011.

Nair, Padmaja. "Historical Analysis of Relationships between the State and the Non-Governmental Sector in India." University of Birmingham, International Development Department, 2007.

Nandy, Ashis. Address to the Nagel Institute Scholars. YMCA International Guest House, New Delhi, August 1, 2015.

------. *Creating a Nationality: The Ramjanmabhumi Movement and Fear of the Self.* Delhi: Oxford University Press, 2010.

------. "The Politics of Secularism and the Recovery of Religious Tolerance." In *Secularism and Its Critics*, edited by Rajeev Bhargava. Delhi: Oxford University Press, 1998.

------. "The Return of the Sacred: The Language of Religion and the Fear of Democracy in a Post-Secular World." *The Mahesh Chandra Regmi Lecture 2007*, December 13, Kathmandu, Nepal.

------. *The Romance of the State and the Fate of Dissent in the Tropics.* New Delhi: Oxford University Press, 2003.

------. *Time Warps: Silent and Evasive Pasts in Indian Politics and Religion.* New Brunswick: Rutgers University Press, 2002.

National People's Tribunal Report on Kandhamal. *Final Report.* August 22-24, 2010. http://www.sabrang.com/cc/archive/2012/jan2012/citizens%20tribunal%20Kandhamal%20Report%20Full.pdf. Accessed August 26, 2011.

Nayak, Rajesh. "I, a Hindu Brahmin Convert to Christianity, Even Though Everyone Thought I Was Already a Catholic." *AsiaNews.it,* March 29, 2017. http://www.asianews.it/news-en/-I,-a-Hindu-Brahmin-convert-to-Christianity,-even-though-everyone-thought-I-was-already-a-Catholic-40331.html. Accessed November 29, 2017.

Newbigin, Lesslie. *The Gospel in a Pluralistic Society.* Grand Rapids, MI: Eerdmans, 1989.

------. *The Household of God.* Eugene, OR: Wipf and Stock, 1954.

------. *The Open Secret: An Introduction to the Theology of Mission.* Rev. ed. Grand Rapids, MI: Eerdmans, 1995.

Nirmal, A. P. "Towards a Christian Dalit Theology." In *Indigenous People: Dalits: Dalit Issues in Today's Theological Debate,* edited by James Massey. New Delhi: ISPCK, 1998.

Nongbri, Brent. *Before Religion: A History of a Modern Concept.* New Haven: Yale University Press, 2012.

Nussbaum, Martha. *The Clash Within: Democracy, Religious Violence, and India's Future.* Cambridge, MA: Belknap Press of Harvard University Press, 2007.

------. *Cultivating Humanity: A Classical Defense of Reform in Liberal Education.* Cambridge, MA: Harvard University Press, 1997.

Obama, Barack. "Remarks by President Obama in Address to the People of India," January 27, 2015. https://www.whitehouse.gov/the-press-office/2015/01/27/remarks-president-obama-address-people-india.

O'Connor, Daniel. *A Clear Star: C. F. Andrews in India, 1904-1914.* 2nd ed. Delhi: DC Books, 2005.

Oddie, G. A. "Christian Conversion among Non-Brahmins in Andhra Pradesh: With Special Reference to the Dornakal Diocese, c.1900-36." In *Religion in South Asia: Religious Conversion and Revival Moments in South Asia in Medieval and Modern Times,* edited by G. A. Oddie, 95-124. New Delhi: Manohar, 1991.

O'Hanlon, Rosalind. *Caste, Conflict, and Ideology: Mahatma Jotirao Phule and Low Caste Protest in Nineteenth-Century Western India.* New York: Cambridge University Press, 1985.

"On Religious Hostilities, India Ranked Just Slightly Better Than Syria: Pew Study. Animosity between Hindus and Muslims Drove India's Poor Ranking in 2015." *Huffington Post*, April 14, 2017, http://www.huffingtonpost.in/2017/04/13/on-religious-hostilities-india-ranked-just-slightly-better-than_a_22037994/. Accessed February 12, 2018.

Ostrowski, Ally. "Found in Translation: From Hollywood Hits to Bollywood Blockbusters." *Journal of Religion and Film* 11, no. 2 (October 2007).

Osuri, Goldie. *Religious Freedom in India: Sovereignty and (anti) Conversion*. London: Routledge, 2013.

Pachuau, Lalsangkima. "A Clash of 'Mass Movements'? Christian Mission and the Gandhian Nationalist Movement in India." *Transformation* 31, no. 3 (2014).

Paloutzian, Raymond F., James T. Richardson, and Lewis R. Rambo. "Religious Conversion and Personality Change." *Journal of Personality* 67, no. 6 (1999): 1047-79.

Pandey, Prashant. "Jharkhand Guv Approves Freedom of Religion Bill, Land Act; BJP Welcomes Move." *Indian Express,* September 6, 2017. http://indianexpress.com/article/india/jharkhand-guv-approves-freedom-of-religion-bill-land-act-bjp-welcomes-move/.

------. "Jhakhand Passes Anti-Conversion Bill, Govt Rejects Demand for More Scrutiny." *India Express,* August 13, 2017. http://indianexpress.com/article/india/jharkhand-passes-anti-conversion-bill-govt-rejects-demand-for-more-scrutiny-4794360/.

------. "Jharkhand Quotes Mahatma Gandhi to Push Its Conversion Bill." *Indian Express*, August 12, 2017. http://indianexpress.com/article/india/jharkhand-quotes-mahatma-gandhi-to-push-its-conversion-bill-4792888/. Accessed January 20, 2018.

Pascale, Richard, Mark Millemann, and Linda Gloja. *Surfing the Edge of Chaos: The Laws of Nature and the New Law of Business*. New York: Three Rivers Press, 2000.

Patil, Prachi. "Jesus's Two Great Commandments: Analysing Indian Theology through Caste and Gender." *Feminist Theology* 25, no. 1 (2006).

Pew Research Center. "Trends in Global Restrictions on Religion," June 23, 2016. http://www.pewforum.org/2016/06/23/trends-in-global-restrictions-on-religion/. Accessed February 13, 2018.

"Photos of Orissa Violence." *Christian Persecution India*, September 10, 2008. http://christianpersecutionindia.blogspot.in/2008/09/photos-of-orissa-violence.html.

Pickett, J. Waskom. *Christian Mass Movements in India: A Study with Recommendations.* New York: Abingdon Press, 1933.

"Politics of Religious Freedom, The." *The Immanent Frame.* https://tif.ssrc.org/category/exchanges/religion-world-affairs/the-politics-of-religious-freedom/.

Puniyani, Ram. *Communal Politics: Facts versus Myths.* New Delhi: Sage Publications, 2003.

------. *Hindu Nationalism versus Indian Nationalism.* http://www.countercurrents.org/puniyani240713.html. Accessed January 23, 2016.

------, ed. *Ghar Wapsi: Conversations and Freedom of Religion.* Delhi: Media House, 2015.

Ragunathan, Susheela. "Jesus, Did You Really Die for Me?" *Conversions in India--Testimonies,* May 8, 2013. https://conversionsinindia.wordpress.com/2013/05/08/susheela-raghunathan/. Accessed November 29, 2017.

Raj, Selva J., and Corinne G. Dempsey, eds. *Popular Christianity in India: Riting between the Lines.* Albany: State University of New York Press, 2002.

Rajkumar, Ramachandran. "Ramachandran Rajkumar." *Conversions in India-Testimonies,* January 1, 2009. https://conversionsinindia.wordpress.com/2009/01/31/ramachandran-rajkumar/. Accessed November 29, 2017.

Rambo, Lewis. *Understanding Religious Conversion.* New Haven: Yale University Press, 1993.

"Religious Freedom Bill Passed in Rajasthan." *The Hindu,* March 21, 2008. http://www.thehindu.com/todays-paper/tp-national/Religious-Freedom-Bill-passed-in-Rajasthan/article15188629.ece.

Report of the Christian Missionary Activities Enquiry Committee, Madhya Pradesh. 2 vols. Nagpur: Madhya Pradesh, 1956.

Reynolds, Amy, and Stephen Offutt. "Global Poverty and Evangelical Action." In *The New Evangelical Social Engagement,* edited by Brian Steensland and Philip Goff. New York: Oxford University Press, 2014.

Richard, H. L. *Following Jesus in the Hindu Context: The Intriguing Implications of N. V. Tilak's Life and Thought.* Pasadena: William Carey Library, 1998.

Richardson, James T. "The Active vs. Passive Convert: Paradigm Conflict in Conversion/Recruitment Research." *Journal for the Scientific Study of Religion* 24, no. 2 (1985).

Robert, Dana L. "Shifting Southward: Global Christianity since 1945." *International Bulletin of Missionary Research* 24, no. 2 (2000): 50-58.

Robinson, Rowena. *Boundaries of Religion: Essays on Christianity, Ethnic Conflict and Violence.* New Delhi: Oxford University Press, 2013.

Roskies, David G. *The Literature of Destruction: Jewish Responses to Catastrophe.* Philadelphia: Jewish Publication Society, 1988.

Safdar Hashmi Memorial Trust (SAHMAT). *Secularism Alert.* Delhi: SAHMAT, 1998.

Sahoo, Sarbeswar. "Religious Violence and the Developmental State." In *Perspectives on Violence and Othering in India*, edited by R. C. Tripathi and Purnima Singh. New Delhi: Springer, 2016.

Salam, Ziya Us. "Peddling Patriotism." *The Hindu*, March 15, 2002. http://www.thehindu.com/thehindu/fr/2002/03/15/stories/2002031500070100.htm.

Salamon, Lester M., Leslie C. Hems, and Kathryn Chinnock. "The Nonprofit Sector: For What and for Whom?" In *Working Papers of the Johns Hopkins Comparative Nonprofit Sector Project.* Johns Hopkins University, 2000.

Samuel, Vinay, and Chris Sugden. "God's Intention for the World." In *Mission as Transformation: A Theology of the Whole Gospel*, edited by Vinay Samuel and Chris Sugden. Oxford: Regnum, 1999.

Sanneh, Lamin O. *Disciples of All Nations: Pillars of World Christianity.* New York: Oxford University Press, 2007.

Sarvarkar, V. D. "The Glories of the Hindu Nation." In *Sources of Indian Tradition*, edited by Wm. Theodore DeBary et al., 881-87. New York: Columbia University Press, 1958.

Scherer, James. "Church, Kingdom, and *Missio Dei*: Lutheran and Orthodox Correctives to Recent Ecumenical Mission Theology." In *The Good News of the Kingdom: Mission Theology for the Third Millennia*, edited by C. Van Engen, D. S. Gilliland, and P. Pierson. Maryknoll, NY: Orbis, 1993.

Sen, Amartya. *The Argumentative Indian.* New York: Picador, 2005.

Shah, Rebecca Samuel. "Christianity among the Marginalized: Empowering Poor Women in India." In *Christianity and Freedom*, vol. 2, *Contemporary Perspectives*, edited by Allen D. Hertzke and Timothy Shah Samuel. New York: Cambridge University Press, 2016.

------. "Religion and Economic Empowerment among the Enterprising Poor." *The Review of Faith and International Affairs* 11, no. 4 (2013): 41-45.

------. "Religious Innovation and Economic Empowerment in India: An Empirical Exploration." In *Religion and Innovation: Antagonists or Partners?* edited by Donald A. Yerxa. London: Bloomsbury Academic, 2016.

Shah, Rebecca Samuel, and Timothy Samuel Shah. "How Evangelicalism--Including Pentecostalism—Helps the Poor: The Role of Spiritual

Capital." In *The Hidden Form of Capital: Spiritual Influences in Societal Progress*, edited by Peter L. Berger and Gordon Redding. London: Anthem, 2011.

------. "Pentecost amid Pujas: Charismatic Christianity and Dalit Women in Twenty-First Century India." In *Pentecostalism in the 21st Century*, edited by Robert W. Hefner. Bloomington: Indiana University Press, 2013.

Sharma, Anuradha. "Dalit Women Writings: Breaking the Stereotypical Annotations of 'Being an Untouchable.'" *International Journal of English Language, Literature, and Humanities* 2, no. 5 (2014).

Sharma, Jyotirmaya. *Hindutva: Exploring the Idea of Hindu Nationalism*. New Delhi: Viking, 2003.

Sharma, Pathika Dhara. "Christianity in the Northeast." *The Telegraph*, Calcutta Edition, September 9, 2011. http://www.telegraphindia.com/1110909/jsp/northeast/story_14484991.jsp. Accessed March 3, 2016.

Sharma, Raj Bahadur. *History of Christian Missions: North India Perspective*. New Delhi: Mittal Publications, 1998.

Sharma, Rajendra. "Conversion Was Mother Teresa's Real Aim, RSS Chief Mohan Bhagwat Says." *The Times of India*, February 24, 2015. http://timesofindia.indiatimes.com/india/Conversion-was-Mother-Teresas-real-aim-RSS-chief-Mohan-Bhagwat-says/articleshow/46348555.cms. Accessed February 18, 2018.

Shirsat, K. R., *Narayan Vaman Tilak: Poet and Patriot*. Bombay: Bombay Tract and Book Society, 1979.

Shourie, Arun. *Missionaries in India: Continuities, Changes, Dilemmas*, New Delhi: ASA, 1994.

Shrestha, Celayne Heaton. "'They Can't Mix Like We Can': Bracketing Differences and the Professionalization of NGOs in Nepal." In *Development Brokers and Translators: The Ethnography of Aid and Agencies*, edited by David Lewis and David Mosse. Bloomfield, CT: Kumarian Press, 2006.

Sider, Richard J. *Rich Christians in an Age of Hunger*. Downers Grove, IL: Intervarsity Press, 1977.

Singh, K. S. "A Note on the Series, Peoples of India—Anthropological Survey of India." http://www.ansi.gov.in/people_india.htm. Accessed September 22, 2015.

Singh, Roja. "Bama's Critical-Constructive Narratives." In *Dalit Theology in the Twenty-First Century: Discordant Voice, Discerning Pathways*, edited by Sathianathan Clarke, Deenabandhu Manchala, and Philip Peacock. New Delhi: Oxford University Press, 2010.

Smith, Christian. *American Evangelicalism: Embattled and Thriving.* Chicago: University of Chicago Press, 1998.

Smith, Donald Eugene. *India as a Secular State.* Princeton: Princeton University Press, 1963.

Smith, Jonathan A., and Mike Osborn. "Interpretive Phenomenological Analysis." In *Qualitative Psychology: A Practical Guide to Research Methods*, edited by Jonathan A. Smith. London: Sage, 2003.

Snow, David A., and R. Machalek. "The Sociology of Conversion." *Annual Review of Sociology* 10 (1984): 167-90.

Stearns, Richard. *The Hole in Our Gospel.* Nashville: Thomas Nelson, 2009.

Steensland, Brian, and Philip Goff, eds. *The New Evangelical Social Engagement.* New York: Oxford University Press, 2014.

Strange, Daniel. "Rooted and Grounded? The Legitimacy of Abraham Kuyper's Distinction between Church as *Institute* and Church and *Organism*, and Its Usefulness in Constructing an Evangelical Public Theology." *Themelios* 40, no. 3 (2015).

Sullivan, Winnifred Fallers. *The Impossibility of Religious Freedom.* Princeton: Princeton University Press, 2005.

Sullivan, Winnifred Fallers, et al. *Politics of Religious Freedom.* Chicago: University of Chicago Press, 2015.

Sunquist, Scott W. *The Unexpected Christian Century: The Reversal and Transformation of Global Christianity, 1900-2000.* Grand Rapids, MI: Baker Academic, 2015.

Svelmoe, Bill. "Evangelism Only? Theory versus Practice in the Early Faith Missions." *Missiology: An International Review* 31, no. 2 (2003): 195-206.

Sykes, Marjorie. *C. F. Andrews: Representative Writings.* New Delhi: National Book Trust, 1973.

Tamadonfar, Mehran, and Ted G. Jelen, eds. *Religion and Regimes.* Lanham, MD: Lexington Books, 2014.

Tambiah, Stanley J. "The Crisis of Secularism in India." In *Secularism and Its Critics*, edited by Rajeev Bhargava. Delhi: Oxford University Press, 1998.

Thapar, Romila. "Syndicated Hinduism." In *Hinduism Reconsidered*, edited by Gunther D. Sontheimer and Hermann Kulke. New Delhi: Manohar, 1991.

------. "Syndicated Moksha?" *Seminar*, no. 313 (September 1985): 21.

Tharu, Susie, and K. Lalita, eds. *Women Writing in India*, vol. 1, *600 B.C. to the Early Twentieth Century.* Delhi: Oxford University Press, 1993.

Thomas, P. N. *Strong Religion, Zealous Media: Christian Fundamentalism and Communication in India.* Thousand Oaks: Sage, 2008.

Tilak, Lakshmibai. *Agadi Step by Step: Testimony of Lakshmibai Tilak in Her Own Words.* Edited by Ashok Tilak. Nasik: M. A. Tilak, 1968.

------. *Bharali Ghagar.* Mumbai: K. B. Devale, 1948.

------. *I Follow After: An Autobiography.* Translated by E. Josephine Inkster. Madras: Oxford University Press, 1950.

------. *Sketches from Memory.* Translated by Louis Menezes. New Delhi: Katha, 2007.

Tilak, Lakshmibai, and Narayan Tilak. *Kristayan.* Nasik: Devadatta Tilak, 1938.

Tinker, Hugh. *A New System of Slavery: The Export of Indian Labour Overseas, 1830-1920.* 2nd ed. London: Hansib Publications, 1993.

------. *Ordeal of Love: C. F. Andrews and India.* Delhi: Oxford University Press, 1979.

Toft, Monica Duffy, Daniel Philpott, and Timothy Samuel Shah. *God's Century: Resurgent Religion and Global Politics.* New York: W. W. Norton, 2011.

Torgovnik, Jonathan. *Bollywood Dreams: An Exploration of the Motion Picture Industry and Its Culture in India.* London: Phaidon Press, 2003.

United Nations Office of the High Commissioner for Human Rights. "Universal Periodic Review—India." http://www.ohchr.org/EN/HRBodies/UPR/Pages/INIndex.aspx. Accessed February 12, 2018.

US Commission on International Religious Freedom. *2017 Annual Report.* http://www.uscirf.gov/sites/default/files/2017.USCIRFAnnualReport.pdf. Accessed February 13, 2018.

Valančiūnas, Deimantas. "Myth in Constructing Contemporary Indian Identity in Popular Hindi Film: The Case of Ashutosh Gowariker." *Acta Orientalia Vilnensia* 9:2 (2010).

van der Veer, Peter. *Imperial Encounters.* Princeton: Princeton University Press, 2001.

Van Gelder, Craig, and Dwight J. Zschelle. *The Missional Church in Perspective: Mapping Trends and Shaping the Conversation.* Grand Rapids, MI: Baker Academic, 2011.

Vanaik, Achin. "Making India Strong: The BJP-Led Government's Foreign Policy Perspectives." In *Hindu Nationalism and Governance,* edited by John McGuire and Ian Copland. New Delhi: Oxford University Press, 2007.

Vinayaraj, Y. T. "Envisioning a Postmodern Method of Doing Dalit Theology." In *Dalit Theology in the Twenty-First Century: Discordant Voices, Discerning Pathways,* ed. Sathianathan Clarke, Deenabandhu Manchala, and Philip Peacock. New Delhi: Oxford University Press, 2010.

Viswanathan, Gauri. *Outside the Fold: Conversion, Modernity, and Belief.* New Delhi: Oxford University Press, 2001.

Vivekananda, Swami. "Paper on Hinduism." First World's Parliament of Religions in Chicago, September 19, 1893. http://www.viveksamity.org/user/doc/CHICAGO-SPEECH.pdf. Accessed July 20, 2017.

Volf, Miroslav. *After Our Likeness: The Church in the Image of the Trinity.* Grand Rapids, MI: Eerdmans, 1998.

------. "Soft Difference: Theological Reflections on the Relation Between Church and Culture in 1 Peter." *Ex Auditu* 10 (1994).

Vorster, J. "Kingdom, Church and Civil Society: A Theological Paradigm for Civil Action." *HTs Teologiese Studies/Theological Studies* 71, no. 3 (2015).

Walls, Andrew F. *The Missionary Movement in Christian History: Studies in the Transmission of Faith.* Maryknoll, NY: Orbis, 1996.

------. "Missionary Societies and the Fortunate Subversion of the Church." In *The Missionary Movement in Christian History*, edited by Andrew F. Walls. Maryknoll, NY: Orbis, 1996.

Wani, Aarti. "Three Films and a Nation." *MR Zine*, October 22, 2005. http://mronline.org/2005/10/22/three-films-and-a-nation/.

Weber, Otto. *Versammelte Gemeinde: Beitrage zum Gesprach die Kirche und Gottesdienst.* Neukirchen, Austria: Buchhandlung des Erziehungsvereins, 1949.

Webster, John C. B. *A History of Dalit Christians in India.* San Francisco: Mellen Research University Press, 1992.

Weedon, Chris, and Glenn Jordan. "Collective Memory: Theory and Politics." *Social Semiotics* 22, no. 2 (April 2012).

Werker, Eric, and Faisal Z. Ahmed. "What Do Nongovernmental Organizations Do?" *Journal of Economic Perspectives* 22, no. 2 (2008).

Wolpert, Stanley. *Tilak and Gokhale: Revolution and Reform in the Making of Modern India.* Berkeley: University of California Press, 1962.

Woodberry, Robert D. "The Origins of the Temperance Movement: A Comparative Historical Analysis." Paper presented at the national meeting of the American Sociological Association, New York. August 16-20, 1996.

Woods, Mark. "India: 8,000 Christians Targeted by Violence and Persecution in 2015." *World.* http://www.christiantoday.com/article/india.8000.christians.targeted.by.violence.and.persecution.in.2015.report.says/77222.htm. Accessed on February 20, 2015.

Wright, Melanie J. *Religion and Film: An Introduction.* London: IB Tauris, 2007.

Wuthnow, Robert. *Boundless Faith: The Global Outreach of American Churches.* Berkeley: University of California Press, 2009.

Zelliot, Eleanor. "A Bibliographical Essay on Women in Maharashtra." In *Images of Women in Maharashtrian Society*, edited by Anne Feldhaus. Albany: State University of New York Press, 1998.

Zuckerman, Gil, and Liat Korn. "Post-Traumatic Stress and World Assumptions: The Effects of Religious Coping." *Journal of Religion and Health* 53 (2014).

Contributors

Aminta Arrington is assistant professor of intercultural studies at John Brown University. Prior to teaching at JBU, she spent eight years teaching in China, where she conducted long-term ethnographic fieldwork among the Lisu Christians in southwest China. She has published a memoir of that experience: *Home is a Roof Over a Pig: An American Family's Journey in China* (2012).

Joel A. Carpenter is a professor of history and director of the Nagel Institute for the Study of World Christianity at Calvin College. He has researched and published in American religious history, Christian higher education, and world Christianity. His best-known book is *Revive Us Again: The Reawakening of American Fundamentalism* (1997); and his most recent one is a co-edited work, *Christianity in Chinese Public Life: Religion, Society and the Rule of Law* (2014).

John Dayal is a journalist, author and occasional film maker, and is now involved full time in freedom of religion advocacy, especially in India and South Asia. Among his works is *For Reasons of State* (1977), *Gujarat* (2002), Untold Stories (2002) and *A Matter of Equity - Interrogating Secularism in India* (2007). He has contributed to, and co-edited, many anthologies.

Sean Doyle is associate professor of world history and humanities at Geneva College. His research specialty is the history of Christian interaction with Hindu spirituality and philosophy. He is the author of a book in that field of inquiry, *Synthesizing the Vedanta: The Theology of Pierre Johanns S.J.* (2006).

Darren Duerksen is associate professor and director of intercultural and religious studies at Fresno Pacific University. Darren also served with Mennonite Brethren Mission in New Delhi, India. His recent publications include *Ecclesial Identities in a Multi-Faith Context: Jesus Truth-Gatherings (Yeshu Satsangs) among Hindus and Sikhs in Northwest India* (2015) and *Discovering Church* (co-authored with William Dyrness, forthcoming).

Joshua Iyadurai is the director of the Marina Centre for Interdisciplinary Studies in Religion, in Chennai. He teaches theology online for the University of Roehampton, London; and is a visiting professor at the University of Madras; the South Asia Institute for Advanced Christian Studies; and at the Centre for Advanced Theological Studies at the Sam Higginbotham University of Agriculture, Technology and Sciences. He is the author of *Transformative Religious Experience: A Phenomenological Understanding of Religious Conversion* (2015).

Karuna John is a Delhi-based independent journalist and editor. She has published in leading newspapers and magazines over the past 20 years. She writes on politics, gender, people, food, travel, books, and the arts.

Vijayesh Lal serves as General Secretary of the Evangelical Fellowship of India (EFI). He initiated and was a leader of Open Doors International in India and Bhutan n 1999 until 2014, while serving as National Director for EFI's Religious Liberty Commission. He speaks and writes frequently on religious freedom issues. He is a member of the National United Christian Forum (NUCF) on religious freedom and is a founder of the Christian Legal Association of India.

Bernardo A. Michael is a professor of history at Messiah College. He is an expert on British colonization of the Indian subcontinent, especially relationships with the kingdom of Gorkha (present-day Nepal). His book in that field is *Statemaking and Territory: Lessons of the Anglo-Gorkha War (1814-1816)* (2012). His current research focuses on the Anglican missionary, educator, and activist, Charles Freer Andrews (1871-1940).

Vikas Ram holds degrees in science, social science and theology, and is currently doing doctoral research on the resilience of persecuted first-generation followers of Christ in India. For a number of years, he has organized research to document persecution of Christians in India. He is the author of *The Role of Understanding in Discipleship* (2010).

Paul S. Rowe is Professor of Political and International Studies and senior research fellow in the Religion, Culture, and Conflict Research Group at Trinity Western University. Dr. Rowe's research focuses on the politics of Christian minorities in the Middle East and South Asia. He is the author of *Religion and Global Politics* (2012) and co-editor of *Whose Will be Done? Essays on Sovereignty and Religion* (2015), and *Christians and the Middle East Conflict* (2014).

Rebecca Samuel Shah is a research professor at Baylor University's Institute for the Studies of Religion. She is currently the principal investigator for the Religion and Economic Empowerment Project (REEP) and serves as senior fellow with the Religious Freedom Institute and as associate director of its South and Southeast Asia Action Team. She is also senior fellow of the DeVoe School of Business at Indiana Wesleyan University. Shah's work has appeared in various journals, including *Transformation, Third Way, Society* and the *Journal of Church and State*.

Timothy Samuel Shah is a senior scholar and project director at Georgetown University's Berkley Center for Religion, Peace & World Affairs; the Religious Freedom Institute; and Baylor University's Institute for Studies of Religion. He is a political scientist specializing in religious freedom and is an authority in the broader field of religion and politics as well. He is an author or editor of many works, most notably *God's Century: Resurgent Religion and Global Politics* (2011), and *Christianity and Freedom* (2 vols., 2016).

Kay Higuera Smith is a professor of biblical and religious studies and program director of the religious studies program at Azusa Pacific

University. She does research and publishes on issues of religion, culture, and scriptural interpretation. She is the chief editor of *Evangelical Postcolonial Conversation: Global Awakenings in Theology and Praxis* (2014).

Samuel Thambusamy is currently the Director of Media and Special Audiences for the Bible Society of India, after several years of service as the Principal of South India Biblical Seminary, Bangarapet. His interests are in theology, politics and popular culture, and the places where they intersect. He is involved in the emerging discipline of film and theology and has made many presentations on it in both academic and secular settings.

INDEX

A

Adivasis 6, 16, 234, 249
Advani, L. K. 166, 192
Agneepath (1990) 164
Alliance Defending Freedom India 194
Ambedkar, B. R. 76, 77, 78, 160, 284
American Marathi Mission 25, 31, 37
Anagol, Padma 37, 47
Andhra Pradesh (state) 14, 15, 292
Andrews, Charles Freer 53, 54, 55, 57, 58, 59, 62, 63, 68, 284, 303
Anglican Church 57, 58
Arrington, Aminta vii, xvi, 107, 301
Assam (state) 4, 270
Athanasian Creed 58
Aurobindo 12
Australia 57, 152, 170
Ayodhya 8, 49, 192, 261, 276
Azariah, V. S. 15, 19, 77, 287

B

Bacote, Vincent 114
Baglur (slum area of Bangalore) 107, 247
Bajrang Dal 13, 20, 51, 184, 210, 215, 276, 277, 282
Bangalore v, viii-xi, xvii, 16, 77, 107, 122-123, 145, 209, 228, 246, 248, 250-251, 271, 275, 284, 287, 290
Barjatya, Sooraj 154, 159
Bauman, Chad 201
Bayly, Christopher 10
Bhandarkar, R. G. 26
Bharali Ghagar (Lakshmibai) 41, 298
Bharatiya Janatha Party (BJP) ix, xv, 3, 51, 70, 78, 151, 180, 202, 230, 258

Bihar (state) 173, 236, 277, 282
Biju Janata Dal 277
Bollywood viii, xvii, 120, 151-152, 153-154, 155-156, 157-158, 159-160, 161-162, 163-164, 165-166, 167-168, 170-171, 172, 175, 176-177, 178, 287, 291, 293, 298
Bombay Association 199
Bombay/Mumbai 41, 153, 159, 160, 185, 201, 253, 298
Border (1997) 160
Brahmins; Chitpavan Brahmin community 29
Brahmo Samaj 26, 59
Bridges of God, The (McGavran) 113, 290
Bright, Bill 111
British Guyana 57
Brosius, Christiane 166
Buddhism 7, 12, 182
Bunch of Thoughts (Golwalkar) 69, 78, 80, 287
Butler, Judith 53

C

Calcutta/Kolkata 153, 270
Calderisi, Robert 273
Calvin, John 135, 289
Campus Crusade 111
Carman, John 273
Catholic Bishops Conference of India (CBCI) 192, 195
Catholic Social Teaching 108
Catholics xiii, 117, 197, 251-252, 253, 273
Chatterjee, Saibal 178
Chennai ix, 64, 95, 153, 271, 273, 288, 302
Chhattisgarh (state) 192, 230, 234, 236
China 49, 301

Chopra, Yash 154, 174
Chowpatty Beach (in Mumbai) 185
Christ at Heart's Door (Sallman) 3
Christ's Faithful Apostle (CFA) 62
Christian Community Development Association 109
Christian developmental organizations (CDOs) 125, 127
Christian Medical College at Vellore 279
Christology 120
Communalism 49, 52, 199, 200, 284
Compassion International 126
Congress Party 3, 4, 152, 191
Constitution (Scheduled Castes) Order (1950) 181
Conversion, religious 41, 127, 181
Corporatism 258, 269-270, 277-278, 279

D

Dalits xvii, 16, 24, 33, 37, 69-70, 71, 73-74, 76-77, 80-81, 82, 101-102, 120-121, 181-182, 183, 188, 190-191, 205-206, 233, 239, 245, 247, 248-249, 255, 285, 292
Danchin, Peter 231, 290
Dass, Arul 187
Daya 36
Dayal, John viii, xvii, 179, 183, 202, 206, 301
Deenabandhu 54, 55, 120, 122, 123, 284, 296, 298
Deewar (2004) 160
Dehradun 209
Delhi ix, xvii, 3-4, 6, 8, 11, 13, 15-16, 20, 27, 35, 37, 41, 43, 49, 51, 54, 55, 57, 58, 60, 62-63, 65, 76, 78, 100, 120, 122-123, 144, 151, 153, 158, 166-167, 170, 181, 186, 192, 199, 200-201, 202-203, 204-205, 207, 209-210, 235, 238, 256, 258, 260, 263, 270, 282-283, 284-285, 286-287, 288, 290-291, 292, 294-295, 296-297, 298-299, 302
Democracy/democracies 53, 262, 278, 285, 287, 291, 292
Dempsey, Corinne 272
Deshpande, Sudhanva 285
Devgan, Kajol 165

Dewick, E. C. 65
Dharma Productions
Dilwaale Dulhaniya Le Jayenge (1995) 155, 164
Diversity xiv, 7, 60, 172, 178, 232, 259, 261-263, 264, 266, 272, 278
Divya Shanthi Christian Association (DSCA) 107, 122, 145
Dostana (1980) 164
Doyle, Sean vii, xv, 23, 301
Dr. Babasaheb Ambedkar (2000) 160
Duerkson, Darren viii, xvii, 125, 302
Duplicate (1998) 164
Duraisingh, Christopher 119
Dywer, Rachel 154

E

Ebrahim, Anloor 128
Economic Lives of the Poor, The (Banerjee and Duflo) 249, 282
Egypt 256, 268, 284
Ekal Vidyalaya 6
Embree, Ainslie 20
Evangelical Fellowship of India (EFI) xvii, 187, 192, 195, 202, 285, 302
Evangelism 5, 109, 111-112, 113, 115, 118-119, 128, 130, 136, 208, 224

F

Fadnavis, Devendra 185
Faith xiii, 5, 7, 9, 11, 12, 13, 18, 19, 24, 31, 32, 34, 35, 36, 46, 47, 48, 60, 61, 64, 65, 66, 68, 72, 73, 88, 91, 95, 100, 102, 103, 113, 114, 115, 117, 119, 123, 124, 138, 162, 169, 179, 180, 181, 183, 186, 187, 189, 193, 194, 196, 204, 206, 208, 213, 214, 217, 218, 221, 226, 228, 229, 241, 243, 249, 254, 257, 259, 263, 264, 265, 266, 268, 272, 274, 281
Fiji 57
Filming the Gods (Dwyer) 154, 162, 176, 285
First World Parliament of Religion 6, 8, 9, 20, 299
France 49
Freedom of Religion Bill (2017) 5
Frykenberg, Robert 6, 7, 13

G

Gadar: Ek Prem Katha (2001) 161
Galanter, Marc 236-237, 238, 240
Gandhi, Mahatma 14, 17, 19, 21, 63, 65, 68-69, 70, 175, 191, 260, 286, 293
George, Ernest V. 275
G. M. Arumugam v. S. Rajagopal (1975) 243
Gokhale, Narayan 28
Golwalkar, M. S. 69, 70, 78, 260
Gowariker, Aushutosh 161
Great Britain; British imperialism 55
Grudem, Wayne 108
Gujarat (state) 152, 186, 202, 230, 261, 276, 281, 301
Guntur (district) 15
Guru Nanak 63
Gurudwara 63

H

Hansen, Thomas Blom 169-170, 262
Harichandra (1913) 156
Harrison, Agatha 54
Hauerwas, Stanley 137
Hedgewar, K. P. 260
Heifetz, Ronald A. 139, 140
Himachal Pradesh (state) 270
Hindoo Christians 7
Hindu Mahasabha 11, 13, 14, 200, 201
Hinduism xvii, 5, 6, 7, 8, 9, 10, 11, 12, 13, 16, 17, 18, 19, 20, 21, 26, 35, 47, 51, 69, 71, 72, 73, 74, 76, 77, 79, 80, 81, 85, 86, 87, 88, 90, 92, 94, 102, 128, 154, 176, 180, 182, 190, 210, 213, 236, 243, 244, 246, 262, 263, 272, 274, 286, 289, 297, 299
Hindutva xv, 6, 8, 11, 12, 22, 151, 152, 153, 161, 172, 173, 189, 190, 200, 201, 211, 226, 255, 258, 259, 260, 261, 262, 263, 274, 276, 277, 279, 289, 296
Hirschl, Ran 262
HIV/AIDS 113
Holism 118, 119
Holy Spirit 77, 94, 101, 114
Houshi 36
Hum Aapke Hair Koun (1994) 154

Human Developmental Index (HDI) 120, 271
Hurd, Elizabeth Shakman 231

I

independent church ministers 209
India as a Secular State (D. E. Smith) 234, 297
Indian diaspora xvii, 151, 153, 159, 166, 177
Indian Muslim League 200
Indian National Congress 56, 199, 200, 260
Indian National Family Health Survey (NFHS) 252
Indian Witness 15
Indian-ness 154, 155, 156, 157, 158, 160, 162, 163, 166, 167, 168, 172, 173, 174, 176, 177, 178, 288
Indonesia 268
Interest aggregation 269
International Missionary Council 15, 64
International Review of Mission 119
interpretive phenomenological analysis (IPA) 297
Islam 5, 7, 11, 14, 20, 21, 69, 81, 182, 200, 240, 244, 288
Iyadurai, Joshua vii, xvi, 69, 83, 95, 102, 302
Iyer, Mani 84, 288

J

Jainism 7, 12
Jesus Christ 18, 27, 34, 58, 91, 92, 100, 111, 112, 226, 274
Jews 49, 221
Jharkhand (state) 5, 70, 228, 229, 230, 233, 277, 290, 293
Jharkhand Freedom of Religion Bill (2017) 5
Jaipur 117, 209, 274, 289
Johar, Karan viii, xvii, 151, 155, 163, 164, 165, 166, 168, 176, 177
Joharnnd, Yash 154, 155, 164
John, Karuna 302
Jordan 221, 225, 268, 299
Judaism 7, 11
Juvenile Justice Act 190

K

Kabhi Alvida Na Kehna (2006) 155, 165
Kabhie Kushie Kabhie Gham (2001) 155
Kabhir, Nasreen Munni 153
Kal Ho Na Ho (2003) 155, 166
Kandhamal (district) 183, 184, 186, 202, 203, 204, 205, 209, 210, 211, 218, 281, 286, 287, 292
Kandhamal Christians 204
Kapoor, Jayasudha 84
Karawan-e-Mohabbat 183
Kargil War 175
Karnataka (state) 192, 211, 212, 248, 270
Kashmir 179, 244
Keonjhar (district of Odisha) 277
Kerala (region) xiii, 205, 270, 273
Khan, Shah Rukh 159, 163, 164, 165, 172, 174, 175
Khasi 275
Khristayan (Narayan) 42, 45, 46
Kishore, Radha Krishna 230
Kosambi, Meera 30, 47
Kuch Kuch Hota Hai (1998) 163
Kuyper, Abraham 135, 138, 297

L

Lagaan (2001) 161, 171
Lal, Vijayesh viii, xvii, 179, 183, 186, 302
Latur 202
Legend of Bhagat Singh, The (2002) 160
Linsky, Marty 139, 140, 287
Lobo, Lancy 117, 273, 274
LOC Kargil (2003) 160
Localism 232
Lofland, John 87
Lok Sabha 242
Luhrmann, T. 96

M

Maatrebhoomi 20
Madhya Pradesh (state) 184, 188, 192, 230, 236, 240, 241, 242, 294
Madras Mahajan Sabha 199
Mahadevan, Anand 83
Maharashtra (state) 23, 24, 25, 28, 37, 38, 43, 45, 47, 185, 202, 282, 289, 300

Maharashtra, social and intellectual context of in the nineteenth century 25
Mahmood, Saba 231
Majhi, Rajini 203
Making of the mahatma, The (1996) 160
Malaysia 163, 268
Mallampalli, Chandra 238
Mallik, Gurdial 54, 62
Mantras 89, 127
"*masdala*" formula 157
Masih, Sultan 195
McGavran, Donald 113
Meek, A. S. 234
Meghalaya (state) 4, 270, 275
Mehra, Aman 169
Melanchthon, M. J. 121
Michael, Bernardo vii, xvi, 48, 302
mission Dei (the mission of God) 126, 131, 132, 133, 134, 136, 139, 141
Mizoram (state) 4, 275
Mizos 275
Modi, Narendra 151, 186
Moltmann, Jürgen 137
Monotheistic Association 26
Monsma, Stephen 266
Mosaic of Christian Belief (Olsen) 108
Mott, John 15, 74
Mudaliar v. Masilamani (1909) 237
Mukherji, Rani 165, 174
Munisa, Shanu 248
Munshi Ram (Swami Shraddhanand) 54
Muslim Brotherhood 256
Muslims ix, 7, 20, 32, 49, 51, 79, 161, 163, 172, 174, 175, 177, 180, 182, 183, 186, 188, 190, 194, 201, 211, 237, 240, 248, 251, 252, 253, 257, 259, 260, 261, 269, 293
My Name is Khan (2010) 177
Myers, Bryant 108, 130

N

Nagaland (state) 4, 275
Nagas 275
Nagpur 41, 51, 78, 240, 287, 294
Nandy, Ashis 11, 48, 49, 52, 53, 199, 262, 263
Narayan xvi, 23, 24, 26, 28, 29, 30, 31, 32, 33, 34, 35, 36, 38, 39, 40, 41, 42, 43,

45, 46, 296, 298
National Council of Churches in India (NCCI) 195
national symbols (Indian) 165, 171
nationalism xv, xvii, 4, 22, 49, 51, 52, 70, 78, 152, 156, 158, 162, 200, 259, 260, 262, 269, 270, 278
Nayak, Rajesh 84
Nehru, Jawaharlal 18, 54, 191, 193
Nepal 48, 53, 129, 268, 291, 296, 302
New Zealand 57, 170
Nirmal, A. P. 120, 121
Niyogi, M. B. 240
non-governmental organizations (NGOs) xix, 129, 232, 296
Nussbaum, Martha 50, 67, 68, 261, 262

O

Obama, Barack 259
Odisha (state [formerly Orissa]) 183, 203, 205, 210, 230, 241, 271, 277, 281
Olsen, Roger 108
Overseas Indian Day 153

P

Padmini 107, 120, 122, 123
Pakistan 49, 50, 158, 161, 163, 174, 175, 176, 177, 178, 180
Parsis 49
Partition of India (1947) 180
Patel, Karsanbhai 171
Patil, Prachi 120, 121
Patna 234, 236
P.E.A.C.E. 109, 110
Pearce, Bob 109
Pentecostal Chistianity 253
Pentecostal churches 117, 197, 212, 246, 254, 274
Pearson, W. W. 54, 56
Philippines 49
Philpott, Daniel 265, 266, 298
Phule, Jyotirao 27
Pickett, J. Waskom 15, 16
Pluralism xv, xviii, xix, 50, 51, 52, 64, 257, 258, 262, 264, 265, 267, 278, 279
Poland 49

Politics (esp. identity politics) 6, 51, 75, 80, 81, 135, 160, 199, 232, 257, 259, 261, 264, 265, 266, 267, 272, 274, 279, 294, 302, 303, 304
Prasad, Rajendra 191
Protestant Social Gospel Movement 112
Pune (city) 23, 27, 36, 199
Pune Sarvajanik Sabha 199
Punjab (state) 195, 213
Pranav (case study) 211, 212, 213, 217, 218, 219, 222, 223, 224, 226
Purpose Driven Life, The (Warren) 109

Q

Quest for the Historical Jesus, The (Schweitzer) 66

R

Rabindranath 54, 60, 61, 63, 68
Rai, Amit 175
Raichand, Yashvardhan 171
Raj, Selva 272
Rajgargh (district)
Rajgargh State Conversion Act (1936) 234
Rajasthan (state) 201, 213, 234, 235, 236, 294
Rajasthan Dharma Swatantrya Bill (2008) 235
Rajunathan, Susheela 85
Ram, Vikas viii, xviii, 198, 303
Ramachandran, Rajkumar 84, 85, 294
Ranchi 235
Rao, Chilkuri Vasantha 273, 283
Rashtriya Swayamsevak Sangh (RSS) 6, 11, 51, 185, 200, 260, 288
Rawal, Paresh 175
Razak Palaya (village) 248
Realization 48, 216, 225
Religion, nature of 8
Remembering/remembrance 221, 225, 286
Report of the Christian Missionary Activities Enquiry Committee 240, 294
Rev. Stanislaus v. State of Madhya Pradesh and Orissa (1977) 242
Richardson, James 90
Road to Sangam (2009) 175

Roskies, David 223
Rowe, Paul viii, xviii, 256, 303
Roy, Ram Mohan 26
Rudra, Susil Kamar 54
Russia 49

S

Safdar Hashmi Memorial Trust 51, 295
Salam, Ziya Us 161
Sallman, Warner 3
Samaj, Arya 11, 12, 17, 59, 64, 65

Samaj, Brahmo 26, 59
Samaritan's Purse 109
Samuel, Colleen v, xi, 145
Samuel, Vinay x, 118, 122, 123, 295
Sangh Parivar 6, 51, 190, 200, 204, 260, 261, 276, 277, 279
Saraswati, Dayanand 12, 65
Saraswati, Swami Lakshmanananda 202
Sarguja 234, 236
Sarguja State Apostasy Act (1945) 234
Sarvarkar, Vinayak Damodar 11
Satyashodhaka Samaj (Society for Truth Seekers) 27
Scheduled Castes 5, 181, 182, 229, 239, 240, 242, 243, 255
Secularism 193, 232, 257, 258, 262, 263, 264, 276, 279
Sen Keshub Chunder 26
Sermon on the Mount 31, 34, 39
Shah Bano case 261s
Shah, Rebecca vii, viii, xv, xviii, 3, 124, 228, 246, 248, 271, 303
Shah, Timothy Samuel viii, x, xviii, 228, 246, 247, 265, 266, 271, 295, 298, 303
Shahdev, Pratul 230
Shaheed-E-Hasam (2002) 160
Shaurya (case study) 198, 209, 210, 211, 212, 217, 218, 219, 221, 223
Shiv Sena 14, 277
short-term mission (STM) 108
Sikhs 177, 183, 192, 201, 211, 237, 240, 259, 260, 302
Singh, Rajnath 242
Slavery, Priestcraft Exposed (Phule) 28

Smith, Christian 112
Smith, Donald Eugene 234
Smith, Kay Higuera viii, xviii, 198, 303
Smriti Chitre (Laksmibai) 28, 29, 43, 44, 46
Society for the teaching of Knowledge to Mahars, Mangs and Other People 27
Sonagachi (district of Kolkata) 270
South Africa 18, 57, 170, 287
South Gujarat 186
Sri Lanka 5, 49, 268
Staines, Graham Stuart 184
Stark, Rodney 87, 290
Strange, Daniel 138
Suffering xvii, 39, 57, 108, 115, 118, 120, 121, 122, 124, 198, 211, 218, 219, 221, 222, 223, 226, 227
Sugden, Chris x, 118, 295
Sullivan, Winnifred Fallers 231, 288
Swades (2004) 175
Swami Vivekananda 8, 9, 73
Swarajya 185
"Syndicated Hinduism" 13, 297
Systematic Theology (Grudem) 108

T

Tagore, Dwijendranath 60
Tagore, Rabindranath 54, 60, 61, 63, 68
Talwar, Samarajit Singh 171
Tambiah, Stanley 263
Tamil Nadu (region) 123, 205, 242, 270, 271, 273
Tamil Nadu Prohibition of Forcible Conversion of Religion Ordinance (2002) 242
Telangana (state) 273
Telugu (region) xiii
Thapar, Romila 7, 8, 13
Thomas, P. N. 273, 275
Tilak, Lakshmibai; conversion of; restrictive upbringing of 28
Tilak, Narayan Waman xvi
Toft, Monica Duffy 265, 266
Transformation: An International Journal of Holistic Mission 118
Trauma 207, 208, 215, 216, 217, 218, 220, 221, 222, 223, 224, 225, 226
Tribal Christians 117, 181

Tribals 6, 70, 101, 181, 182, 205, 234, 245

U

Udaipur (city and district) 234, 235, 236, 255
Udaipur Anti-Conversion Act (1946) 234
Udupi 223
Ullah, Munshi Zaka 54
United Christian Forum (UCF) 194, 195, 201, 302
United Kingdom 13, 151, 152, 153, 166, 170
United Nations Human Rights Council (UNHRC) 179
United Nations Rapporteur on Freedom of Religion or Belief 182
United States ix, 13, 31, 48, 49, 67, 110, 112, 151, 152, 153, 166, 170, 171, 177, 204, 232

Universal Periodic Review (UPR) 179
Urbanization 158
Uttar Pradesh (state) 173, 180, 185
Uttarakhand (state) 214

V

Vaishnavites 12
Vajpayee, Atal Bihari 192
Vallamattom, John 192
Vanavasi Kalyan Ashram 6, 202
Varanasi 270
varnashrama (caste system) 73
Vedas 8, 26, 88
Vedic Magazine 64
Veer (case study) 51, 160, 163, 174, 178, 200, 208, 213, 214, 215, 217, 218, 219, 222, 223, 224, 225, 226, 227, 289, 298

Veer Zara (2004) 174, 178
Vellore 123, 271, 279
Vemula, Rohith 255
Vigilantism 258, 262, 277
Vihan (case study) 214, 215, 216, 217, 218, 220, 221, 222, 224, 225
Vinayaraj, Y. T. 121
Vineyard 96, 97, 100
Vishwa Hindu Parishad (VHP) 6, 13
Volf, Miroslav 135, 137

W

Walls, Andrew 116, 131
Wanni, Aarti 160
Warren, Kay 113
Warren, Rick 109, 110, 113, 284, 291
We or Our Nationhood Defined (Golwalkar) 51, 78, 79, 287
West Bengal (state) 59, 61, 65, 68, 244, 270
Westcott, Brooke Foss 57, 58
When God Talks Back (Luhrmann) 97, 290
World's Parliament of Religions 6, 8, 9, 20, 299
World Relief 109
World Vision 109, 130, 271
Wright, Melanie 154
Wuthnow, Robert 109

Y

Young Men's Christian Association (YMCA) 3

Z

Zoroastrain Institute 62
Zoroastrianism 7